# THE TAO OF JESUS

# THE TAO OF JESUS

*A Book of Days for the Natural Year*

JOHN BEVERLEY BUTCHER

HarperSanFrancisco
*A Division of* HarperCollins*Publishers*

Permissions acknowledgments begin on page 414.

Text design by Jaime Robles

FIRST EDITION
Library of Congress Cataloging-in-Publication Data
The tao of Jesus : a book of days for the natural year / [compiled by] John Beverley Butcher. — 1st ed.
    p. cm.
Includes bibliographic references.
ISBN 0-06-061188-x (pbk. : alk. paper)
1. Devotional calendars. 2. Jesus Christ—Devotional literature.
3. Taoist meditations. I. Butcher, John Beverley.
BV4810.T35 1994
242'.2—dc20                    94-6371
                                          CIP
94 95 96 97 98 ❖ BANWI 10 9 8 7 6 5 4 3 2 1
This edition is printed on acid-free paper that meets the American National Standards Institute Z39.48 Standard.

*This anthology is dedicated to the Tao manifesting in Jesus the Nazarene, Mary the Magdalene, Sarah the Egyptian, Lao-tzu, Socrates, Brigid of Kildare, Richard Rolle, George Berkeley, Carl Gustav Jung, Elizabeth Boyden Howes, Sadie Gregory, John Sanford, Edward Edinger, Joseph Campbell, William Temple, Lansing Hicks, Edward Rochie Hardy, Alan Watts, Barry Wood, Kilmer Myers, Wee Chong Tan, Paul Clasper, Elaine Pagels, Matthew Fox, Starhawk, Riane Eisler, Margaret Starbird, and John Bartlett, anthologist.*

*And to those whose vital energy is present in* The Tao of Jesus *through participating in my CoCreators Study Group and shaping the Taoist Eucharist: Patrick Andersen, Greg Brown, Charles Brandon, Patricia Casey, Patrisa DiFrancesca, Elaine Gilmer, Bruce Huston, Joyce Huston, Kendra Langer, Claire Lofgren, Connie Milliken, Christine Nadeau, Ray Patch, Joanna Percival, Mark Tyx, Grace Vilez, Robert Virgil, Stephen Ward, Robin Wirthlin, Shari Young, and the Episcopal congregation of St. Peter's, San Francisco.*

*And with special thanksgiving to the Tao for Alfred James Butcher and Clara Buckingham, Harold Butcher and Elizabeth Ford, Geoffrey Butcher, Tertia West, Connie Jones, Grace Vilez, and Marie Butcher.*

# Contents

✧

**And the Tao Becomes Flesh and Dwells Among Us**

JOHN 1:14

# Introduction

&

Life is a journey from birth to death and beyond. As we move through life, our outer travels are paralleled by inner spiritual journeys. We human beings are traveling together on spaceship Earth, making our annual free trip around the sun. We are entering a new age that requires a new awareness and consciousness on our part, both individually and collectively. As we travel, will ancient wisdom be useful to us?

In this book, travelers on inner and outer journeys will find creation-centered spirituality, a balancing of feminine and masculine energy, and the wisdom of the *Tao Te Ching*. Selections are arranged according to the natural year that begins with the eve of November 1. Yes, Halloween is the beginning of the natural year! (See the Appendix for the rationale.)

The themes in *The Tao of Jesus* proceed in a natural, logical way. Out of the Tao come creation stories that tell us who we are. Then comes a section on *Hun Tun,* the simultaneous coexistence of chaos and order. Out of *Hun Tun* comes the need for rebirth and new beginning illustrated with the prototype for being fully human contained in stories of Jesus' birth and baptism.

Spring selections focus on what comes from rebirth: new ways of relating and fresh, insightful teachings, particularly in the *Gospel of Thomas*. There follows the archetypal springtime theme of resurrection and empowerment with a new Spirit.

Summer readings are devoted to everyday living: the way of the Tao as it relates to ourself, our country, the Mystery of life, whole-earth consciousness, relationships, sexuality, finances, work, and leadership.

Autumn includes attention to the inevitable conflict with the prevailing social order and ways of living with that conflict by belonging to a community of the Tao. Then follow readings on grieving, dying, and returning to the Tao. This completes the cycle and brings us to the beginning of another natural year. All begins and ends in the Tao.

After the annual cycle of daily readings, this book of days provides a collection of CoCreator chants and songs followed by a Taoist Eucharist as a climax for celebrating what we are discovering. The soul of this anthology is contained in one sentence: "The Tao becomes flesh and dwells among us" (John 1:14). The purpose of this book is fulfilled as you *experience* the Tao who is within, around, and beyond us.

You may find *The Tao of Jesus* useful in a number of ways:

- Take it slowly and meditatively one day at a time through the year.
- Read it straight through, cover to cover.
- Scan the table of contents and select the topic that particularly interests you at the time.
- Open it at random and see if something speaks to you.

The same Spirit who inspired the original writers lives within you. You may find the ancient wisdom resonating in your own mind and heart and soul. Your body may also begin moving in new ways.

## Sources for *The Tao of Jesus*

For the past forty years I have been searching for and collecting all the ancient documents I can find, giving special attention to the time before Jesus and the three hundred years following him. This brings us to the time when Constantine took over the church, and controls were put in place that began stifling free thought and expression of the Spirit.

In addition to the conventional biblical collections, we now have more ancient wisdom available to us than ever before because of recent discoveries of early documents and intense work by reliable scholars. The two most notable collections are *The Dead Sea Scrolls,* discovered in 1947 in caves at Qumran on the northwest shore of the Dead Sea; and *The Nag Hammadi Library,* discovered in 1945 in a large jar buried at the foot of a cliff not far from the big bend of the Nile River in Egypt. One of these documents contains this remarkable statement: "The Great Seth wrote this book, . . . placed it in the mountain, . . . in order that, at the end of the times and eras, . . . it may come forth!" (*Gospel of the Egyptians* 68:11–20).

Besides these two collections of holy writings there are others of great value, including the *Tao Te Ching,* Inanna, the Apocrypha, the Old Testament Pseudepigrapha, the New Testament Apocrypha, and Ante-Nicene Fathers. I include stories from ancient oral tradition, some of which have only recently been put into written form. Among these are myths from Africa, the Haida Indians of British Columbia, and aboriginal people of Australia. For a complete list of the material I have been researching, see the "Sources" section at the end of this book.

As a boy in Arizona, I enjoyed going on field trips with our local rock club looking for interesting gems, crystals, and unusual natural formations. Drawing on my rockhound instincts, I have been going through this ancient material page by page looking for the gems, the useful Holy Scriptures, for us as we seek to live creatively in the time given to us. I am gathering gems of wisdom and arranging them in a natural setting for others to see. Usually these gems stand on their own. Once in a while I provide background, comments, or questions.

The treasures I found appear to me to be holy ones, worth carrying in our mind and heart while on our journey. There are others that I have no doubt missed or overlooked or been too blind to see. After you have worked meditatively with the gems I offer here, you may wish to do some fieldwork of your own, studying the various collections of ancient wisdom now available in the English language.

# QUESTIONS TO USE WITH THE STORIES

꿍

1. Who are the characters in the story? What parts of yourself might each character in the story represent?

   What other symbols do you see in the story? How might the symbols also be parts of you?

2. What dialogue occurs? What dialogue do you hear going on within yourself?

3. What questions appear? What responses are given? What responses are surfacing within you?

4. What interaction do you see between the characters? How do you feel the interacting going on within you?

5. Walk each character through the story: How is this character feeling at each step?

6. How do the characters relate to each other and to the symbols? What feelings is the story evoking from you?

7. How does the story as a whole illustrate spiritual processes going on within you now?

# Dated Entries

~  ~  ~

OCTOBER 31 THROUGH FEBRUARY 1

# New Year's Eve

❧

## OCTOBER 31, NEW YEAR'S EVE

### Opposites Need Each Other

*Your first association with October 31 may be Halloween with its masks, witches, and pumpkins. But there is more. Sundown of this day is the beginning of the natural year, which is in rhythm with the natural cycles of Mother Earth in her revolutions around the sun.*

Light and Darkness, Life and Death, Right and Left, are brothers of one another. They are inseparable. Because of this neither are the good good, nor the evil evil, nor is life life, nor death death. For this reason each will dissolve into its original nature. But those who are exalted above the world are indissoluble, eternal.

**GOSPEL OF PHILIP 53:14–23 (ROBINSON, 3D ED.)**

*In conventional Western thinking, the opposites in life are often separated into good and bad, for instance, light is good, dark is evil; strong is good, weak is bad; spirit is good, body and sex are bad. In the Tao Te Ching, the opposites are understood as necessary to each other and complementary. Night and day complete each other; death and life complete each other.*

# Tao of Creating
## (Chinese, Hebrew, and Greek Stories)

↬

### NOVEMBER 1

---

*Unspeakable Mystery*

The Tao that can be spoken of is not the eternal Tao.
The name that can be named is not the eternal name.

The nameless is the beginning of heaven and earth.
The named is the mother of the ten thousand things.

Send your desires away and you will see the mystery.
Be filled with desire
　　and you will see only the manifestation.

As these two come forth they differ in name.
Yet at their source they are the same.
This source is called a mystery.

Darkness within darkness,
　　the gateway to all mystery

TAO TE CHING, 1 (MCCARROLL)

## November 2

---

### *Before the Universe Was Born*

There was something undifferentiated and yet complete,
Which existed before heaven and earth.
Soundless and formless, it depends on nothing and does not change.
It operates everywhere and is free from danger.
It may be considered the mother of the universe.
I do not know its name; I call it Tao.
If forced to give it a name, I shall call it Great.
Now being great means functioning everywhere.
Functioning everywhere means far-reaching.
Being far-reaching means returning to the original point.

TAO TE CHING 25, PART ONE (CHAN)

Therefore, the Tao is great.
Heaven is great.
Earth is great.
Humankind is also great.
The four are great in the Universe,
and one of the four is humankind.

Humans follow the Way of the Earth,
The Earth follows the Way of Heaven,
Heaven follows the Way of the Tao,
Tao follows its own nature.

TAO TE CHING, 25, PART TWO (TAN, 1992)

## NOVEMBER 3

———

### *The Tao Gives Birth*

The Tao gives birth to One.
One gives birth to Two.
Two gives birth to Three.
Three gives birth to all things.

TAO TE CHING, 42 (MITCHELL)

All things in the universe carry the Yin and embrace the Yang,
to produce harmony through their dynamic interactions.

TAO TE CHING, 42 (TAN, 1983)

## NOVEMBER 4

———

### *All Things Arise from Tao*

All things arise from Tao.
They are nourished by Virtue.
They are formed from matter.
They are shaped by environment.
Thus the ten thousand things all respect Tao
    and honor Virtue.
Respect of Tao and honor of Virtue are not
    demanded,
but they are in the nature of things.

Therefore all things arise from Tao.
By virtue they are nourished,

Developed, cared for,
Sheltered, comforted,
Grown, and protected.
Creating without claiming,
Doing without taking credit,
Guiding without interfering,
This is Primal Virtue.

TAO TE CHING, 51 (FENG AND ENGLISH)

# NOVEMBER 5

## *The Great Tao Flows Everywhere*

The Great Tao flows everywhere.
    It may go left or right.
All things depend on it for life,
    and it does not turn away from them.
It accomplishes its task,
    but does not claim credit for it.
It clothes and feeds all things
    but does not claim to be master over them.
Always without desires, it may be called The Small.
All things come to it and it does not master them;
    It may be called The Great.
Therefore (the sage) never strives himself for the great,
    and thereby the great is achieved.

TAO TE CHING, 34 (CHAN)

## NOVEMBER 6

### *The Root of Everything*

It is fitting that we begin with the Father who is the Root of everything. . . . He is the one called "without a beginning" and "without an end," because he is unbegotten and immortal. But just as he has no beginning and no end, so he is unattainable in his greatness, inscrutable in his wisdom, incomprehensible in his power, and unfathomable in his sweetness. . . .

He is sustenance; he is joy; he is truth; he is rejoicing; he is rest. That which he conceives, that which he sees, that about which he speaks, the thought which he has, transcends all wisdom, and is above all intellect, and is above all glory, and is above all honor, and all sweetness, and all greatness, and any depth, and any height.

But since he is as he is, he is like a spring which is not diminished by the water which abundantly flows from it. . . . The Father brought forth everything, like a little child, like a drop from a spring, like a blossom from a vine, like a planting.

TRIPARTITE TRACTATE (ROBINSON, 3D ED.)

## NOVEMBER 7

### *Bursting from the Hen's Egg (First Version)*

Aeons ago heaven and earth were commingled like a big egg. Inside the "Egg" was a man named Pan Gu, who kept growing slowly until he became a giant of 90,000 miles high.

Pan Gu slept for 18,000 years, but one day he woke up. Pan Gu opened his eyes but all he could see was darkness. Feeling bored, he picked up an axe and swung it. Boom! The big "egg" was split into two parts.

The lighter part rose high and became heaven. The heavier part sank and became earth. Pan Gu feared that heaven and earth would reunite so he stood up and propped them apart like a pillar.

Tens of thousands years later, heaven was so high it was impossible for it to reunite with earth. Pan Gu was exhausted by then so he slumped to the ground.

Pan Gu was dead. His left eye became the sun and his right eye the moon. His body turned into mountains. His blood became rivers and his hair turned into trees and flowers. His bones became metals and hard rocks, and his sweat produced rain and dew.

Pan Gu not only separated heaven and earth, his body became the new world.

A CHINESE CREATION MYTH FROM 600 B.C. (JIN)

## NOVEMBER 8

*Bursting from the Hen's Egg (Second Version)*

The space of the universe was in the shape of a hen's egg. Within the egg was a great mass called *no thing*. Inside *no thing* was something not yet born. It was not yet developed, and it was called Phan Ku.

In no time, Phan Ku burst from the egg. He was the first being. He was the Great Creator. Phan Ku was the size of a giant. He grew ten feet a day and lived for eighteen thousand years.

Hair grew all over Phan Ku. Horns curved up out of his head, and tusks jutted from his jaw. In one hand he held a chisel; and with it he carved out the world.

Phan Ku separated sky from earth. The light, pure sky was *yang*, and the heavy, dark weight of earth was *yin*. The vast Phan Ku himself filled the space between earth and sky, yin and yang.

He chiseled out earth's rivers; he scooped out the valleys. It was easy for him to layer the mountains and pile them up on high.

Then Phan Ku placed the stars and moon in the night sky and the sun into the day. He put the great seas where they are now, and he showed the people how to fashion ships, how to build bridges.

Only when Phan Ku died was the world at last complete. The dome of the sky was made from Phan Ku's skull. Soil was formed from his body. Rocks were made from his bones; rivers and seas, from his blood. All of plant life came from Phan Ku's hair. Thunder and lightning are the sound of his voice. The wind and the clouds are his breath. Rain was made from his sweat. And from the fleas that lived in the hair covering him came all of humankind.

The form of Phan Ku vanished in the making of the world. After he was gone, there was room then for pain, and that is how suffering came to human beings.

A CHINESE CREATION MYTH FROM 600 B.C. (HAMILTON AND MOSER)

## NOVEMBER 9

### *Nu Wa Creates Human Beings as a Reflection of Her*

Nu Wa was a goddess and one day she arrived in the world created by Pan Gu. As she travelled across mountains and rivers, she decided that something should be added to enliven the new world.

When Nu Wa felt tired, she sat down by the side of a pond, which reflected her figure like a mirror. Wouldn't it be nice to make something living like me? she thought.

Nu Wa then began to mould a doll very carefully with water and mud. The clay figure became alive the minute it was put on the ground.

He could walk, jump, and speak. Nu Wa called him a "human being." Ah! This was the first human being.

Nu Wa moulded more clay figures and each one became alive. Moulding clay figures took a lot of time so she picked a rattan and dipped it into the mud. Afterwards, each drip of mud which fell from the rattan turned into a human being when it touched the ground.

A Chinese creation myth from 600 b.c. (Jin)

*In the Genesis creation story, human beings are made in the "image of God." Here they are made in her reflection. You are in the image of God, and you are a reflection of her.*

## NOVEMBER 10

### A Facsimile of God's Face

The Lord with his own two hands created mankind;
    in a facsimile of his own face, both small and great, the Lord
    created them.
And whoever insults a person's face, insults the face of a king,
    and treats the face of the Lord with repugnance.
He who treats with contempt the face of any person treats the face of the
    Lord with contempt.

2 Enoch 44:1–2 (Charlesworth)

## NOVEMBER 11

---

### *Nothing Is Hidden from the Face of the Lord*

For the Lord sees everything that a person thinks in his heart. . . .
If you look upon the sky, behold the Lord is there;
   for the Lord created the sky.
If you look upon the earth, then the Lord is there;
   for the Lord founded the earth, and placed upon it all his creatures.
If you meditate upon the depths of the ocean and all that is beneath
   the earth,
   then the Lord is there. Because the Lord created all things.
Do not bow down to anything created by man,
   nor to anything created by God, so committing apostasy against
   the Lord of all creation.
For no kind of deed is hidden from the face of the Lord.

2 ENOCH 66:3–5 (CHARLESWORTH)

## NOVEMBER 12

---

### *A Valentinian Myth of Creation*

Within invisible and unnameable heights there was—they say—a pre-existent, perfect entity; this they call the prior source, ancestor, and the deep. And it existed uncontained, invisible, everlasting, and unengendered. Within infinite eternal realms it was in great stillness and rest.

And within it coexisted thought, which they also call loveliness and silence.

And eventually the aforementioned deep took thought to emit a source of the entirety. And it deposited this emanation that it had thought to emit, like sperm, in the womb of silence that coexisted with it. And the latter received this sperm, conceived, and brought forth intellect, which was like and equal to the emitter and was the only being that comprehended the magnitude of its parent. And this intellect they call also only-begotten, parent, and source of the entirety.

And truth was emitted along with it.

And this is equivalent to the first, primal *tetraktys* of Pythagorean philosophy. They call it also the root of entirety. For it consists of the deep; silence; and then intellect; truth.

Now when this only-begotten perceived the ends for which it had been emitted, it emitted the Word and Life (Zoe)—a parent of the entirety of beings that were to exist after it and a source and forming of the entire fullness.

And from the Word and Life (Zoe) emanated the human being and the church, as a pair.

And these constitute the primal octet—a root and source of the entirety. It is designated by them with four names: the deep; intellect; the Word; human being. For each of them is androgynous, as follows:

first, the ancestor united with its thought—called also loveliness and silence—forming a pair;

the only begotten, i.e. intellect, united with truth;

the Word united with Life (Zoe);

the human being united with the church.

A Valentinian creation myth from the writings of Irenaeus, second century c.e. (Layton)

## NOVEMBER 13

### *Tao Speaking*

"At the beginning of the circle of the Earth,
before the portals of the world were in place,
and before the assembled winds blew,
and before the rumblings of thunder sounded,
and before the flashes of lightning shone,
and before the foundations of paradise were laid,
and before the beautiful flowers were seen,
and before the powers of earthquakes were established,
and before the innumerable hosts of angels were gathered together,
and before the heights of the air were filled up,
and before the measures of the heavens were named,
and before the footstool of Zion was established,
and before the present years were reckoned,
and before the imaginations of those who now sin were estranged,
and before those who stored up treasures of faith were sealed—
then I planned these things,
and they were made through me alone and not through another;
just as the end shall come through me alone and not through another."

2 ESDRAS 6:1–66 (NEW REVISED STANDARD VERSION)

## NOVEMBER 14

### *Tao Speaking*

Before anything existed at all, from the beginning, whatever exists I created from the non-existent, and from the invisible the visible. . . . For not even to my angels have I explained my secrets, nor related to them my origin, nor my endlessness and inconceivableness, as I devise the creatures, for I am making them known to you today.

For, before any visible things had come into existence, I the ONE, moved around in the invisible things, like the sun, from east to west, and from west to east. But the sun has rest in himself; yet I did not find rest, because everything was not yet created. And I thought up the idea of establishing a foundation, to create a visible creation.

2 ENOCH 24:2–5 (CHARLESWORTH)

## NOVEMBER 15

### Tao's Riddle: Who Am I?

I am the one who is, but you consider in your heart:
I am robed with heaven, draped around with sea,
the earth is the support for my feet, around my body is poured the air,
the entire chorus of stars revolves around me.
I have nine letters, I am four syllables. Consider me.
The first three have two letters each.
The last has the rest, and five are consonants.
The entire number is: twice eight plus three hundred, three tens
    and seven.
If you know who I am you will not be uninitiated in my wisdom.

SIBYLLINE ORACLES, BOOK 1, LINES 137–45 (CHARLESWORTH)

## November 16

*Wisdom Creates Human Beings from Seven Components*

On the sixth day I commanded my Wisdom to create man out of seven components

his flesh from the earth;
his blood from dew and the sun;
his eyes from the bottomless sea;
his bones from stone;
his reason from the mobility of the angels and from clouds;
his veins and hair from grass of the earth;
his spirit from my spirit and from wind.

And I gave him 7 properties:

| hearing | to the flesh; |
| sight | to the eyes; |
| smell | to the spirit; |
| touch | to the veins; |
| taste | to the blood; |
| to the bones | endurance; |
| to the reason | sweetness. |

Behold, I have thought up an ingenious poem to recite:
From invisible and visible substances I created man.
From both his natures come both death and life.
And as my image he knows the word like no other creature
But even at his greatest he is small,
And again at his smallest he is great.

And on the earth I assigned him to be a second angel, honored and great and glorious. And I assigned him to be a king, to reign on the earth, and to have my wisdom. And there was nothing comparable to him on earth, even among my creatures that exist.

2 ENOCH 30:8–16 (CHARLESWORTH)

## November 17

---

### *The Eighth Day*

*Tao speaking to Enoch:*

On the eighth day I likewise appointed, so that the eighth day might be
    the first,
the first-created of my week. . . .
And now, Enoch, whatever I have told you, and whatever you have
    understood, and whatever you have seen in the heavens, and
    whatever you have seen on the earth, and whatever I have written in
    the books—by my supreme wisdom all these things I planned to
    accomplish.
And I created them from the highest foundation to the lowest, and to
    the end.
And there is no adviser and no successor to my creation.
I am self-eternal and not made by hands.
My thought is without change.
My Wisdom is my adviser and my deed is my word.
And my eyes look at all things.
If I look at all things, then they stand still and shake with terror;
but, if I should turn my face away, then all things would perish.
Apply your mind, Enoch, and acknowledge the One who is speaking
    to you.

2 ENOCH 33:1–5 (CHARLESWORTH)

## NOVEMBER 18

---

### *Hours of Night and Day*

The first hour of the night is the praise of demons; and at that hour they
do not injure or harm any human being.

The second hour is the praise of the doves.

The third hour is the praise of the fish and of fire and of all the lower
depths.

The fourth hour is the "holy, holy, holy" praise of the seraphim. . . .

The fifth hour is the praise of the waters that are above heaven.

The sixth hour is the construction of clouds and of the great fear which
comes in the middle of the night.

The seventh hour is the viewing of their powers while the waters are
asleep.

And at that hour the waters can be taken up and the priest of God mixes
them with consecrated oil and anoints those who are afflicted and
they rest.

The eighth hour is the sprouting of the grass of the earth while the dew
descends from heaven.

The ninth hour is the praise of the cherubim.

The tenth hour is the praise of human beings, and the gate of heaven is
opened through which the prayers of all living things enter, and they
worship and depart.

And at that hour whatever a man will ask of God is given to him when
the seraphim and the roosters beat their wings.

The eleventh hour there is joy in all the earth when the sun rises from
Paradise and shines forth upon creation.

The twelfth hour is the waiting for incense, and silence is imposed on all
the ranks of fire and wind until the priests burn incense to his
divinity.

And at that time all the heavenly powers are dismissed.
The End of the Hours of the Night.

The Hours of the Day:
The first hour is the petition of the heavenly ones.
The second hour is the prayer of angels.
The third hour is the praise of birds.
The fourth hour is the praise of the beasts.
The fifth hour is the praise which is above heaven.
The sixth hour is the praise of the cherubim who plead against the inequity of human nature.
The seventh hour is the entry and exit from the presence of God, when the prayers of all living things enter, and they worship and depart.
The eighth hour is the praise of fire and of the waters.
The ninth hour is the entreaty of those angels who stand before the throne of majesty.
The tenth hour is the visitation of the waters when the spirit descends and broods upon the waters and upon the fountains.
And if the spirit of the Lord did not descend and brood upon the waters and upon the fountains, human beings would be injured, and everyone the demons saw they would injure.
And at that hour the waters are taken up and the priest of God mixes them with consecrated oil and anoints those who are afflicted and they are restored and healed.
The eleventh hour is the exultation and joy of the righteous.
The twelfth, the hour of the evening, is the entreaty of human beings, for the gracious will of God, the Lord of all.

THE TESTAMENT OF OUR FATHER ADAM,
CHAPTERS 1 AND 2 (CHARLESWORTH)

## NOVEMBER 19

### *Why Human Beings Were Cut in Half*

The original human nature was not like the present, but different. The sexes were not two as they are now, but originally three in number. There was man, woman, and the union of the two, having a name corresponding to this double nature, which had once a real existence, but is now lost, and the word, "Androgynous" is only preserved as a term of reproach.

In the second place, the primeval man was round, his back and sides forming a circle; and he had four hands and four feet, one head with two faces, looking opposite ways, set on a round neck and precisely alike; also four ears, two privy members, and the remaining to correspond. He could walk upright as men now do, backwards or forwards as he pleased, and he could also roll over and over at a great pace, turning on his four hands and four feet, eight in all, like tumblers going over and over with their legs in the air; this was when he wanted to run fast. Now the sexes were three, and such as I have described them, because the sun, moon, and earth are three; and the man was originally the child of the sun, the woman of the earth, and the man-woman of the moon, which is made up of sun and earth, and they were all round and moved round and round like their parents.

Terrible was their might and strength, and the thoughts of their hearts were great, and they made an attack upon the gods; of them is told the tale of Otys and Ephialtes who, as Homer says, dared to scale heaven, and would have laid hands upon the gods. Doubts reigned in the celestial councils. Should they kill them and annihilate the race with thunderbolts, as they had done the giants, then there would be an end of the sacrifices and worship which men offered to them; but, on the other hand, the gods could not suffer their insolence to be unrestrained.

At last, after a good deal of reflection, Zeus discovered a way. He said: "Methinks I have a plan which will humble their pride and improve their manners; men shall continue to exist, but I will cut them in two and then they will be diminished in strength and increased in numbers; this will have the advantage of making them more profitable to us. They shall walk upright on two legs, and if they continue insolent and will not be quiet, I will split them again and they shall hop about on a single leg."

He spoke and cut men in two, like a sorb-apple which is halved for pickling, or as you might divide an egg with a hair; and as he cut them one after another, he bade Apollo give the face and the half of the neck a turn in order that the man might contemplate the section of himself; he would thus learn a lesson of humility.

Apollo was also bidden to heal their wounds and compose their forms. So he gave a turn to the face and pulled the skin from the sides all over that which in our language is called the belly, like the purses which draw in, and he made one mouth at the center, which he fastened in a knot (the same which is called the navel); he also molded the breast and took out most of the wrinkles, much as a shoemaker might smooth leather upon a last; he left a few, however, in the region of the belly and navel, as a memorial of the primeval state. After the division the two parts of man, each desiring his other half, came together, and throwing their arms about one another, entwined in mutual embraces, longing to grow into one, they were on the point of dying from hunger and self-neglect, because they did not like to do anything apart; and when one of the halves died and the other survived, the survivor sought another mate, man or woman as we call them, being the sections of entire men or women, and clung to that.

They were being destroyed when Zeus in pity of them invented a new plan: he turned the parts of generation round to the front, for this had not always been their position, and they sowed the seed no longer as hitherto like grasshoppers in the ground, but in one another; and after the transposition the male generated in the female in order that by mutual embraces of man and woman they might breed, and the race might continue; or if man came to man they might be satisfied, and rest, and

go their ways to the business of life; so ancient is the desire of one another which is implanted in us, reuniting our original nature, making
one of two, and healing the state of man.

PLATO, THE SYMPOSIUM 189–91A (HUTCHINS)

## NOVEMBER 20

### *The Desire and the Pursuit of the Whole*

Each of us when separated, having one side only, like a flat fish, is but the
indenture of a man, and he is always looking for his other half. Men who
are a section of that double nature which was once called Androgynous
are lovers of women; adulterers are generally of this breed, and also adul-
terous women who lust after men.

The women who are a section of the woman do not care for men, but
have female attachments; the female companions are of this sort.

But they who are a section of the male follow the male, and while
they are young, being slices of the original man, they hang about men
and embrace them, and they are themselves the best of boys and youth,
because they have the most manly nature. Some indeed assert that they
are shameless, but this is not true; for they do not act thus from any
want of shame, but because they are valiant and embrace that which is
like them.

And these when they grow up become our statesmen, and these only,
which is great proof of the truth of what I am saying. When they reach
manhood they are lovers of youth, and are not naturally inclined to
marry or beget children, if at all, they do so only in obedience of the law;
but they are satisfied in that they may be allowed to live with one another unwedded; and such a nature is prone to love and ready to return
love, always embracing that which is akin to him. And when one of them

meets with his other half, the actual half of himself, whether he be a lover of youth or a lover of another sort, the pair are lost in an amazement of love and friendship and intimacy, and will not be out of the other's sight, as I may say, even for a moment: these are the people who pass their whole lives together; yet they could not explain what they desire of one another. For the intense yearning which each of them has towards the other does not appear to be the desire of lover's intercourse, but of something else which the soul of either evidently desires and cannot tell, and of which she has only a dark and doubtful presentiment.

Suppose Hephaestus, with his instruments, were to come to the pair who are lying side by side and to say to them, "What do you people want of one another?" They would be unable to explain. And suppose further, that when he saw their perplexity he said: "Do you desire to be wholly one; always day and night to be in one another's company? For if this is what you desire, I am ready to melt you into one and let you grow together, so that being two you shall become one, and while you live in a common life as if you were a single human being, and after your death in the world below still be one departed soul instead of two, I ask whether this is what you lovingly desire, and whether you are satisfied to attain this?" There is not one of them who when he heard the proposal would deny or would not acknowledge that this meeting and melting into one another, this becoming one instead of two, was the very expression of this ancient need. And the reason is that human nature was originally one and we were a whole, and the desire and pursuit of the whole is called love.

There was a time, I say, when we were one, but now because of the wickedness of humankind God has dispersed us. . . .

For if we are friends of God and at peace with God we shall find our own true loves, which rarely happens in this world at present. . . .

I believe that if our loves were perfectly accomplished, and each one returning to his primeval nature had his original true love, then our race would be happy. . . .

We must praise the God Love, who is our greatest benefactor, both leading us in this life back to our own nature, and giving us high hopes for the future, for he promises if we are spiritually devoted, God will restore us to our original state, and heal us and make us happy and blessed.

PLATO, THE SYMPOSIUM 189–91A (HUTCHINS)

*Here in mythic form we have acknowledgment of the naturalness of straight and gay and lesbian relationships. All three are natural. The majority of human beings may be heterosexual and a minority homosexual and lesbian, just as the majority appear to be right-handed and a minority left-handed. All are part of the diversity of nature.*

## NOVEMBER 21

### Sibyl's Version of the Creation Story

First God bids me tell truly how the world came to be . . .
The Most High created the whole world, saying, "Let it come
    to be"
and it came to be.
For he established the earth, draping it around with Tartarus,
and he himself gave sweet light.
He elevated heaven, and stretched out the gleaming sea,
and he crowned the vault of heaven amply with bright-shining
    stars
and decorated the earth with plants.
He mixed the sea with rivers, pouring them in, and with the air he
    mingled fragrances, and dewy clouds.

He placed another species, fish, in the seas, and gave birds to the
    winds.
To the woods, also, shaggy wild beasts, and creeping serpents to
    the earth;
and all things which are now seen.
He himself made these things with a word, and all came to be,
    swiftly and truly.
For he is self-begotten looking down from heaven.
Under him the world has been brought to completion.
And then later he again fashioned an animate object,
making a copy from his own image, youthful man, beautiful,
    wonderful.
He bade him live in an ambrosial garden, so that he might be
    concerned with beautiful works.
But he being alone in the luxuriant plantation of the garden
    desired conversation, and prayed to behold another form like
    his own.
God himself indeed took a bone from his flank and made Eve, a
    wonderful maidenly spouse, whom he gave to this man to live
    with him in the garden.
And he, when he saw her, was suddenly greatly amazed in spirit,
    rejoicing,
such a corresponding copy did he see.
They conversed with wise words which flowed spontaneously,
for God had taken care of everything.
For they neither covered their minds with licentiousness nor felt
    shame,
but were far removed from evil heart;
and they walked like wild beasts with uncovered limbs.

THE SIBYLLINE ORACLES, BOOK 1, LINES 5–25 (CHARLESWORTH)

## November 22

---

### *Eve Gives Soul to Adam*

After the day of rest Sophia sent her daughter Zoe, being called Eve, as an instructor in order that she might make Adam, who had no soul, arise so that those whom he should engender might become containers of light.

When Eve saw her male counterpart prostrate she had pity upon him, and she said, "Adam! Become alive! Arise upon the earth!" Immediately her word became accomplished fact. For Adam, having arisen, suddenly opened his eyes. When he saw her he said, "You shall be called 'Mother of the Living.' For it is you who have given me life."

ON THE ORIGIN OF THE WORLD (ROBINSON, 3D ED.)


The rulers took counsel with one another and said, "Come, let us cause a deep sleep to fall upon Adam." And he slept. Now the deep sleep that they "caused to fall upon him, and he slept" is Ignorance. They opened his side like a living Woman. And they built up his side with some flesh in place of her, and Adam came to be endowed only with soul.

And the spirit-endowed woman came to him and spoke with him, saying, "Arise Adam." And when he saw her, he said, "It is you who have given me life; you will be called 'Mother of the living.' For it is she who is my mother. It is she who is the Physician, and the Woman, and She who has given Birth."

THE HYPOSTASIS OF THE ARCHONS (ROBINSON, 1977)

## NOVEMBER 23

### *The Instructor Comes to Adam and Eve*

Then the Female Spiritual Principle came in the Serpent, the Instructor; and she taught them, saying, "What did he say to you? Was it, 'From every tree in the Garden shall you eat; yet do not eat from the Tree of recognizing evil? Do not eat from the tree of Knowledge?' "

The earthy Woman said, "He not only said, 'Don't eat from them' but 'Don't touch them, lest you die.' " The Serpent the Instructor, said to her, "Don't be afraid. You certainly shall not die; for it was out of jealousy that he said this to you. Rather your eyes shall open, your mind will become sober, and you will come to be like gods, recognizing the distinctions which exist between evil and good." And the Female Instructing Principle was taken from the Snake, and she left it behind, merely a thing of the earth.

Now Eve had confidence in the words of the Instructor. She gazed at the two trees and saw that they were beautiful and appetizing, and liked them; she took some of the fruit and ate it; and she gave some also to her husband, and he too ate it.

Then their intellect became open. For when they had eaten, the light of knowledge (gnosis) had shone upon them. When they clothed themselves with shame, they knew they were naked with regard to knowledge. They recognized that they were naked of the Spiritual Element, and took fig leaves and bound them upon their loins. When they sobered up, they saw they were naked and they became enamored of one another. They understood very much. . . .

Now when God saw that Adam and Eve nad acquired a different knowledge, God desired to test them. God gathered all of the domestic animals and wild beasts of the earth and the birds of the heaven. God brought them to Adam and Eve to see what they would call them. When they saw them, they named their creatures. God was troubled because Adam and Eve had sobered from every ignorance.

CONFLATED AND ADAPTED FROM THE HYPOSTASIS OF THE ARCHONS AND ON THE ORIGIN OF THE WORLD (ROBINSON, 1977)

## NOVEMBER 24

*"Adam! Where Are You?"*

Then God came; and said, "Adam! Where are you?" For he did not understand what had happened. And Adam said, "I heard your voice and I was afraid because I was naked and I hid."

God said, "Why did you hide, unless it is because you have eaten from the tree from which alone I commanded you not to eat? And you have eaten!" Adam said, "The woman that you gave me, she gave to me and I ate."

They turned to the snake and cursed its shadowy reflection, . . . powerless, not comprehending that it was a form they themselves had modelled. From that day, the snake came to be under the curse of the authorities; until the all-powerful man was to come, that curse fell upon the snake.

God turned to Adam, took him and expelled him from the garden along with his wife; for they have no blessing, since they too are beneath the curse. Moreover they threw human beings into great distraction and into a life of toil, so that their humankind might be occupied with worldly affairs, and might not have the opportunity of being devoted to the Holy Spirit.

THE HYPOSTASIS OF THE ARCHONS, ADAPTED (ROBINSON, 3D ED.)

*One of those persistent questions that comes to us repeatedly in our lives is "Where are you?"*

## November 25

*Cain and Abel*

Now afterwards, she bore Cain, their son; and Cain cultivated the land. Thereupon he knew his wife; again becoming pregnant, she bore Abel; and Abel was a herdsman of sheep. Now Cain brought in from the crops of the field, but Abel brought in an offering from among his lambs. God looked upon the votive offerings of Abel; but he did not accept the votive offerings of Cain. And carnal Cain pursued Abel his brother.

And God said to Cain, "Where is Abel your brother?"

He answered, saying, "Am I, then, my brother's keeper?"

God said to Cain, "Listen! The voice of your brother's blood is crying up to me! You have sinned with your mouth. It will return to you: anyone who kills Cain will let loose seven vengeances, and you will exist groaning and trembling upon the earth."

And Adam knew his female counterpart Eve, and she became pregnant and bore Seth to Adam. And she said, "I have borne another man through God, in place of Abel."

Again Eve became pregnant, and she bore Norea. And she said, "He has begotten on me a virgin as an assistance for many generations of mankind." She is the virgin whom the forces did not defile.

Then mankind began to multiply and improve.

THE HYPOSTASIS OF THE ARCHONS (ROBINSON, 3D ED.)

## NOVEMBER 26

### Eve's Daughter, Norea

*Norea is the daughter of Adam and Eve. She is sister-wife of Seth. In* The Thought of Norea, *quoted in full here, "Thought" means more than rational thinking; it is the awareness of knowing the Source directly, immediately, personally. It means centering in and resting in the All. The word* pleroma *means "fullness" or "all."*

*Norea shows what is possible for everyone who discovers and becomes aware of the Tao. This passage opens with Norea offering the heartfelt praise that springs out of her knowing Tao.*

Father of All, Ennoia of the Light dwelling in the heights above the regions below, Light dwelling in the heights, Voice of Truth, upright Nous, untouchable Logos, and ineffable Voice, incomprehensible Father!

It is Norea who cries out to them. They heard, and they received her into her place forever. They gave it to her in the Father of Nous, Adamas, as well as the voice of the Holy Ones, in order that she might inherit the first mind which she had received, and that she might rest in the divine Autogenes, and that she too might generate herself, just as she also has inherited the living Logos, and that she might be joined to all of the Imperishable Ones, and speak with the mind of the Father.

And she began to speak with words of Life, and she remained in the presence of the Exalted One, possessing that which she had received before the world came into being. She has the great mind of the Invisible One, and she gives glory to her Father, and she dwells within those who [ . . . ] within the Pleroma, and she beholds the Pleroma.

There will be days when she will behold the Pleroma, and she will not be in the deficiency, for she has the four holy helpers who intercede on her behalf with the Father of the All, Adamas. He it is who is within all of the Adams, possessing the thought of Norea who speaks concerning the two names which create a single name.

THE THOUGHT OF NOREA (COMPLETE) (ROBINSON, 3D ED.)

*Interesting to notice that even though Adam and Eve's first children, Cain and Abel, are in such disharmony that one kills the other, their second pair, Seth and Norea, rediscover the original harmony!*

*And who might the four holy helpers be? The Great Mind, the Glory, the Dwelling in the Presence, and the Pleroma. Do you understand this? If so, nothing more needs to be said. If not, there is no way to explain it now. Later you may know and understand. Then you may find it just as difficult to explain. You may know it but not have the words to say it. This is the "peace that passes all understanding" (Philippians 4:7).*

## NOVEMBER 27

### *Adam Tells His Son Seth What Happened*

The revelation which Adam taught his son Seth in the seven hundredth year, saying, "Listen to my words, my son Seth. When God had created me out of the earth along with Eve your mother, I went about with her in a glory which she had seen in the aeon from which we had come forth. She taught me a word of knowledge of the eternal God. And we resembled the great eternal angels, for we were higher than the God who created us and the powers with him, whom we did not know.

"Then God, the ruler of the aeons and the powers, divided us in wrath. Then we became two aeons. And the glory in our hearts left us, me and your mother Eve, along with the first knowledge that breathed within us. And glory fled from us. . . . The eternal knowledge of the God of truth withdrew from me and your mother Eve. . . . And after these events we became darkened in our hearts. Now I slept in the thought of my heart.

"And I saw three men before me whose likeness I was unable to recognize, since they were not the powers of the God who had created us. They surpassed glory. . . . [They were] saying to me, 'Arise, Adam, from the sleep of death, and hear about the aeon and the seed of that man to whom life has come, who came from you and from Eve, your wife.'

"When I heard these words from the great men who were standing before me, then we sighed, I and Eve, in our hearts. And the Lord, the God who had created us, stood before us. He said to us, 'Adam, why were you sighing in your heart? Do you not know that I am the God who created you? And I breathed into you a spirit of life as a living soul.' Then darkness came upon our eyes.

"Then the God, who created us, created a son from himself and Eve, your mother, . . . I knew a sweet desire for your mother. Then the vigor of our eternal knowledge was destroyed in us, and weakness pursued us. Therefore the days of our life became few. For I knew that I had come under the authority of death."

THE APOCALYPSE OF ADAM (ROBINSON, 3D ED.)

# Tao of Creating

## (African, Native American, and Aboriginal Stories)

&#x21ac;

### Mawu-Lisa the Creators

Nana Buluku, the Great Mother, created the world. She had twins, Mawu and Lisa. She did nothing after that. Mawu was the moon who had power over the night and lived in the west. Lisa was the sun, who made his home in the east. At first Mawu and Lisa had no offspring. But then, when there was an eclipse—when one of them was in the shadow of the other or another heavenly body—they came together and created children.

Mawu and Lisa were Mother and Father of all the other gods. And there were fourteen of these gods, who were seven pairs of twins. The gods of earth, storm, and iron were born first.

One day, Mawu-Lisa called all of her children to come around them. When they all came, Mawu-Lisa gave each pair of twins a good place to rule.

The first twins were told to rule the earth.

"Take what you wish from our heaven," Mawu-Lisa told them.

The second pair of twins were told to stay in the sky.

"You will rule over thunder and lightning," said Mawu-Lisa.

The third pair, who were iron, were the strength of their parents.

"You will clear the forests and prepare the land," Mawu-Lisa said, "and you will give humans their tools and weapons."

The next twins were to live in the sea.

"Children, rule all waters and all fishes," Mawu-Lisa commanded.

Other twins would rule over the birds and beasts of the bush country. They would take care of all of the trees everywhere.

More twins were to take care of the space between the earth and sky. "And you will also make the length of time that humans shall live," said Mawu-Lisa.

Then Mawu said, "Come visit me. You will tell me everything that goes on in the world." Mawu-Lisa took care that none of the lesser gods were ever seen by human beings. That is why people speak of the sky as a spirit, and speak of storms and lightning as spirits, too. And all of it is because of the power of the sky gods, Moon and Sun, Mawu-Lisa.

MAWU-LISA THE CREATORS (HAMILTON)

## NOVEMBER 29

### Raven and the First Humans—Part 1

The great flood which had covered the earth for so long had at last receded and even the thin strip of sand stretching north from Naikun, which we now call Rose Spit, lay dry. The Raven had flown there to gorge himself upon the delicacies left by the falling water, and so for a change wasn't hungry.

But his other appetites, lust, curiosity, the unquenchable desire to interfere and change things, to play tricks on the world and its creatures, these remained unsatisfied.

He had recently stolen the light from the old man who had kept it hidden in a box in his house in the middle of the darkness, and scattered it throughout the sky where it spattered across the night and dazzled the day with a simple bright shining. Under it now, the long beach that curved between the spit where he stood and Tao Hill lay quiet and deserted, and to the Raven, infinitely boring. He walked along the sand, his shiny head cocked, his sharp eyes and ears alert for any unusual sight or sound. In frustration he called petulantly to the empty sky and to his delight heard an answering cry, though from his great height it was no more than an obscure muffled squeak.

At first he saw nothing, but as he looked again a flash of white caught his eye, and there right at his feet, half buried in the sand, was a gigantic clamshell.

He looked more closely and saw that the shell was full of little creatures cowering in terror in his enormous shadow.

Well, here was a diversion, something to break the monotony of his day. But it wasn't much fun as long as the silly things stayed in their shell. And they certainly weren't going to come out in their present terrified state. So he leaned his great head close and with the smooth trickster's tongue that had got him into and out of so many misadventures during his troubled and troublesome existence, he coaxed and cajoled and coerced them to come out and play in his wonderful new shiny world.

As you know, the Raven speaks in two voices, one harsh and strident; the other, which he used now, a seductive bell-like croon, certainly one of the most beautiful sounds in the world. So it wasn't long until first one, and then another of the little shell dwellers emerged. Some of them immediately scurried back when they saw the immensity of the sea and the sky and the overwhelming blackness of the Raven. But eventually curiosity overcame caution and they all clambered out. Very curious creatures they were: two legged like the Raven, but there the resemblance ended. No glossy feathers, no thrusting beak, but pale skin, naked except for long black hair on their round, flat-featured heads; instead of strong wings, thin stick-like appendages that waved and fluttered constantly—the original Haida, the first humans.

THE HAIDA LEGEND OF THE RAVEN AND THE FIRST HUMANS (REID)

## NOVEMBER 30

---

### *Raven and the First Humans—Part 2*

For a long time the Raven amused himself with his new playthings, watching them as they explored their suddenly expanded world, sometimes helping each other in new discoveries, as often squabbling over some novelty they found on the beach. He taught them clever tricks at which they were very adept.

But the Raven's attention span was very brief and soon he was again bored in spite of the strange antics of his little companions. For one thing, he noticed they were all males. And no matter how hard he looked, he failed to find any females to make his games with the Haida more interesting.

Suddenly he had an idea and lost no time in putting it into practice. He picked up the men, one by one, and in spite of their struggles and cries of fright, put them on his broad back where they hid themselves among his feathers. When he had picked up the last one, the Raven spread his wings and flew rapidly to North Island and landed on a beach near a high rock which at low tide was covered with red chitons. He shook himself gently and the men slid down his back to the sand. He left them there and flew to the rock, and with his strong beak pried a chiton from its surface. Now if any of you have ever examined the underside of a chiton,* you may begin to get an idea of what the Raven had in his devious, libidinous mind. He threw back his head and flung the chiton at the nearest of the men. His aim was as unerring as only that of a great magician's can be, and the chiton found its mark in the delicate groin area of the shellborn creature, where it attached itself firmly. As rapidly as spray falls on the shore after the breaking of a wave, the Raven showered the rest of the group with chitons, each inexorably flying to its own target.

Nothing remotely like this had ever happened to the men during their long childhood in the clamshell. They were astounded, embarrassed, confused by a rush of new sensations, emotional and physical. They became more and more agitated, uncertain whether it was pain or pleasure or both they were experiencing. They threw themselves on the beach and suddenly a great storm seemed to break over them, followed just as suddenly by an intense calm. One by one, the chitons dropped off. The men staggered to their feet and began slowly to walk down the beach, followed by the raucous laughter of the Raven which re-echoed all the way to the great island to the north which we now call Prince of Wales.

They eventually disappeared behind the nearest headland and passed out of the games of the Raven and the story of mankind. Whether they found their way back to the shell or lived out their lives elsewhere, or perished in the strange environment in which they found themselves, nobody remembers or cares. They had played their parts and gone their way.

Meanwhile, the chitons had been making their way back to the rock where they attached themselves as before. But they too had been changed. As high tide followed low, and the great storms of winter gave way to the softer rains and warm sun of spring, the chitons grew, many times larger than their kind had ever been before. It seemed as though their jointed shells were about to fly apart from enormous pressure inside them. And one day a huge wave swept over the rock and tore them from their footholds and carried them to the beach. As the water receded, the warm sun dried the sand, and soon there was a great stirring among the chitons. From each emerged a brown-skinned, black-haired human, and this time there were both males and females, and the Raven could begin his greatest game, one that still goes on.

THE HAIDA LEGEND OF THE RAVEN AND THE FIRST HUMANS (REID)

---

*A chiton is a kind of mollusk that adheres strongly to rocks.

## DECEMBER 1

### *Raven and the First Humans—Part 3*

No timid shell dwellers these, children of the wild coast, born between the sea and the land, to challenge the strength of the stormy North Pacific and wrest from it a rich livelihood. Their descendants would build on its beaches the strong, beautiful homes of the Haida and embellish them with the powerful heraldic carvings that told of the legendary beginnings of the great families, all the heroes and heroines, the gallant beasts and monsters that shaped their world and their destinies. For many, many generations they grew and flourished, built and created, fought and destroyed, lived according to the changing seasons and the unchanging rituals of their rich and complex lives.

It's nearly over now. Most of the villages are abandoned and in ruins. The people who remain are changed. The sea has lost much of its richness and great areas of the land itself lie in waste. Perhaps it's time that the Raven or someone found a way to start again.

THE HAIDA LEGEND OF THE RAVEN AND THE FIRST HUMANS (REID)

## DECEMBER 2

### *Kala Creates the Sea*

Before the first sunrise, all was darkness. The surface of the earth was smooth and without feature. No hills, valleys or watercourses broke its surface, no trees covered its nakedness, no calls of birds punctuated its silence.

Then, during those far-off times, Mudungkala, old and blind, rose out of the ground. She carried three infants in her arms: a boy and two girls. No one knows from where she came—nor, after she had finished the creation of the land of the Tiwis, to what place she went.

Crawling on her hands and knees, she began to travel northward in a wide arc. The water that bubbled up in her track became Dundas Strait, the swiftflowing channel that now separates the east coast of Melville Island from the mainland.

Then she turned westward, forming the northern shores of Melville Island and making occasional journeys inland to create bays and rivers. And so she continued, her track becoming the waterways of the land, until she reached her starting point. On her last journey she created Clarence Strait, thus completely separating the land of the Tiwis from the rest of Australia.

KALA CREATES THE SEA (ROBERTS)

## DECEMBER 3

### The First Birth

Long before the dawn of time, the earth was uninhabited. There was no light, no living creature, not even a blade of grass to disturb that dim, featureless immensity.

Then, at some time during the period of darkness, an old blind woman, Mudungkala, rose out of the ground somewhere on southeast Melville Island. She clasped in her arms three infants: two girls, Wuriupranala and Murupiangkala, and a boy, Purukupali. She had come to create the land of the Tiwis.

Carrying her children, she crawled along the land, in the process forming all the watercourses. When she had finished she disappeared. But before she left, she decreed that the bare land she had created should be clothed with vegetation and populated with creatures so that her children, whom she was leaving behind, and the generations to come, should have ample food and shelter.

And so her two daughters and son established themselves in the new land. Purukupali visited the homes of the spirit-children and brought some of them back to his sisters so that they could become mothers. Thus Mudungkala's family multiplied.

The creation of the peoples of the world had begun.

THE FIRST BIRTH (ROBERTS)

## DECEMBER 4

### Origin of the Platypus

Naruni, youngest and most beautiful woman in her tribe, had been promised in marriage to a tribal elder. But she was attracted to the younger and more attractive Kuralka, who persuaded her to run away with him to the hill country. After many months the pair became conscience-stricken and returned to the tribe in disgrace. Naruni was transformed into a duck, and Kuralka was punished by being changed into a giant water-rat. Both were banished to a far-distant river.

Rejected by the land of her people, Naruni in due course hatched two eggs. To her horror, she found that they did not contain ducklings, but strange creatures with bodies of fur, webbed feet and duckbills. So great was Naruni's disappointment, and so strong was her yearning for the solid ground and her lost tribal life, that she pined away and died. But her two children thrived in their watery home, and multiplied to establish the platypus family.

This is how the Aborigines explained the origin of the platypus to the early settlers of New South Wales, Australia. They also described its habits and how it reproduced. When the first platypus skin was shown to European scientists it caused a sensation, and they were so astonished that they said the beak and the feet of a water bird had been sewn to the skin of some animal. After that, controversy raged for eighty years over how the platypus produced its young, until it was proved that the creature laid eggs and suckled its offspring. This strange link in the biological chain is unique to Australia.

The myth that explains the origin of the platypus is characteristic of the way Aborigines used fantasy to account for natural phenomena which, later, were to baffle European scientists for many years.

ORIGIN OF THE PLATYPUS (ROBERTS)

*The unusual, the different, the puzzling—all are inherent in nature. Yet why do human beings so often have difficulty accepting that which is different or unusual? Instead of dismissing the different, wouldn't we do better to try to accept it as natural even if we do not fully understand it?*

## DECEMBER 5

### The Blessing of Fire

One of the many variations on the origin of fire is the Aboriginal myth which relates how in the beginning there was no warmth and the only light was from the stars. This was the way of life for the Aborigines until the time came when a man and his wife, after a heavy thunderstorm, saw a strange glow where a bolt of lightning had struck an old log.

Puzzled by this weird sight, they covered it with bark in an attempt to hide it, but the bark suddenly burst into flame. This frightened them so much that they went to their tribal chief, a noted man of magic, and asked him to destroy the unknown thing they had found.

But when they returned to the now blazing log, and felt the comfort of its warmth, the chief realized that his companions had found something that would give his people light to dispel their darkness, and heat to keep them warm.

He gave a large torch of blazing wood to the woman and a smaller torch to the man, and so that the twin blessings of light and warmth would never be lost he sent them up into the sky to become the sun and the moon. He divided the rest of the burning log among the members of the tribe, and told them to place a coal in every tree so that the spirit of fire would always be available to everyone.

With fire to cook their food, keep them warm and light their darkness, life suddenly became so much easier that the Aborigines increased in numbers and gradually spread over their new land. The use of fire not only altered man's way of life, but set him apart from the rest of creation as nothing else could have done.

THE BLESSING OF FIRE (ROBERTS)

## DECEMBER 6

### The Capture of the First Fire

One of the most important factors in Aboriginal life was fire and its benefits. There are many different stories explaining how it was first obtained. Some stories say that a bird brought it to the people, others describe a tribesman's dangerous journey to obtain fire from a burning mountain, and in some myths the gift of fire resulted from lightning setting fire to a tree.

Most fire-myth variations share common themes of greed and reprisal. There is a selfish person who discovers the secret of fire, but keeps it to himself, and there are those who use courage and ingenuity to take it from him so that it can be shared.

A fire-myth from the Murrumbidgee region is typical of this construction. It tells how Goodah, a noted magician, captured a piece of lightning as it struck a dead tree during a storm. He imprisoned it as a convenient way to make fire for his own use, and ignored demands that he share this wonderful discovery.

At last the tribe became so enraged with Goodah that a group of elders called up a whirlwind just when Goodah had made a fire with his piece of lightning. The whirlwind picked up the fire and scattered it all over the country, and fire became common property when members of the tribe gathered up enough burning wood to make fires for themselves.

To escape the jeers and laughter of the tribe, Goodah fled to the hills to sulk, and to plan revenge.

THE CAPTURE OF THE FIRST FIRE (ROBERTS)

## DECEMBER 7

### The Fighting Brothers

Long ago, on what is now known as the western coast of Victoria, Australia, there lived two brothers who had hunted and fished together since childhood. Pupadi, the elder, was the one who always speared the most game, knew the best fishing spots, and was looked upon as the camp favourite. Gerdang, the younger, secretly resented his secondary role. His jealousy increased when Pupadi took a wife, because she was the woman Gerdang most desired.

Gerdang's longing for his brother's wife became so fierce that he begged her to run away with him. When she refused, Gerdang took her by force and carried her far to the east, where a great shelf of rock runs into the sea.

Pupadi returned from hunting, and realized what had taken place because he was aware of Gerdang's envy. In a violent rage he followed their tracks and found his wife and brother. He attacked Gerdang, and they fought for many hours until the younger brother ran into a scrub and hid. Pupadi climbed a rock to gain a better view, but Gerdang circled behind him and threw a boomerang with such force that it buried itself deep between his brother's shoulder-blades and knocked him into the bushes at the cliff's edge.

Reckless with triumph, and expecting to find his brother dead, Gerdang leapt into the bushes. But Pupadi, calling on the last of his strength, lay on his stomach with his spear held upwards. Gerdang jumped straight unto it, to die with the barbed point sticking out through his back.

The impact carried them over the cliff, and Pupadi fell into the sea and became the shark. The big fin on his back is his brother's boomerang, still deeply embedded. Gerdang hit a shelf rock with such force that his body was flattened, and in this form the tide carried it away as the stingray, with Pupadi's spear changed into the barbed sting at the base of the tail. The blowholes along the clifftop were made by the stamping feet of the fighting brothers.

THE FIGHTING BROTHERS (ROBERTS)


*Fighting brothers—a common theme! The stories abound in many cultures, not just in the well-known Hebrew tales of Cain and Abel, Jacob and Esau. Instead of killing one another, how can we find the Tao of conflict resolution?*


## DECEMBER 8

### Banishment of the Goanna

There have always been mean and selfish people, even among the Aborigines who first lived in Australia. This myth relates how the selfish Goanna-men were outwitted by their wives, the Gecko-women.

During a great drought, the Goanna-men had a secret waterhole which they would share with no-one but their own tribe. But their wives, seeing so many others, young and old, dying of thirst, determined to find the waterhole in order that everyone could share it.

So the wives told their men that one of the women—who was actually hiding in the hills—had been stolen by a stranger. The Goanna-men immediately suspected the men of the neighbouring Emu tribe and set off to do battle with them.

With their men out of the way, the women began their search. They were aided in this by a magical stick given to one of them the previous night by her dead grandmother—for the dead sometimes help living relatives who are in serious trouble.

When they found the spring that fed the waterhole, the women drove the stick deep into the opening in the hillside. Immediately the water poured out in a torrent to form a huge river, and all the people from the tribes drank their fill of the sweet liquid.

The evil Goanna-men were enraged—they had lost not only their secret waterhole, but their power to hurt others. The Gecko-women climbed to the top of a large gum tree where, to escape their husbands' wrath, they changed themselves into the little gecko lizards that live under the bark of trees today.

For their sins, the spirits banished the men from the area, destined to live forever as goannas in the great red sandhills and the dry open plains.

This story was told to Aboriginal children to teach them that water belongs to everybody, and that those who disobey this law must be punished.

BANISHMENT OF THE GOANNA (ROBERTS)

## DECEMBER 9

*The Weeping Opal*

A myth of central Queensland (Australia) relates that in the days of the Dreamtime, when the world was young and the great creation events were taking place, a giant opal ruled over the destinies of men and women.

This ancestral being lived in the sky, made the laws under which the tribes should live, and dictated the punishments to be inflicted on law-breakers.

The creation of this Aboriginal ancestor came about as a result of a war between two tribes. The fighting had gone on for so long that, at last, the combatants had broken or lost all their weapons. So they began hurling boulders at each other, and a tribesman threw one so hard that it flew upwards and lodged in the sky.

The boulder grew rapidly as the frightened warriors watched, until it burst open and revealed the flashing colours of a huge opal. The opal saw the dead and wounded warriors lying on the ground below, and it wept in sorrow.

Tears streamed from the opal in such profusion that they became a great rainstorm, and when the sun shone on the opal-coloured tears the Aborigines saw their first rainbow.

From that time on, the Aborigines of the area believed the rainbow to be a sign that someone had committed a crime against the tribal laws laid down so long ago, and that the tears of opal were again falling in sorrow.

THE WEEPING OPAL (ROBERTS)

*The rainbow symbol appears at the end of the story of Noah and the flood as a sign of the covenant between God and people. It continually speaks to people as a symbol of unity and harmony. In recent years we have in this country the Rainbow Nation with its annual gatherings around the Fourth of July, the Rainbow Coalition seeking to bring all people together, and the Rainbow flag affirming all people and sexual orientations.*

*A rainbow is a bridge, a colorful way of connecting us with one another.*

# Hun Tun in Creating

↔

## DECEMBER 10

### We Exist in This World Like Fish

We exist in this world like fish. The adversary spies on us, lying in wait for us like a fisherman, wishing to seize us, rejoicing that he might swallow us. For he places many foods before our eyes, things which belong to this world. He wishes to make us desire one of them and to taste only a little, so that he may seize us with his hidden poison and bring us out of freedom and take into slavery. For whenever he catches us with a single food, it is necessary for us to desire to rest. Finally, then, such things become the food of death.

Now these are the foods with which the devil lies in wait for us. First he injects a pain into your heart until you have heartache on account of a small thing of this life, and he seizes you with his poisons. And afterwards he injects the desire of a tunic so that you will pride yourself in it, and love of money, pride, vanity, envy that rivals another envy, beauty of body, fraudulence. The greatest of all these are ignorance and ease.

Now all such things the adversary prepares beautifully and spreads out before the body, wishing to make the mind of the soul incline her toward one of them and overwhelm her, like a hook drawing her by force in ignorance, deceiving her until she conceives evil, and bears fruit of matter, and conducts herself in uncleanness, pursuing many desires, covetousness, while fleshly pleasure draws her in ignorance.

But the soul—she who has tasted these things—realized that sweet passions are transitory.

AUTHORITATIVE TEACHING (ROBINSON, 3D ED.)

*Western thought looks at what goes on in the world and sees what is commonly called the problem of evil. If creation and the Creator are good, why is there so much injustice, pain, and suffering?*

*Some minds see order and chaos as mutually exclusive opposites and would choose to affirm order and seek to be rid of chaos; one is good and the other bad. In contrast, the Chinese concept of hun tun (pronounced "hoon toon") is that order and chaos exist together simultaneously and cannot be separated. In the midst of order is chaos, and in the midst of chaos is order. Attempts to destroy chaos are futile, because the chaos, ironically, contains the emerging new order. Our task is to learn ways of recognizing and accepting hun tun.*

## DECEMBER 11

### Interfering with the Tao

In harmony with the Tao,
the sky is clear and spacious,
the earth is solid and full,
all creatures flourish together,
content with the way they are,
endlessly repeating themselves,
endlessly renewed.

When human beings interfere with the Tao,
the sky becomes filthy,

the earth becomes depleted,
the equilibrium crumbles,
creatures become extinct.

The Master views the parts with compassion,
because he understands the whole.
His constant practice is humility,
He doesn't glitter like a jewel
but lets himself be shaped by the Tao,
as rugged and common as a stone.

TAO TE CHING, 39 (MITCHELL)

## DECEMBER 12

### *Eternal Questions*

Men, who have the form which God molded in his image, why do you wander in vain, and not walk the path of the Way ever mindful of the Eternal Creator?

SIBYLLINE ORACLES, BOOK 3, LINES 8–9 (CHARLESWORTH)

*Why chaos in the midst of order? Why hun tun? Why do people not follow the Way of the Tao? Why suffering? Why injustice? Why me? The questions go on and on. Answers of various kinds abound in the writings and hearts of people of all ages. Are there definitive answers, or only perennial questions and provisional answers?*

## December 13
---

### *The Logos Is Embarrassed*

In the manner of a reflection are they beautiful. For the face of the copy normally takes its beauty from that of which it is a copy.

They thought of themselves that they are beings existing by themselves and are without a source, since they do not see anything else existing before them. Therefore, they live in disobedience and acts of rebellion, without having humbled themselves before the one because of whom they came into being. They wanted to command one another, overcoming one another in their vain ambition, while the glory which they possess contains a cause of the system which was to be.

They are likeness of the things which are exalted. They are brought to a lust of power in each one of them, according to the greatness of the name of which each is a shadow, each one imagining that it is superior to his fellows. The thought of these others was not barren, but just like those of which they are shadows, all that they thought about they had as offspring. Therefore it happened that many offspring came forth from them, as fighters, as warriors, as troublemakers, as apostates. They are disobedient beings, lovers of power.

The Logos was a cause of those who came into being and he continued all the more to be at a loss and he was embarrassed and astonished. Instead of perfection, he saw a defect; instead of unification, he saw division; instead of stability, he saw disturbances; instead of rests, tumults.

TRIPARTITE TRACTATE (ROBINSON, 1977)


*If you feel that facing the questions is difficult for you, how do you think it must be for the Logos, the Tao?*

# *Hope for Reconciling in the Tao*

☙

*Pandora's Box*

Pandora is the name of woman made in heaven. The name means "all's gift." After Zeus had wrapped her in a robe of innocence, other gods placed flowers in her hair.

Before Pandora left heaven, Zeus made the gods give her a box with a surprise inside. "She won't be able to stop herself from looking in the box," Zeus said.

It was Apollo who gave Pandora the present from Zeus. "The great God sends this box," he said. Then he whispered to her, "Pandora, don't ever, ever open it!"

"Oh, I won't if you say not to," she said to Apollo. Pandora was so shy and as good as she could be. But she had one weakness which put a shadow in her eyes. She was curious about everything. Pandora had to look into all she saw. She had to touch this jar and that bottle.

"Oh!" she would exclaim, seeing something new. And she would peer under its cover and breathe deeply of its scent in order to know what it was.

"One look in the box, perhaps," she said to Venus, smiling her winning smile. "Just to see what might be inside?"

"No! No!" warned Venus. "Never, never look inside the box!"

"Pandora, Zeus made us give it to you. He swore us to a terrible fate if we told you what was inside," Apollo said. "All we can do is give you fair warning."

"Yes, I heed the warning. I will not look," said Pandora. But she thought that somehow she must find a way to see what was inside the box. . . .

All of the days she was with Epimetheus, she waited for a time when both he and Prometheus were away. Then she wandered around the making shop. She looked at all the molds for making man that were now rusting, for man was made and doing well on earth. Finally her eyes rested on the box, high up on the shelf. She climbed the stool and stood on the very tips of her toes, but she could not reach the box.

"I know," she said, "I will put something sturdy on the stool. She climbed up on the chest. Unsteadily, she stood on her toes, peering at the box.

"Just to bring it down and shake it and listen to it," she murmured to herself. "I won't open it. I promised I wouldn't."

"Oh! Oh!" cried Pandora, stepping down before she, too, fell. The lid of the box came off and sailed through the air. The box tumbled. As it did, there was a great jumble of noise—roars and screams, howls and cries. For a moment the room was dark.

"What? Oh! No!" screamed Pandora.

For out of the box came awful things, the gifts of Zeus. Winged things and crawling things. Slithering things and creeping things, bringing with them a slime of dark and gray despair. Some creatures had pointed ears; some had flat, furry heads. Some had wicked eyes. Some were fanged, with scaly arms and hands. Some were tiny. Others were giant size. There were plagues of sorrow and pain. There was misery, holding its dripping head. Envy took hold of Pandora and tried to tear her hair out. Poverty slid hungrily across the floor and melted into the air.

Pandora flung herself at the box. She caught the lid and managed to fit it on.

But it was too late. All of the awful things were out of the box. They clamored through the house and on and out into the street, the town, the whole world, it seemed.

There was one thing left quivering on the floor. It was a small thing. It must have been on the very bottom of the box. It was not as musty-smelling or as damp and horrible as the rest had been. To Pandora, its scent was quite sweet.

"You're not a bad one, I can tell," she said to it. "You're hurt, aren't you?" she asked it, swallowing her fear.

It didn't answer, so sick it seemed.

"Here, let me help you," she said. Pandora took hold of the thing by its wings. It felt warm, trembling. She could see its great heart swell and sink in its chest.

It sat up and rested against her.

"There, there," soothed Pandora. "That's better. Now tell me who you are."

"Ahhhh," sighed the thing. "I must go!" It rose weakly to its crooked feet.

"No, don't go," Pandora pleaded. "I need company. It is so lonely here."

"If I do not go, what will become of humans without me?"

"But who are you?" Pandora asked.

The thing smiled a wan smile. It seemed to gather strength within. Its brightly colored wings unfolded, bringing a fresh breeze.

"I am Hope," it said. "If I do not hurry, humans will have so little reason to live." With one great leap, Hope sprang from the room, from the house, and into the world. Pandora stood at the door holding the empty box from Zeus in her hands. She saw Hope gather light around it, brightening the day.

PANDORA'S BOX (HAMILTON)

## DECEMBER 15

*Adam's Deathbed Hope for CoCreators*

Adam said to his son, Seth, "You have heard, my son, that God is going to come into the world after a long time, he will be conceived of a virgin and put on a body, be born like a human being, and grow up as a child. He will perform signs and wonders on the earth, will walk on the waves of the sea. He will rebuke the winds and they will be silenced. He will motion to the waves and they will stand still. He will open the eyes of the blind and cleanse the lepers.

"He will cause the deaf to hear, and the mute to speak. He will straighten the hunchbacked, strengthen the paralyzed, find the lost, drive out evil spirits, and cast out demons.

"He spoke to me about this in Paradise after I picked some of the fruit in which death was hiding: 'Adam, Adam do not fear. You wanted to be a god; I will make you a god, not right now, but after a space of many years. I am consigning you to death, and the maggot and the worm will eat your body.'

"And I answered and said to him, 'Why, my Lord?' And he said to me, 'Because you listened to the words of the serpent, you and your posterity will be food for the serpent. But after a short time there will be mercy on you because you were created in my image, and I will not leave you to waste away in Sheol.

" 'For your sake I will be born of the Virgin Mary. For your sake I will taste death and enter the house of the dead. For your sake I will make a new heaven, and I will be established over your posterity. And after three days, while I am in the tomb, I will raise up the body I received from you. And I will set you at the right hand of my divinity. And I will make you a god just like you wanted. And I will receive favor from God and I will restore to you and to your posterity that which is the justice of heaven. . . .' "

And I, Seth, wrote this testament. And my father died, and they buried him at the east of Paradise opposite the first city built on the earth, which was named after Enoch. And Adam was borne to his grave by the angels and powers of heaven because he had been created in the image of God. And the sun and the moon were darkened, and there was thick darkness for seven days.

And we sealed the testament and we put it in the cave with the treasures with the offerings Adam had taken out of Paradise, gold and myrrh and frankincense. And the sons of kings, the magi, will come and get them, and they will take them to the son of God, to Bethlehem of Judea, to the cave.

TESTAMENT OF ADAM, CHAPTER 3 (CHARLESWORTH)

*Notice that the hope lies in a cave.*

## DECEMBER 16

### *An Interpretation of Jacob's Ladder Dream*

And as for the angels you saw descending and ascending the ladder, in the last years there will be a man from the Most High, and he will desire to join the upper [things] with the lower. And before his coming your sons and daughters will tell about him and your young men will have visions about him.

Such will be the signs at the time of his coming.

A tree cut with an ax will bleed, three-month-old babes will speak understanding; a baby in the womb of his mother will speak this way; a youth will be like an old man. And then the unexpected will come, whose path will not be noticed by anyone.

Then the earth will be glorified, receiving heavenly glory. What was above will be below also. And from your seed will bloom a root of kings;

it will emerge and overthrow the power of Eve. And he himself will be the Savior for every land and rest for those who toil, and a cloud shading the whole world from the burning heat. For otherwise the uncontrolled will not be controlled. If he does not come, the lower [things] cannot be joined with the upper.

At his coming the idols of brass, stone, and any sort of carving will give voice for three days. They will give wise men news of him and let them know what will be on earth. By a star, those who wish to see on earth him whom the angels do not see above will find the way to him.

Then the Almighty will be on earth in body, and embraced by corporeal arms, he will restore human nature. And he will revive Eve, who died by the fruit of the tree. Then the deceit of the impious will be exposed and all the idols will fall face down. For they will be put to shame by a dignitary. For because [they were] lying by means of hallucinations, henceforth they will not be able to rule or prophesy. Honor will be taken from them and they will remain without glory.

For he who comes will take power and might and will give Abraham the truth which he previously told him. Everything sharp he will make dull, and the rough will be smooth. And he will cast all the iniquitous into the depths of the sea. He will work wonders in heaven and on earth. And he will be wounded in the midst of his beloved house. And when he is wounded, then salvation will be ready, and the end to all perdition. For those who have wounded him will themselves receive a wound which will not be cured in them forever. And all creation will bow to him who was wounded, and many will trust in him. And he will become known everywhere in all lands, and those who acknowledge his name will not be ashamed. His own dominion and years will be unending forever.

LADDER OF JACOB 7:1–35 (CHARLESWORTH)

*The ladder connects heaven and earth, the human and the divine, the conscious and the unconscious of every person. Make use of the ladder!*

## DECEMBER 17

### *Jacob's Psalm of Praise After His Ladder Dream*

Lord God of Adam your creature and Lord God of Abraham and Isaac my fathers and of all who have walked before you in justice! You sit firmly on the cherubim and the fiery throne of Glory

and the many-eyed [ones] just as I saw in my dream,

Holding the four-faced cherubim, bearing also the many-eyed seraphim,

carrying the whole world under your arm, yet not being borne by anyone;

you who have made the skies firm for the glory of your name, stretching out on two heavenly clouds the heavens which gleam under you, that beneath it you may cause the sun to course and conceal it during the night so that they too might not seem gods.

Before the face of your glory the six-winged seraphim are afraid, and they cover their genitals and faces with their wings, while flying with their other wings, and they sing unceasingly a hymn: . . .

Twelve-crested, twelve-faced, many-named, fiery one! Lightning-eyed holy one! Holy, Holy, Holy, Yao, Yaova, Yaoil, Yao, Kados, Chavod, Savaoth,

Omlemlech il avir amismi varich, eternal king, mighty, powerful, most great, patient, blessed one! You who fill heaven and earth, the sea and abysses and all the ages with your glory, hear my song which I sing to you and grant me the request I ask of you. Tell me the interpretation of my dream, for you are a god who is mighty, powerful and glorious, a god who is holy; my Lord and Lord of my fathers.

LADDER OF JACOB 2:6–22 (CHARLESWORTH)

## DECEMBER 18

*Advent of Christ*

Then indeed the son of the great God will come, incarnate, likened to mortal men on earth. . . . Consider in your heart Christ, the son of the most high, immortal God. He will fulfill the law of God—not destroy it—bearing a likeness which corresponds to types, and he will teach everything.

Priests will bring gifts to him, bringing forward gold, myrrh, and incense. For he will also do all these things.

But when a certain voice will come through the desert land bringing tidings to mortals, and will cry out to all to make the paths straight and cast away evils from the heart, and that every human person may be illumined by waters, so that being born from above they may no longer in any respect at all transgress justice—but a man with barbarous mind, enslaved to dances will cut out this voice and give it as a reward—then there will suddenly be a sign to mortals when a beautiful stone which has been preserved will come from the land of Egypt. Against this the people of the Hebrews will stumble. But the gentiles will be gathered under his leadership. For they will also recognize God who rules on high on account of this man's path in common light.

For he will show eternal life to chosen men but will bring fire upon the lawless for all ages. Then indeed he will cure the sick and all who are blemished, as many as put faith in him. The blind will see, the lame will walk. The deaf will hear. Those who cannot speak will speak. He will drive out demons. There will be a resurrection of the dead. He will walk the waves, and in a desert place he will satisfy five thousand from five loaves and a fish of the sea, and the leftovers of these will fill twelve baskets for the hope of the peoples.

SIBYLLINE ORACLES, BOOK 1, LINES 324–55 (CHARLESWORTH)

## DECEMBER 19

### *Sybil on the Incarnation*

In the last times he changed the earth and, coming late as a new light, he rose from the womb of the Virgin Mary. Coming from heaven, he put on a mortal form. First, then Gabriel was revealed in his strong and holy person. Second, the archangel also addressed the maiden in speech:

"Receive God, Virgin, in your immaculate bosom." Thus speaking, he breathed in the grace of God, even to one who was always a maiden. Fear and, at the same time, wonder seized her as she listened. She stood trembling. Her mind fluttered while her heart was shaken by the unfamiliar things she heard.

But again she rejoiced, and her heart was healed by the voice. The maiden laughed and reddened her cheek, rejoicing with joy and enchanted in her heart with awe. Courage also came over her. A word flew to her womb. In time it was made flesh and came to life in the womb, and was fashioned in mortal form and became a boy by virgin birth.

For this is a great wonder to men, but nothing is a great wonder for God the Father and God the Son. The joyful earth fluttered to the child at its birth. The heavenly throne laughed and the world rejoiced. A wondrous, new shining star was venerated by Magi. The newborn child was revealed in a manger to those who obey God: cowherds and goatherds and shepherd of sheep. And Bethlehem was said to be the divinely named homeland of the Word.

SIBYLLINE ORACLES, BOOK 10, LINES 456–79 (CHARLESWORTH)

# Nativity Stories

*Rebirthing the Tao*

*Birth of Melchizedek*

*Mythic stories specialize in impossible births: Either the woman is past menopause, too old to have a child, or a virgin, too young and inexperienced. This story adds yet another component: A child is born from a woman who has died. Can new life come out of even death?*

*The child born is Melchizedek, the same name as the priest who was with Abraham and Sarah, a priestess of the fertility religion preceding the patriarchal god. This priesthood is more rooted in the natural Way of the Tao.*

*The New Testament epistle of Hebrews focuses on Christ as from the "order of Melchizedek." All these great symbols converge in the one through whom the healing of ancient splits begins.*

*If you try to understand this story literally, your credulity will be stretched beyond belief. But if you take it symbolically, you will find tremendous potential and meaning.*

Behold, the wife of Nir, whose name was Sopanim, being sterile and never having at any time given birth to a child by Nir. And Sopanim was in the time of her old age, and in the day of her death. She conceived in her womb, but Nir the priest had not slept with her, nor had he touched her, from the day that the Lord had appointed him to conduct the liturgy in front of the face of the people. And when Sopanim saw her pregnancy, she was ashamed and embarrassed, and she hid herself during all the days until she gave birth. And not one of the people knew about it.

And when 282 days had been completed, and the day of birth had begun to approach, and Nir remembered his wife, and he called her to himself in his house, so that he might converse with her. And Sopanim came to Nir, her husband; and behold, she was pregnant, and the day appointed for giving birth was drawing near. And Nir saw her, and he became very ashamed. And he said to her, "What is this that you have done, O wife? And why have you disgraced me in front of the face of these people? And now, depart from me, and go where you began the disgrace of your womb, so that I might not defile my hand on account of you, and sin in front of the face of the Lord."

And Sopanim spoke to Nir, her husband, saying, "O my lord! Behold, it is the time of my old age, and the day of my death has arrived. I do not understand how my menopause and the barrenness of my womb has been reversed." And Nir did not believe his wife, and for the second time he said to her, "Depart from me, or else I might assault you, and commit a sin in front of the face of the Lord."

And it came to pass, when Nir had spoken to his wife, Sopanim, that Sopanim fell down at Nir's feet and died. Nir was extremely distressed; and he said in his heart, "Could this have happened because of my word, since by word and thought a person can sin in front of the face of the Lord? Now may God have mercy upon me! I know in truth in my heart that my hand was not upon her. And so I say, Glory to you, O Lord, because no one among mankind knows about this deed which the Lord has done."

And Nir hurried, and he shut the door of his house, and he went to Noe his brother, and he reported to him everything that had happened in connection with his wife.

And Noe hurried. He came with Nir his brother; he came into Nir's house, because of the death of Sopanim, and they discussed between themselves how her womb was at the time of giving birth. And Noe said to Nir, "Don't let yourself be sorrowful, Nir, my brother! For the Lord this day has covered up your scandal, in that nobody from the people knows this. Now, let us go quickly and let us bury her secretly, and the Lord will cover up the scandal of our shame."

And they placed Sopanim on the bed, and they wrapped her around with black garments, and shut her in the house, prepared for burial. They dug a grave in secret. And a child came out from the dead Sopanim. And he sat on the bed at her side. And Noe and Nir came in to bury Sopanim, and they saw the child sitting beside the dead Sopanim, and wiping his clothing. And Noe and Nir were very terrified with a great fear, because the child was fully developed physically, like a three-year-old. And he spoke with his lips, and he blessed the Lord.

And Noe and Nir looked at him, and behold, the badge of priesthood was on his chest, and it was glorious in appearance. And Noe and Nir said, "Behold, God is renewing his priesthood from blood related to us, just as he pleases." And Noe and Nir hurried, and they washed the child, and they dressed him in the garments of priesthood, and they gave him holy bread and he ate it. And they called his name Melchizedek.

And Noe and Nir lifted up the body of Sopanim, and divested her of the black garments, and they washed her, and they dressed her in exceptionally bright garments, and they built a shrine for her. Noe and Nir and Melchizedek came, and they buried her publicly.

And Noe said to his brother Nir, "Look after this child in secret until the time, because people will become treacherous in all the earth, and they will begin to turn away from God, and having become totally ignorant, they will put him to death."

And then Noe went away to his own place.

2 ENOCH 71:1–23 (CHARLESWORTH)

## DECEMBER 21, WINTER SOLSTICE

### Mary's Time for Delivery Approaches

*On the winter solstice, the shortest day and longest night of the year, we begin the wonderful story of the birth of the child in a cave.*

*There are three main nativity stories about Jesus. In Matthew's version, the child is born in a house to which the wise men come. In Luke's version, the child is born in a stable to which the shepherds come. And in this story from the Infancy Gospel of James, the child is born in a cave, a natural womb of Mother Earth. Adam's deathbed hope is being lived out.*

*A house, a stable, a cave—each setting for the birth conveys its own special symbolic context: the familiar, the earthy, the deeply centered. Likewise the rebirth of anyone can occur in a variety of contexts: at home in familiar surroundings, out in nature, or anytime and anyplace where you are in touch with the life within you.*

Now an order came from the Emperor Augustus to enroll everybody in Bethlehem of Judea in the census. And Joseph wondered, "I will enroll my sons, but what am I going to do with this child? How will I enroll her? As my wife? I am ashamed to do that. Or as my daughter? My countrymen know she's not my daughter. This event will turn out the way the Lord wants it to."

And so he saddled his donkey and had her get on it. His son led it and Samuel brought up the rear. As they neared the three mile marker, Joseph turned around and saw that she was upset. And he said to himself, "Perhaps the child she is carrying is causing her discomfort." And Joseph turned around again and saw her laughing and said to her, "Mary, what is going on with you? One minute you're laughing and the next minute you're upset."

And she replied, "Joseph, it is because I imagine two peoples in front of me, one weeping and mourning and the other celebrating and jumping for joy."

Halfway through the trip Mary said to him, "Joseph, help me down from the donkey because the child inside me is about to be born."

And he helped her down and said to her, "Where will I take you to give you some privacy, since this place is out in the open?"

INFANCY GOSPEL OF JAMES 17:1–11 (MILLER)

*Laughing one moment, sad the next—how true of the process of birth and rebirth!*

## DECEMBER 22

### Birth of the Child in a Cave

Joseph found a cave nearby and took her inside. He stationed his sons to guard her and went to look for a Hebrew midwife in the country around Bethlehem.

"Now I, Joseph, was walking along and yet not going anywhere. I looked up at the vault of the sky and saw it standing still, and then at the wind, and saw it arrested in amazement; and the birds of the sky stopped in mid-air. As I looked on the earth, I saw a bowl lying there and workers reclining around it with their hands in the bowl; some were chewing and yet did not chew; some were picking up something to eat and yet did not pick it up; and some were putting food in their mouths and yet did not do so. Instead, they were all looking upward.

"I saw sheep being driven along and yet the sheep stood still; the shepherd was lifting his hand to strike them, and yet his hand did not fall. And I observed the current of the river and saw goats with their mouths in the water and yet they were not drinking. And suddenly everything and everybody went on with what they were doing.

"And I saw a young woman coming down from the hill country, and she asked, 'Where are you going, sir?'

"And I replied, 'I am looking for a Hebrew midwife.'

"And she inquired, 'Are you an Israelite?'

"And I told her, 'Yes.'

"And she said, 'And who's the one having a baby in the cave?'

"And I said, 'My fiancee.'

"And she continued, 'She isn't your wife?'

"And I said to her, 'Her name is Mary, and she was raised in the temple of the Lord; I obtained her by lot as my wife. But she is not really my wife; she is pregnant by the holy spirit.'

"And the midwife said, 'Really?'

"And Joseph said, 'Come and see.' "

And she went with him. As she stood in front of the cave, a bright cloud overshadowed it. The midwife said, "Today I've really been privileged, because my eyes have seen a miracle in that salvation has come to Israel."

Suddenly the cloud withdrew from the cave and a great light appeared inside the cave, so that her eyes could not bear to look. And a little later that light receded until an infant became visible; he went and took the breast of his mother Mary.

Then the midwife shouted: "What a great day this is for me because I have seen this new miracle!"

INFANCY GOSPEL OF JAMES 18:1–19:18 (MILLER)

## DECEMBER 23

*Salome Does Not Believe a Virgin Has Borne a Child*

And the midwife left the cave and met Salome and said to her, "Salome, Salome, I have a new marvel to tell: a virgin has given birth, something physically impossible for a virgin!"

And Salome replied, "As the Lord my God lives, unless I insert my finger and examine her, I will never believe that a virgin has given birth."

The midwife entered and said, "Mary, position yourself for an examination. You are facing a serious test."

And so Mary, when she heard these instructions, positioned herself, and Salome inserted her finger into Mary. And then Salome cried aloud and said, "I am damned because of my transgression and my disbelief, since I have put the living God on trial. Look! I am losing my hand! It is being eaten by the flames!"

Then Salome fell on her knees in the presence of the Lord, with these words, "God of my ancestors, remember me because I am a descendant of Abraham, Isaac, and Jacob. Do not make an example out of me for the people of Israel, but restore me to the poor. For you yourself know, Lord, that I have been healing people in your name and have been receiving my payments from you."

And suddenly a messenger of the Lord appeared, saying to her, "Salome, Salome, the Lord of all has heard your prayer. Hold out your hand to the child and pick him up, and then you'll have salvation and joy."

Salome approached the child and picked him up with these words, "I'll worship him because he has been born king on behalf of Israel." And Salome was instantly healed and left the cave vindicated.

Then a voice said abruptly, "Salome, Salome, don't report the marvels you have seen until the child goes to Jerusalem."

INFANCY GOSPEL OF JAMES 19:19–20:12 (MILLER)

*Doubt is a natural part of the process. Doubting our doubts moves us further along in the process toward new life.*

## DECEMBER 24

### *The Animals Come to the Child*

On the third day after the birth of our Lord Jesus Christ holy Mary went out from the cave, and went into a stable and put her child in a manger, and an ox and an ass worshipped him. Then was fulfilled that which was said through the prophet Isaiah: "The ox knows his owner and the ass his master's crib."

Thus the beasts, ox and ass, with him between them, unceasingly worshipped him. Then was fulfilled what was said through the prophet Habakkuk: "Between two beasts are you known." And Joseph remained in the same place with Mary for three days.

THE GOSPEL OF PSEUDO-MATTHEW 14
(HENNECKE AND SCHNEEMELCHER)

# Tao Becoming Flesh

❧

## DECEMBER 25, CHRISTMAS DAY

*The Tao Becomes Flesh and Dwells Among Us*

In the beginning was the Tao, and the Tao was with God, and the Tao was God. All things came into being through him, and without him not one thing came into being. What has come into being in him was Life, and the Life was the Light of all people. The light shines in darkness, and the darkness did not overcome it.

There was a man sent from God, whose name was John. He came as a witness to testify to the Light, so that all might believe through him. He himself was not the Light, but he came to testify to the Light. The true Light, which enlightens everyone, was coming into the world.

He was in the world, and the world came into being through him; yet the world did not know him. He came to what was his own, and his own people did not accept him. But to all who received him, who believed in his name, he gave power to become children of God, who were born, not of human stock or human desire or of human will, but of God.

And the Tao became flesh and lived among us, and we have seen his glory, the glory as of a father's only son, full of grace and truth. . . . From his fullness we have all received grace upon grace.

THE GOSPEL ACCORDING TO JOHN 1:1–16 (NEW REVISED STANDARD VERSION, WITH ADAPTATION BY WEE CHONG TAN)

*"In the beginning was the Tao." This is the very best translation possible. Conventional English translations read, "In the beginning was the Word." The Scholars version is better and translates, "In the beginning was the divine word and wisdom," which is more balanced but requires too many words. All are lacking the fullness of Tao.*

*When the English language fails us, the Chinese word* Tao *comes to our rescue, providing the single word we need.*

## DECEMBER 26, SECOND DAY OF CHRISTMAS

*In the Beginning Was the Tao*

In the beginning was the Tao,
All things issue from it;
all things return to it.

TAO TE CHING, 52 (MITCHELL)

All things under heaven had a common beginning,
    and that beginning could be considered
    the Mother of all things.
When you know the Mother,
    you will also know the children.
*Having known the children, we can return into the*
    *embrace of the Mother,*\*
    and to the end of your days,
    you will be free from danger. . . .
See the small and develop clear vision.
Practice yielding and develop strength.
Use the outer light to return to the inner light,

and save yourself from harm.
This is known as following the Always-so.

TAO TE CHING, 52 (MCCARROLL)

*Italics: Wee Chong Tan's translation.

## DECEMBER 27, THIRD DAY OF CHRISTMAS

### *Tao Is Like an Empty Bowl*

Tao is empty like a bowl.
It may be used but its capacity is never exhausted.
It is bottomless, perhaps the ancestor of all things.
It blunts its sharpness.
It unties its tangles.*
It softens its light.
It becomes one with the dusty world.
Deep and still, it appears to exist forever.
I do not know whose son it is.
It seems to have existed before the Lord.

TAO TE CHING, 4 (CHAN)

*It transcends conflicts (Wee Chong Tan's translation).

It is not there yet it is there.
I do not know whose Son it is,
Image proceeding before God.

TAO TE CHING, 4 (TAN, 1992)

# Nativity Stories

## Young Life in the Tao

✧

### DECEMBER 28, FOURTH DAY OF CHRISTMAS

---

#### *Circumcision and Naming*

After eight days had passed, it was time to circumcise the child; and he was called Jesus, the name given by the angel before he was conceived in the womb.

THE GOSPEL ACCORDING TO MATTHEW 2:21
(NEW REVISED STANDARD VERSION)

And when the time of his circumcision was come, namely, the eighth day, on which the law commanded the child to be circumcised, they circumcised him in the cave.

And the old Hebrew woman took the foreskin (others say she took the navel-string), and preserved it in an alabaster box of old oil of spikenard. And she had a son who was a druggist, to whom she said, Take heed thou sell not this alabaster box of spikenard ointment, even if you are offered three hundred pence for it.

Now this is the alabaster box which Mary the sinner procured, and poured forth the ointment out of it upon the head and the feet of our Lord Jesus Christ, and wiped it off with the hairs of her head.

THE FIRST GOSPEL OF THE INFANCY OF JESUS CHRIST (CRANE)

*Circumcision is an ancient way of marking permanently the ones who belong. Baptism, which is readily available to both females and males, serves a comparable function as a way of marking those who are entering into the Way of the Tao.*

### DECEMBER 29, FIFTH DAY OF CHRISTMAS

*Mother and Child Come to the Temple*

When the time came for their purification according to the law of Moses, they brought him up to Jerusalem to present him to the Lord (as it is written in the law of the Lord, "Every firstborn male shall be designated as holy to the Lord"), and they offered a sacrifice according to what is stated in the law of the Lord, "a pair of turtledoves or two young pigeons."

Now there was a man in Jerusalem whose name was Simeon; this man was righteous and devout, looking forward to the consolation of Israel, and the Holy Spirit rested on him. It had been revealed to him by the Holy Spirit that he would not see death before he had seen the Lord's Messiah. Guided by the Spirit, Simeon came into the temple; and when the parents brought in the child Jesus, to do for him what was customary under the law, Simeon took him in his arms and praised God, saying,

> "Lord, now lettest thou thy servant depart in peace,
>> according to thy word.
> For mine eyes have seen thy salvation
> Which thou hast prepared before the face of all people;
> To be a light to lighten the Gentiles
> and to be the glory of thy people Israel."

And the child's father and mother were amazed at what was being said about him. Then Simeon blessed them and said to his mother, Mary, "This child is destined for the falling and the rising of many in

Israel, and to be a sign that will be opposed so that the inner thoughts of many will be revealed—and a sword will pierce your own soul too."

There was also a prophet, Anna, the daughter of Phanuel, of the tribe of Asher. She was of a great age, having lived with her husband seven years after her marriage, then as a widow to the age of eighty-four. She never left the temple but worshiped there with fasting and prayer night and day. At that moment she came, and began to praise God and to speak about the child to all who were looking for the redemption of Jerusalem.

THE GOSPEL ACCORDING TO LUKE 2:22–38
(NEW REVISED STANDARD VERSION, EXCEPT SIMEON'S SONG,
WHICH IS FROM THE *BOOK OF COMMON PRAYER*, 1928 ED.)

## DECEMBER 30, SIXTH DAY OF CHRISTMAS

### The Visit of the Wise Men

Joseph was soon ready to depart for Judea, but a great disturbance took place in Bethlehem in Judea. Astrologers came inquiring, "Where is the king of the Jews? You see, we saw his star in the east and have come to pay him homage."

When Herod heard about their visit, he was terrified and sent agents to the astrologers. He also sent for the high priests and questioned them: "What has been written about the Anointed? Where is he supposed to be born?"

And they said to him, "In Bethlehem in Judea is what the scripture says."

And he dismissed the high priests. Then he questioned the astrologers: "What sign have you seen regarding the one who has been born king?"

And the astrologers said, "We saw a star of exceptional brilliance and it so dimmed the other stars that they disappeared. Consequently, we know that a king was born for Israel. And we have come to pay him homage."

Herod instructed them: "Go and begin your search, and if you find him, report back to me, so that I can also come and pay him homage."

The astrologers departed. Would you believe it, the star they had seen in the east went before them until they came to the cave; then the star stopped over the head of the child. After the astrologers saw him with his mother Mary, they took gold, frankincense, and myrrh out of their bag.

(Then the lady Mary took one of his swaddling cloths in which the infant was wrapped, and gave it to them instead of a blessing, which they received from her as a most noble present.)

Since they had been warned in a dream by the heavenly messengers not to go into Judea, they returned to their country by another route.

INFANCY GOSPEL OF JAMES 21:1–12 (MILLER;
SENTENCE IN PARENTHESES IS FROM THE FIRST GOSPEL
OF THE INFANCY OF JESUS CHRIST III:2 [CRANE])

*When the holy child is born, immediately there is an attempt to snuff out the new life. The archetypal story is found with the birth of Moses, Jesus, and other hero figures. Why does the structure in power fear the new life? Whenever an individual experiences a new birth, the former structure quickly seeks to kill it by doubt, criticism, even violence.*

## DECEMBER 31, SEVENTH DAY OF CHRISTMAS

### The Journey of the Wise Men Home

On their return their kings and princes came to them inquiring, What they had seen and done? What sort of journey and return they had? What company they had on the road?

But they produced the swaddling cloth which St. Mary had given to them, on account whereof they kept a feast. And having, according to the custom of their country, made a fire, they worshipped it. And casting the swaddling cloth into it, the fire took it, and kept it. And when the fire was put out, they took forth the swaddling cloth unhurt, as much as if the fire had not touched it. Then they began to kiss it, and put it on their heads and their eyes, saying, "This is certainly an undoubted truth and it is really surprising that the fire could not burn it, and consume it." Then they took it, and with the greatest respect laid it up among their treasures.

THE FIRST GOSPEL OF THE INFANCY OF JESUS CHRIST (CRANE)

## JANUARY 1, EIGHTH DAY OF CHRISTMAS

### *The Threat to the Lives of the Children*

When Herod realized that he had been tricked by the astrologers, he flew into a rage and dispatched his executioners with instructions to kill all the infants two years old and younger.

And when Mary heard that the infants were being killed, she was frightened and took her child, wrapped him in strips of cloth, and laid him in a feeding trough used by cattle.

When Elizabeth heard that they were looking for John, however, she took him and went up into the hill country. She kept searching for a place to hide him, but there was none to be had. Then she groaned and said, "Mountain of God, please take in a mother with her child." You see, Elizabeth was unable to keep on climbing. Suddenly the mountain split open and let them in. That mountain was a transparent light to her, since a heavenly messenger of the Lord was with them for protection.

INFANCY GOSPEL OF JAMES 22:1–9 (MILLER)

Now after the wise men had left, an angel of the Lord appeared to Joseph in a dream and said, "Get up, take the child and his mother, and flee to Egypt, and remain there until I tell you; for Herod is about to search for the child to destroy him." Then Joseph got up, took the child and his mother by night, and went to Egypt, and remained there until the death of Herod. This was to fulfill what had been spoken by the Lord through the prophet, "Out of Egypt have I called my son."

THE GOSPEL ACCORDING TO MATTHEW 2:13–15
(NEW REVISED STANDARD VERSION)

## JANUARY 2, NINTH DAY OF CHRISTMAS

### The Flight into Egypt—Part 1

*In the story of the exodus, Moses leads the people out of slavery in Egypt through the waters (baptism of the people as a community), and after this new beginning, their forty-year journey through the wilderness begins. Jesus is seen as the one who leads the new birth of the renewed people of God and of each individual. The pattern is clear: first the rebirth, then the journey in the Way of the Tao.*

[On their journey to Egypt,] when they came to a cave and wished to rest in it, holy Mary dismounted and sat down the child Jesus in her lap. And on the journey there were with Joseph three boys and with Mary some maidens. And behold, suddenly many dragons came out of the cave. When the boys saw them they cried out in terror. Then Jesus got down from his mother's lap, and stood on his feet before the dragons; thereupon they worshipped Jesus, and then went back from them. Then was fulfilled that which was spoken through the prophet David: "Praise the Lord, you dragons from the earth, you dragons and all deeps." And the child Jesus himself went before the dragons and commanded them not to harm anyone.

But Mary and Joseph had great fear lest the child should be hurt by the dragons. And Jesus said to them, "Have no fear, and do not think that I am a child; for I have always been and even now am perfect; all wild beasts must be docile before me."

Likewise lions and leopards worshipped him and accompanied them in the desert. Wherever Joseph and holy Mary went, they went before them, showing them the way and lowering their heads in worship; they showed their servitude by wagging their tails and honored him with great reverence. But when Mary saw the lions and leopards and all kinds of wild beasts surrounding them, she was at first gripped by violent fear.

But the child Jesus looked at her face with a happy countenance, and said: "Do not fear, mother; for they do not come to harm you, but they hasten to obey you and me." With these words he removed all fear from her heart. And the lions went along with them, and with the oxen and asses and the beasts of burden which carried what they needed, and they harmed no one, although they remained with them. Rather they were docile among the sheep and rams which they had brought with them from Judaea and had with them. They walked among the wolves without fear, and neither was harmed by the other. Then was fulfilled that which was said by the prophet: "The wolves pasture with the lambs; lions and oxen eat straw together." And the lions guided on their journey the two oxen and the wagon in which they carried what they needed.

THE GOSPEL OF PSEUDO-MATTHEW (HENNECKE AND SCHNEEMELCHER)

## JANUARY 3, TENTH DAY OF CHRISTMAS

### The Flight into Egypt—Part 2

*This delightful story continues on the theme of being in harmony with the natural.*

Now on the third day of their journey, as they went on, it happened that blessed Mary was wearied by too great heat of the sun in the desert, and seeing a palm-tree, she said to Joseph: "I should like to rest a little in the shade of this tree." And Joseph led her quickly to the palm and let her dismount from her animal. And when blessed Mary had sat down, she looked up at the top of the palm-tree and saw that it was full of fruits, and said to Joseph: "I wish someone would fetch some of these fruits of the palm-tree."

And Joseph said to her: "I wonder that you say this; for you see how high this palm-tree is, and I wonder that you even think about eating of the fruits of the palm. I think rather of the lack of water, which already fails us in the skins, and we have nothing with which we can refresh ourselves and the animals."

Then the child Jesus, who was sitting with a happy countenance in his mother's lap, said to the palm: "Bend down your branches, O tree, and refresh my mother with your fruit." And immediately at this command the palm bent its head down to the feet of blessed Mary, and they gathered from it fruits with which they all refreshed themselves. But after they had gathered all its fruits, it remained bent down and waited to raise itself again at the command of him at whose command it had bent down. Then Jesus said to it: "Raise yourself, O palm, and be strong and join my trees which are in the paradise of my Father. And open beneath your roots a vein of water which is hidden in the earth, and let the waters flow so that we may quench our thirst from it." And immediately it raised itself, and there began to gush out by its root a fountain of water very clear, fresh, and completely bright. And when they saw the fountain of water, they rejoiced greatly, and quenched their thirst, and also all the beasts of burden and all the animals, and gave thanks to God.

THE GOSPEL OF PSEUDO-MATTHEW
(HENNECKE AND SCHNEEMELCHER)

## JANUARY 4, ELEVENTH DAY OF CHRISTMAS

### *The Murder of Zechariah the Priest*

*The power struggle continues. The new life, the Way of the Tao, is perceived as a threat; power structures of the world and within the psyche seek to kill and destroy it.*

Herod, though, kept looking for John and sent his agents to Zechariah serving at the altar with this message: "Where have you hidden your son?"

But he answered them, "I am a minister of God and am attending to his temple. How should I know where my son is?"

And so the agents went away and reported all this to Herod, who became angry and said, "Is his son going to rule over Israel?"

And he sent his agents back with this message: "Tell me the truth. Where is your son? Don't you know that I have your life in my power?"

And the agents went and reported this message to him.

Zechariah answered and said, "I am a martyr for God. Take my life. The Lord, though, will receive my spirit because you are shedding innocent blood at the entrance to the temple of the Lord."

And so at daybreak Zechariah was murdered, but the people of Israel did not know that he had been murdered.

At the hour of formal greetings the priests departed, but Zechariah did not meet and bless them as was customary. And so the priests waited around for Zechariah, to greet him with prayer and to praise the Most High God.

But when he did not show up, they all became fearful. One of them, however, summoned up his courage and entered the sanctuary and saw dried blood next to the Lord's altar. And he heard a voice saying, "Zechariah has been murdered! His blood will not be cleaned up until his avenger appears."

When he heard this he was afraid and went out and reported to the priests what he had seen and heard. And they summoned up their courage, entered, and saw what had happened. And the panels of the temple cried out, and the priests ripped their robes from top to bottom. They didn't find a corpse, but they did find his blood, now turned to stone. They were afraid and went out and reported that Zechariah had been murdered. And all the tribes of the people listened and began to mourn him, and they beat their breasts for three days and three nights.

INFANCY GOSPEL OF JAMES 23:1–24:11 (MILLER)

## JANUARY 5, TWELFTH DAY OF CHRISTMAS

### *Return from Egypt*

*Guidance for ways of protecting the new life comes from angels in the day and dreams during the night. Our spiritual life requires us to pay attention to those who may have messages for us during our waking hours and dream figures while we sleep.*

When Herod died, an angel of the Lord suddenly appeared in a dream to Joseph in Egypt and said, "Get up, take the child and his mother, and go to the land of Israel, for those who were seeking the child's life are dead." Then Joseph got up, took the child and his mother, and went to the land of Israel. But when he heard that Archelaus was ruling over Judea in place of his father Herod, he was afraid to go there. And after being warned in a dream, he went away to the district of Galilee. There he made his home in a town called Nazareth, so that what had been spoken through the prophets might be fulfilled, "He will be called a Nazorean."

THE GOSPEL ACCORDING TO MATTHEW 2:19–23
(NEW REVISED STANDARD VERSION)

# The Baptism of Jesus in the Tao

↩

### He Came up Laughing

John the Baptizer appeared in the wilderness calling for baptism and a change of heart that lead to forgiveness of sins. And everyone from the Judean countryside and all the residents of Jerusalem streamed out to him and were baptized by him in the Jordan river, admitting their sins. And John was dressed in camel hair and wore a leather belt around his waist and lived on locusts and raw honey. And he began his proclamation by saying:

"Someone more powerful than I will succeed me, whose sandal straps I am not fit to bend down and untie. I have been baptizing you with water, but he will baptize you with holy spirit."

During that same period Jesus came from Nazareth in Galilee and was baptized in the Jordan by John. And just as he got up out of the water, he saw the skies torn open and the spirit coming down toward him like a dove. There was also a voice from the skies: "You are my favored son—I fully approve of you."

And right away the spirit drives him out into the wilderness, where he remained for forty days, being put to the test by Satan. While he was living there among the wild animals, the heavenly messengers looked after him.

GOSPEL OF MARK 1:4–13 (MILLER)

As soon as Christ went down into the water he came out laughing at everything of this world, not because he considers it a trifle, but because he is full of contempt for it.

GOSPEL OF PHILIP 74:29–31 (ROBINSON, 1977)

*According to the stories, Jesus is thirty years old when he goes to hear John's preaching and is baptized. What in John's preaching is Jesus responding to? Why does he ask to be baptized? What happens to him during his baptism? How is he changed by this experience? As he comes out of the water, why is he laughing? Has his way of seeing changed?*

## JANUARY 7

### *The Dove Flutters over the Head of Jesus*

The Dove flutters over the head of Jesus, because he is her head.
    And she sings over Jesus, and her voice is heard.
The bird begins to fly,
    and every creeping thing awakes in its hole.
And the chasms are opened and closed;
    and they are seeking the Lord as those who are about to give birth.
For the Lord reveals his Way,
    and spreads out his grace.
And those who recognized it
    know his holiness. Hallelujah.

ODES OF SOLOMON 24 (CHARLESWORTH, ADAPTED)

*This ode focuses on the dove, symbol of the Holy Spirit. As in creation stories with the Spirit hovering over the deep, the flood story with the dove of peace returning to Noah with an olive branch, so the Spirit flutters over Jesus' head, and all creation is awake and aware. Compare this ode with the story of the birth of the child in the cave in the reading for December 22.*

## JANUARY 8

---

*Paradox of Water*

Under heaven nothing is more soft and yielding than water.
Yet for attacking the solid and strong, nothing is better;
it has no equal.
The weak can overcome the strong;
the supple can overcome the stiff.
Under heaven everyone knows this,
yet no one puts it into practice.
Therefore the sage says: he who takes upon himself the
    humiliation of the people is fit to rule them.
He who takes upon himself the country's disasters deserves
    to be king of the universe.
The truth often sounds paradoxical.

TAO TE CHING, 78 (FENG AND ENGLISH)

## JANUARY 9

---

*The Tao Doesn't Take Sides*

Heaven and earth are not humane. They regard all things as
    straw dogs.
The sage is not humane. He regards all people as straw dogs.

TAO TE CHING, 5 (CHAN, 1992)

Heaven and earth are ruthless; They see the ten thousand things
   as dummies.
The wise are ruthless; They see the people as dummies.

TAO TE CHING, 5 (FENG AND ENGLISH)

The Tao doesn't take sides; it gives birth to both good and evil.
The Master doesn't take sides; she welcomes both saints and sinners.

TAO TE CHING, 5 (TAN, 1992)

The Tao is like a bellows; it is empty yet infinitely capable,
The more you use it, the more it produces; the more you talk of it, the
   less you understand. Hold on to the center.

TAO TE CHING, 5 (MITCHELL)

## JANUARY 10

### The Tao Is the Great Mother

The valley Spirit never dies.
It is the unknown* first mother,
   whose gate is the root,
      from which grew heaven and earth.
It is dimly seen, yet always present.
Draw from it all you wish,
   it will never run dry.

TAO TE CHING, 6 (McCARROLL)

*Wee Chong Tan translates *unknown* as *mysterious*.

## JANUARY 11

_____

### *The Tao Is Everlasting and Eternal*

The Heaven is everlasting and the Earth eternal.
The secret for all this is that the Heaven and the Earth
do not live for themselves;
Therefore they are living forever.
Likewise, the Saint is willing to put oneself behind,
and finds oneself leading others;
Disregarding oneself and finds oneself preserved.
Is it not because the Saint is selfless?
That the true-self is fulfilled.

TAO TE CHING, 7 (TAN, 1992)

*Which is it, "everlasting" or "eternal"? One suggests length, the other depth.*
*Which is more important, how long you live or how deep your living?*

## JANUARY 12

_____

### *Being at One with the Tao*

The Great Virtue is to follow the Tao and only the Tao.

The Tao is shadowy and intangible.
Intangible and evasive, and yet within it is a form.
Evasive and intangible, and yet within it is a substance.
Shadowy and dark, and yet within it is a vital force.
This vital force is real and can be relied upon.

From ancient times to the present, the Tao's instructions
   have not been forgotten.

Through it can be perceived the beginning of the story of life.
How do I know it was at the beginning of the story of life?
Because of what is within me.

TAO TE CHING, 21 (MCCARROLL)

The Master keeps her mind always at one with the Tao;
that is what gives her her radiance.
The Tao is ungraspable. How can her mind be at one with it?
Because she doesn't cling to ideas.

The Tao is dark and unfathomable. How can it make her radiant?
Because she lets it.

Since before time and space were, the Tao is. It is beyond *is* and *is not*.
How do I know this is true? I look inside myself and see.

TAO TE CHING, 21 (MITCHELL)

## JANUARY 13

*Disciple of Life in Gentleness and Strength*

A human being is born gentle and weak.
At death he is hard and stiff.
Green plants are tender and filled with sap.
At their death they are withered and dry.
Therefore the stiff and unbending is the disciple of
     death.
The gentle and yielding is the disciple of life.
Thus an army without flexibility never wins a battle.

A tree that is unbending is easily broken.
The hard and the strong will fall.
The soft and the weak will overcome.

TAO TE CHING, 76 (FENG AND ENGLISH)

The most yielding of all things
    overcomes the hardest of all things.
That which has no substance
    enters where there is no crevice.
Hence, I know the value of action without striving.
Few things under heaven bring more benefit than
    the lessons learned from silence and
    the actions taken without striving.

TAO TE CHING, 43 (McCARROLL)

## JANUARY 14

*Opposites Create and Define Each Other*

When the people of the world all know beauty as beauty,
there arises the recognition of ugliness.
When they all know the good as good,
there arises the recognition of evil.
Therefore: being and nonbeing produce each other;
difficult and easy complete each other;
long and short contrast each other;
high and low distinguish each other;
sound and voice harmonize each other;

front and behind accompany each other.
Therefore the sage manages affairs without action
and spreads *teaching*\* without words.
All things arise, and he does not turn away from them.
He produces them but does not take possession of them.
he acts but does not rely on his own ability.
He accomplishes his task but does not claim credit for it.
It is precisely because he does not claim credit
that his accomplishment remains with him.

TAO TE CHING, 2 (CHAN)

\*"Doctrine."

# The New Identity of Jesus
# in the Way of the Tao

↬

### *Jesus Asks, "Who Do You Say That I Am?"*

Jesus went on with his disciples to the villages of Caesarea Philippi; and on the way he asked his disciples, "Who do people say that I am?" And they answered him, "John the Baptist;" and others, "Elijah;" and still others, "one of the prophets." He asked them, "But who do you say that I am?" Peter answered him, "You are the Messiah." And he sternly ordered them not to tell anyone about him.

THE GOSPEL ACCORDING TO MARK 8:27–30
(NEW REVISED STANDARD VERSION)

### *Jesus Says, "Compare Me to Someone"*

Jesus said to his disciples, "Compare me to someone and tell me whom I am like."

Simon Peter said to him, "You are like a righteous angel."

Matthew said to him, "You are like a wise philosopher."

Thomas said to him, "Master, my mouth is totally incapable of saying whom you are like."

Jesus said, "I am not your master. Because you have drunk, you have become intoxicated from the bubbling spring that I have measured out."

GOSPEL OF THOMAS 13 (ROBINSON, 3D ED.)


## JANUARY 17

Disciples Ask, "Who Are You?"

They said to him, "Tell us who you are so that we may believe in you."

He said to them, "You read the face of the sky and of the earth, but you have not recognized the one [or that which is] before you, and you do not know how to read this moment."

GOSPEL OF THOMAS 91 (ROBINSON, 3D ED.)


*Be here now! Pay attention!*


## JANUARY 18

*Salome Asks Jesus, "Who Are You Really?"*

Salome said, "Who are you, man, that you . . . have come up on my couch and eaten from my table?"

Jesus said to her, "I am he who exists from the undivided. I was given some of the things of my father."

[Salome said,] "I am your disciple."

GOSPEL OF THOMAS 61 (ROBINSON, 3D ED.)

*Bed and board are two of the most intimate ways through which we human be-*
*ings come to relate to and to know one another. When we share these experiences,*
*the relationship changes, and once again we ask each other, "Who are you?"*

## JANUARY 19

### *The Importance of Naming*

Names given to the worldly are very deceptive, for they divert our thoughts from what is correct to what is incorrect. Thus one who hears the word "God" does not perceive what is correct, but perceives what is incorrect. So also with "the father" and "the son" and "the holy spirit" and "life" and "light" and "resurrection" and "the church" and all the rest—people do not perceive what is correct but they perceive what is incorrect, unless they have come to know what is correct. . . .

One single name is not uttered in the world, the name which the father gave to the son; it is the name above all things: the name of the father. For the son would not become father unless he wore the name of the father. Those who have this name know it, but they do not speak it. But those who do not have it do not know it.

But truth brought names into existence in the world for our sakes because it is not possible to learn it without these names. Truth is one single thing; it is many things and for our sakes to teach about this one thing in love through many things. . . .

"Jesus" is a hidden name, "Christ" is a revealed name. For this reason "Jesus" is not particular to any language; rather he is always called by the name "Jesus." While as for "Christ," in Syriac it is "Messiah," in Greek it is "Christ." Certainly all the others have it according to their own language. "The Nazarene" is he who reveals what is hidden. Christ has everything in himself, whether man or angel or mystery, and the father. . . .

"The father" and "the son" are single names, "the holy spirit" is a double name. For they are everywhere: they are above, they are below;

they are in the concealed, they are in the revealed. The holy spirit is in the revealed: it is below. It is in the concealed: it is above.

GOSPEL OF PHILIP 53:24–54:18, AND 56:3–15
AND 59:12–17 (ROBINSON, 3D ED.)

*Embodied in the name is the all you need to know: The holy name of God who speaks with Moses from the burning bush (Exodus 3:14) is the Eternal YHWH (English transliteration with vowels added is Yahweh.) In Hebrew the word is four letters: yod, hé, vav, hé. Yod is masculine, and hé is feminine; here is the essential Tao. From their essence springs forth vau, masculine, and a second hé, feminine. The holy name is a Quaternity with the essential Tao giving expression in a second Tao. The name of Jesus in Hebrew is composed of the same four Hebrew letters plus an additional letter, shin, placed in the center and making the word yod, hé, shin, vau, hé.*

*Do you see what is happening here? The name Jesus is an expression of the Eternal, a further evolution of the Eternal, a fresh centering of the Eternal! Jesus is a prototype of the new human being. In Jesus "the Tao is made flesh and dwells among us" (John 1:14). Here is shown the potential for you, me, and every human being. Do you know that the Eternal Tao is to be given full expression in you? You can experience this full expression through the centering of shin! By centering, you become aware of who you are: the Eternal manifesting in this moment!**

*For a further discussion of these ideas, you may wish to read these two books: Migene Gonzáles-Wippler, *A Kaballah for the Modern World* (New York: Julian Press, 1974); Stephan A. Hoeller, *Jung and the Lost Gospels* (Wheaton, IL: Quest Books, 1989).

## JANUARY 20

### *Transitions*

[In Baptism, I move]
from the world into the Jordan,

and from the blindness of the world into the sight of God,
from the carnal into the spiritual, from the physical into the angelic,
from the created into the Pleroma,
from the world into the Aeon,
from the servitudes into sonship, from entanglements into one another,
from the desert into our village,
from the cold into the hot,
from seminal bodies into the bodies with perfect form.

Indeed I entered by way of example the remnant for which the Christ rescued us in the fellowship of his Spirit. And he brought us forth who are in him, and from now on souls will become perfect spirits.

ON BAPTISM B, VALENTINIAN ORIGIN IN THE MIDDLE OF THE
SECOND CENTURY (ROBINSON, 3D ED.)

## JANUARY 21

### *Being Called into a New Way of Living*

#### *Becoming a Medicine Man*

The medicine-man is a person in whom the Aborigines have much faith.

Yet he has a family, he hunts with his companions, he takes part in the secular and ceremonial life of his tribe, and he is subject both to sickness and to death.

But he is a man apart, because the spirits of the dead medicine-men, the Wulgis, have admitted him into their world of healing and magic; a world that few Aborigines can enter.

When the Wulgis notice an Aborigine who shows more than ordinary interest in the psychic life of the tribe, they choose him to become a medicine-man.

The Wulgis wait until the initiate is asleep, take the spirit from his body, and change it into the form of an eaglehawk. Then they conduct it into the sky, where it is shown many wonders and the secrets of magic and healing which are known only to the medicine-men. At dawn, the spirit of the initiate is taken back to his camp, transformed from that of an eaglehawk to that of an Aborigine, and returned to his own body. Those journeys are repeated many times before the initiate has learnt all the secrets of his profession.

On return to his ordinary life, the newly initiated medicine-man has many new powers; he can heal the sick, find the spirits of children who have lost themselves in the darkness, and hunt the malignant night spirits from the camps.

Occasionally the medicine-man will seek the help of a Wulgi to cure an Aborigine suffering severe bodily pains. The Wulgi goes inside the patient and searches until it finds an object such as a stick or stone, which has been placed there by an enemy. The Wulgi gives this to the medicine-man who shows it as evidence that the cause of the pain has been removed.

It is said that the patient always recovers. No Aborigine ever doubts the ability of a medicine-man to cure most forms of sickness, or to overcome the effects of evil spirits.

(ROBERTS)

# Jesus Living the Way of the Tao in Personal Relationships

☙

## JANUARY 22

---

### John Who Baptized Him

Jesus said, "From Adam to John the Baptist, among those born of women, no one is so much greater than John the Baptist that his eyes should not be lowered before him. But I have said that whoever among you becomes a child will recognize the *Way of the Tao*\* and will become greater than John.

**GOSPEL OF THOMAS 46 (MILLER)**

\*Original has here "the (Father's) imperial rule."

[Jesus said,] "What do members of this generation remind me of? What are they like? They are like children sitting in the market place and calling out to one another:

> We played the flute for you,
> but you wouldn't dance;
> We sang a dirge,
> but you wouldn't weep.

"Just remember, John the Baptist appeared on the scene, eating no bread and drinking no wine and you say, 'He is demented.' The son of

Adam appeared on the scene both eating and drinking, and you say, 'There is a glutton and a drunk, a crony of toll collectors and sinners!' Indeed, Wisdom is vindicated by all her children."

GOSPEL OF LUKE 7:31–35 (MILLER)

*Jesus lived the Way of the Tao in his life, just as John was living the Way in his. Both were criticized by people who were resisting and opposing the Way of the Tao living in them.*

A dispute over purification broke out between John's disciples and one of the Judeans. They came to John and reported: "Rabbi, that fellow who was with you across the Jordan—you spoke about him earlier—guess what! He's now baptizing and everyone is flocking to him."

John answered, . . . "I am content. He can only grow in importance; my role can only diminish."

GOSPEL OF JOHN 3:25–27, 29B–30 (MILLER)

## JANUARY 23

---

### *The People Who Traveled with Him*

[Jesus] traveled through towns and villages, preaching and announcing the good news of the *Way of the Tao.** The twelve were with him, and also some women whom he had cured of evil spirits and diseases: Mary, the one from Magdala, from whom seven demons had taken their leave, and Joanna, the wife of Chuza, Herod's steward, and Susanna, and many others, who provided for them out of their resources.

GOSPEL OF LUKE 8:1–3 (MILLER)

*Miller's version has here "God's imperial rule."

## JANUARY 24

### Peter's Family Provides Jesus with a Home

Some days later Jesus went back to Capernaum and was rumored to be at home. And many people crowded around so that there was no longer any room, even outside the door.

GOSPEL OF MARK 2:1–2 (MILLER)

And when Jesus came to Peter's house, he noticed his mother-in-law lying sick with a fever. He touched her hand and the fever disappeared. Then she got up and started looking after him.

GOSPEL OF MATTHEW 8:14 (MILLER)

## JANUARY 25

### Mary Magdalene, Companion of Jesus

There were three who always walked with the Lord: Mary his mother and her sister and Magdalene, the one who was called his companion. His sister and his mother and his companion were each a Mary. . . .

And the companion of the Savior is Mary Magdalene. But Christ loved her more than all the disciples and used to kiss her often on her mouth. The rest of the disciples were offended by it and expressed disapproval. They said to him, "Why do you love her more than all of us?" The Savior answered and said to them, "Why do I not love you like her?" . . .

For it is by a kiss that the perfect conceive and give birth. For this reason we also kiss one another. We receive conception from the grace which is in each other.

GOSPEL OF PHILIP 59:6–11; 63:32–64:5; 59:2–6 (ROBINSON, 3D ED.)

## JANUARY 26

---

### *The Young Man Whom Jesus Loved*

And they [came] into Bethany, and this woman was there whose brother had died. She knelt down in front of Jesus and says to him, "Son of David, have mercy on me." But the disciples rebuked her. And Jesus got angry and went with her into the garden where the tomb was. Just then a loud voice was heard from inside the tomb. Then Jesus went up and rolled the stone away from the entrance to the tomb. He went right in where the young man was, stuck out his hand, grabbed him by the hand, and raised him up. The young man looked at Jesus, loved him, and began to beg him to be with him. Then they left the tomb and went into the young man's house. (Incidentally, he was rich.) Six days later Jesus gave him an order; and when evening had come, the young man went to him, dressed only in a linen cloth. He spent that night with him, because Jesus taught him the mystery of the *Tao*.* From there Jesus got up and returned to the other side of the Jordan.

**SECRET GOSPEL OF MARK 1:1–13 (MILLER)**

*"God's domain" in Miller's edition.

## JANUARY 27

---

### *Jesus in Conversation with a Leper*

Just then a leper comes up to him and says, "Teacher, Jesus, in wandering around with lepers and eating with them in the inn, I became a leper myself. If you want to, I'll be made clean." The master said to him, "Okay—you're clean!" And at once his leprosy vanished from him. Jesus says to him, "Go and have the priests examine (your skin). Then offer for your cleansing what Moses commanded—and no more sinning."

**THE EGERTON GOSPEL 2:1–4 (MILLER)**

*The Egerton Gospel is a scrap of an unknown Gospel named after the English-man who funded the purchase of this first-century fragment.*

*Did Jesus heal? Or was he the catalyst for healing, enabling people to release within themselves the powers that bring wholeness?*

## JANUARY 28

### Jesus in Confrontation with the Legal Experts

They [the legal experts] come to him and interrogate him as a way of putting him to the test. They ask, "Teacher, Jesus, we know that you are from God, since the things you do put you above all the prophets. Tell us, then, is it permissible to pay to rulers what is due them? Should we pay them or not?" Jesus knew what they were up to, and became indignant. Then he said to them, "Why do you pay me lip service as a teacher, but not do what I say? How accurately Isaiah prophesied about you when he said, 'This people honors me with their lips, but their heart stays far from me; their worship of me is empty, because they insist on teachings that are human commandments.'"

THE EGERTON GOSPEL 3:1–6 (MILLER)

*Resistance to the Way of the Tao manifesting in Jesus as the human ideal comes from all directions, including the accepted laws of the time. Legal experts are upset when their rules cannot control the freedom of the Spirit.*

## JANUARY 29

---

### Jesus in Confrontation with a Priest

And taking the disciples along, Jesus led them into the inner sanctuary itself, and began walking about in the temple precinct.

This Pharisee, a leading priest, Levi by name, also entered, ran into them, and said to the savior, "Who gave you permission to wander around in this inner sanctuary and lay eyes on these sacred vessels, when you have not performed your ritual bath, and your disciples have not even washed their feet? Yet in a defiled state you have invaded this sacred place, which is ritually clean. No one walks about in here, or dares lay eyes on these sacred vessels, unless they have bathed themselves and changed clothes."

And the savior stood up immediately, with his disciples, and replied, "Since you are here in the temple, I take it you are clean."

He replies to Jesus, "I am clean. I bathed in the pool of David, you know, by descending into it by one set of steps and coming up out of it by another. I also changed to white and ritually clean clothes. Only then did I come here and lay eyes on these sacred vessels."

In response the savior said to him: "I feel sorry for the blind who can't see. You bathe in these stagnant waters where dogs and pigs wallow day and night. And you wash and scrub the outer layers of skin, just like prostitutes and dance-hall girls, who wash, and scrub, and anoint, and paint themselves to entice men, while inwardly they are crawling with scorpions and filled with all sorts of corruption. But my disciples and I—you say we are unbathed—have bathed in lively, life-giving water that comes down from above.

GOSPEL OXYRHYNCHUS 840 (MILLER)

*Oxyrhynchus is a place in Upper Egypt where a scrap of an unknown Gospel was found. This Gospel dates from about 200 C.E. and is a copy of a small portion of another Gospel that appears to have originated in the first century.*

## JANUARY 30

*Jesus Mixing with tne Wrong People*

When the scholars and Pharisees and priests observed him, they were indignant because he reclined at table in the company of sinners. But Jesus overheard them and said, Those who are well don't need a doctor.

And pray for your enemies. For the one who is not against you is on your side. The one who today is at a distance, tomorrow will be near you.

GOSPEL OXYRHYNCHUS 1224 (MILLER)

## JANUARY 31

*Jesus Took Them All by Stealth*

Jesus took them all by stealth, for he did not appear as he was, but in the manner in which they would be able to see him. He appeared to them all. He appeared to the great as great. He appeared to the small as small. He appeared to the angels as an angel, and to men as a man. Because of this his word hid itself from everyone. Some indeed saw him, thinking that they were seeing themselves, but when he appeared to his disciples in glory on the mount he was not small.* He became great, but he made the disciples great, that they might be able to see him in his greatness.

GOSPEL OF PHILIP 57:28–58:10 (ROBINSON, 3D ED.)

*The mount refers to the story of Jesus' transfiguration. See the entry for August 6.

## FEBRUARY 1, ST. BRIGID'S DAY

---

### *"Ask Your Mother"*

A disciple asked the Lord one day for something of this world. He [Jesus] said to him, "Ask your Mother and she will give you of the things which are another's."

The apostles said to the disciples, "May our whole offering obtain salt." They called Sophia "salt." Without it no offering is acceptable. But Sophia is barren, without child. For this reason she is called "a trace of salt." But where they will be in their own way, the Holy Spirit will also be, and her children are many."

GOSPEL OF PHILIP 59:26–60:1 (ROBINSON, 3D ED.)

*Wisdom comes from the Yin, the feminine of the Tao, who is manifesting through symbolic figures such as Brigid, who emerges from the Celtic tradition, rooted in the natural Way of the Tao. She is known as a scholar, lover of arts and music, and founder of a community of men and women known for their warm hospitality to strangers and people on spiritual pilgrimage. Her deep spirituality manifests in practical living. Here is a portion of one of her writings:*

I should like great lakes of ale* for the King of Kings.
I should like the family of Heaven to be drinking it through time
    eternal
I should like the food to be portions of faith and true devotion.
I should like flails of repentance at my house.
I should like the men of Heaven in my own house.
I should like barrels of peace to be at their disposal.
I should like vessels of love for sharing.
I should like caves of compassion for their company.
I should like cheerfulness to be in their drinking.

I should like Jesus to be there among them.
I should like the three Marys of illustrious renown.
I should like the people of Heaven there from all parts.
I should like to be a rent-payer to the Lord.
that should I suffer distress, He would bestow on me a blessing.

"ON HOSPITALITY" BY ST. BRIGID, 453–523 C.E.

*There is evidence that in the earliest versions of this piece the lakes were not of ale but of milk from the breast of Mother Earth, who feeds all of life from herself. Later versions under masculine influence were translated "ale." Which is it, milk as sustenance from Mother Earth, or ale in celebration of the gift of life? Must we choose between them? Why not use both versions—lakes of milk and of ale!

# Daily Readings Between February 1 and June 15

↩

*If you have been using the readings in this book on a daily basis, you will now discover that the fixed dates have stopped.*

*The next set of readings runs from Ash Wednesday through the forty days of Lent, then Holy Week, and the fifty days of Easter climaxing with Pentecost. I call this season "Ashes to Fire." These days are not fixed to calendar dates but move each year according to natural rhythms. In the Appendix you will find a discussion of the natural liturgical year and how these days are arranged.*

*The season of Ashes to Fire begins whenever Ash Wednesday begins. To find the date of Ash Wednesday in a particular year, consult the Appendix.*

*Each year will have some days between February 1 and Ash Wednesday. For these days I suggest you use one or two of the CoCreator chants and songs at the back of this book. Also, please note that there are several significant fixed days that come between February 1 and May 1 as follows:*

> *March 21  Spring Equinox*
> *March 25  Annunciation*
> *May 1  May Day*

*Readings for these days follow next.*

# Fixed Dates Between
# February 1 and June 15

✦

## MARCH 21, SPRING EQUINOX

### *Birth of the Butterflies*

When the world was very young, the birds and animals had a common language and there was no death. No creature had any experience of death's mystery, until one day a young cockatoo fell from a tree and broke its neck. The birds and animals could not wake it, and a meeting of the wise ones decided that the spirits had taken back the bird to change it into another form.

Everyone thought this a reasonable explanation but to prove the theory the leaders called for volunteers who would imitate the dead cockatoo by going up into the sky for a whole winter. During this time, they would not be allowed to see, hear, smell, or taste anything. In the spring they were to return to earth to relate their experiences to the others. The caterpillars offered to try this experiment, and went up into the sky into a huge cloud.

On the first warm day of spring a pair of excited dragonflies told the gathering that the caterpillars were returning with new bodies. Soon the dragonflies led back into the camp a great pageant of white, yellow, red, blue, and green creatures—the first butterflies, and proof that the spirits had changed the caterpillars' bodies into another form.

They clustered in large groups on the trees and bushes, and everything looked so gay and colourful that the wise ones decided this was a good and happy thing that had happened, and decreed that it must always be so. Since then, caterpillars always spend winter hidden in cocoons, preparing for their dramatic change into one of spring's most beautiful symbols.

BIRTH OF THE BUTTERFLIES (ROBERTS)

## MARCH 25, THE ANNUNCIATION

### *"Mary, the Lord God Has Extolled Your Name"*

There was a council of the priests, which agreed: "Let's make a veil for the temple of the Lord."

And the high priest said, "Send for the uncontaminated virgins from the tribe of David." And so the temple assistants left and searched everywhere and found seven. And the high priest then remembered that the child Mary was from the tribe of David and was uncontaminated before God. And so the temple assistants went out and got her.

And they took the maidens into the temple of the Lord. And the high priest said, "Cast lots for me to decide who will spin threads for the veil: the gold, the white, the linen, the silk, the violet, the scarlet, and the true purple."

And the true purple and scarlet threads fell to Mary. And she took them and returned home. Now it was at this time that Zechariah became mute, and Samuel took his place until Zechariah regained his speech. Meanwhile, Mary had taken up the scarlet and was spinning it.

And she took her water jar and went out to fill it with water. Suddenly there was a voice saying to her, "Greetings, favored one! The Lord is with you. Blessed are you among women." Mary began looking around, both right and left, to see where this voice was coming from. She became terrified and went home. After putting the water jar down and taking up the purple, she sat down in her house and began to spin.

A messenger of the Lord suddenly stood before her: "Do not be afraid, Mary. You see, you have found favor in the sight of the Lord of all. You will conceive by means of his word."

But as she listened, Mary was doubtful, saying to herself, "If I actually conceive by the Lord, the living God, will I also give birth the way women usually do?"

And the messenger of the Lord said, "No, Mary, because the power of God will overshadow you. Therefore, the child to be born will be called holy, the son of the Most High. And you will name him Jesus. For he alone will save his people from their sins."

And Mary said, "Here I am, the Lord's slave before him. May it happen with me just as you have said."

And she finished the purple and the scarlet and took them up to the high priest, and the high priest accepted them and congratulated her and said, "Mary, the Lord God has extolled your name and so you will be congratulated by all the generations of the earth."

INFANCY GOSPEL OF JAMES 10:1–12:2 (MILLER)

*Mary is working on the veil of the temple, the one that separates the people from the holiest place. With the crucifixion, the veil of the temple is split apart and the Way is opened into the holy.*

*As she conceives, she is preparing herself for the new life that will be born from her, grow, and break through into the holiness of God by suffering and the cross.*

Mary rejoiced and left to visit her relative Elizabeth. She knocked at the door, and Elizabeth heard it, tossed aside what she was doing, and ran to the door and opened it for her. And she congratulated her and said,

"Who am I that the mother of the Lord should visit me? You see, the baby inside me has jumped for joy and blessed you."

But Mary forgot the mysteries which the heavenly messenger Gabriel had spoken, and she looked up to the sky and said, "Who am I that every generation on earth will congratulate me?"

Then she spent three months with Elizabeth and returned home. Day by day her womb kept swelling, and so she hid herself from the Israelite public. Now she was sixteen years old when these mysterious things happened to her.

INFANCY GOSPEL OF JAMES 12:3–9 (MILLER)

*When one is spiritually pregnant, there is great advantage to having a spiritual friend, someone with whom to share what is going on in one's soul.*

## MAY 1, MAY DAY

### *Wisdom's Invitation*

"Come to me, you who desire me,
    and eat your fill of my fruits.
For the memory of me is sweeter than honey,
    and the possession of me sweeter than the honeycomb.
Those who eat of me will hunger for more,
    and those who drink of me will thirst for more.
Whoever obeys me will not be put to shame,
    and those who work with me will not sin."

SIRACH 24:19–22 (NEW REVISED STANDARD VERSION)

# Season of Ashes to Fire

∼ ∼ ∼

FORTY DAYS OF LENT:
*Jesus Teaching the Way of the Tao*

# Ash Wednesday and the Days Immediately Following

↭

## ASH WEDNESDAY

---

### *You Have Wrought a Wonder with Dust*

I give thanks unto Thee, O Lord, for you have wrought a wonder
  with dust
    and have shown forth your power in that which is molded of clay.
For you have made me to know Your deep, deep, truth,
    and to divine your wondrous works,
You have put in my mouth the power to praise,
    and songs on my tongue.
You have given me lips unmarred and readiness of songs,
    that I may sing of Your loving kindness
and rehearse Your might all the day
    and continually bless your Name.

#### THE BOOK OF HYMNS (GASTER)

*A common custom on Ash Wednesday is to receive ashes on one's forehead with the words "Remember, you are dust and to dust you shall return." Do we know who we really are? We are clay with life breathed into it! We are from the earth, and we return to the earth. Do we feel connected?*

*Everything that sustains us is from the earth. Eat a piece of bread or drink a glass of water and what was in the environment is now in you. Ecology is an intensely personal matter. Surely anyone who understands the meaning of being dust will know that environmental matters and personal concerns cannot be separated.*

## THURSDAY AFTER ASH WEDNESDAY

### Introducing the Gospel of Thomas

*Daily readings for the next forty days are taken from the* Gospel of Thomas, *one of the most important discoveries in the Nag Hammadi Library. Thomas is composed entirely of sayings attributed to Jesus and relies heavily on oral tradition. The first edition of the* Gospel of Thomas *was written about 50 C.E., roughly the same time as the Gospel of Q (thought to be the canonical Gospels' source for many of Jesus' sayings) and is earlier than the four Gospels of Matthew, Mark, Luke, and John. There is a strong movement among scholars to expand the conventional four Gospels to five. For an in-depth discussion, you may wish to consult* The Five Gospels: A New Translation and Commentary *by Robert W. Funk, Roy W. Hoover, and the Jesus Seminar (New York: Macmillan, 1993).*

*Between now and Holy Week you will find 98 percent of the* Gospel of Thomas, *arranged thematically. The text opens as follows:*

These are the secret sayings that the living Jesus spoke and which Didymos Judas Thomas recorded.

And he said, "Whoever discovers the interpretation of these sayings will not taste death."

GOSPEL OF THOMAS PROLOGUE AND SAYING 1 (MILLER)

*What is meant here by the secret sayings that the living Jesus spoke? Is this material like children who sometimes enjoy saying, "I know something you don't* know"? Or is it like adults joining secret societies that keep information only among those who belong? Or is it rather teachings that are open secrets?

Jesus teaches openly, but many simply do not get the message because they are unable to understand when they first hear it. The information in the Gospel of Thomas is open and available to anyone who will read and ponder the meaning.

Sometimes the meaning becomes clear only after we have progressed spiritually to the point where it becomes clear. The words on the page are clear as a bell when they resonate with the sounds of the heart.

## FRIDAY AFTER ASH WEDNESDAY

### Welcome to the Search

Jesus said, "Let him who seeks continue seeking until he finds. When he finds, he will become troubled. When he becomes troubled, he will be astonished, and he will rule over the all."

GOSPEL OF THOMAS 2 (ROBINSON, 3D ED.)

Jesus said, "Seek and you will find. In the past, however, I did not tell you the things about which you asked me then. Now I am willing to tell them, but you are not seeking them."

GOSPEL OF THOMAS 92 (MILLER)

Jesus said, "One who seeks will find, and for one who knocks it will be opened."

GOSPEL OF THOMAS 94 (MILLER)

The Gospel of Matthew has the phrase "Seek and you shall find." Thomas reveals more of the process that is involved. Have you ever looked or searched for something or someone? When you found what you thought you were looking for, what happened?

For example, a new person in your life can be exciting and also troubling: Your life, your time, and your priorities are all influenced and rearranged. Or a new concept may cause you to rethink many others.

When the time of troubling is over, you may feel rather amazed, surprised! Keep moving further with the process and you may reach the higher point of "ruling over the all"—that is the fresh perspective.

Once the cycle is completed, it may be time to begin with fresh seeking, finding, troubling, being amazed, and having a commanding perspective once again.

## SATURDAY

### Where Do You Start Looking?

Jesus said, "If those who lead you say to you, 'See, the *Way of the Tao*\* is in the sky,' then the birds of the sky will precede you. If they say to you, 'It is in the sea,' then the fish will precede you. Rather, the *Way of the Tao* is inside of you, and it is outside of you. When you come to know yourselves, then you will become known, and you will realize that it is you who are the sons of the living father. But if you will not know yourselves, you dwell in poverty and it is you who are that poverty."

**GOSPEL OF THOMAS 3 (ROBINSON, 3D ED.)**

\*Robinson edition has "kingdom."

*This teaching from Jesus springs from ancient sayings:*

"For this Law which I am laying down for you today is neither obscure for you nor beyond your reach. It is not in heaven so that you need to wonder, 'Who will go up to heaven for us and bring it down for us, so that we can hear and practice it?' Nor is it beyond the seas, so that you need to wonder, 'Who will cross the seas for us and bring it back to us, so that we can hear and practice it?'

"No the word is very near you, it is in your mouth and in your heart for you to put into practice."

DEUTERONOMY 30:11–14 (NEW JERUSALEM BIBLE)

Who has gone up into heaven, and taken her [Wisdom],
    and brought her down from the clouds?
Who has gone over the sea, and found her,
    and will buy her for pure gold?
No one knows the way to her,
    or is concerned about the path to her.
But the one who knows all things knows her."

BARUCH 3:29–31 (NEW REVISED STANDARD VERSION)

*A corollary to this teaching, from Jesus, is found a bit later in Thomas:*

Jesus said, "That which you have will save you if you bring it forth from yourselves. That which you do not have within you will kill you if you do not have it within you."

GOSPEL OF THOMAS 70 (ROBINSON, 3D ED.)

*There is even further use of this passage by Paul:*

"Do not say in your heart, 'Who will ascend into heaven?'" (that is, to bring Christ down) "or 'Who will descend into the abyss?'" (that is, to bring Christ up from the dead). But what does it say?

> "The word is very near you,
> on your lips and in your heart"

that is, the word of faith that we proclaim); because if you confess with your lips that Jesus is Lord and believe in your heart that God raised him from the dead, you will be saved.

**ROMANS 10:6B–10 (NEW REVISED STANDARD VERSION)**

*Do you see what is happening here? Paul projects the process onto the incarnation, death, and resurrection of Christ, which is a further development of the thought. There is nothing wrong with that as long as we recognize it as a projection. The process must still occur within us, or nothing in fact happens of any real value.*

# First Week of Lent

‹›

## SUNDAY

*Fishing in the Unconscious*

And he [Jesus] said, "The human one is like a wise fisherman who cast his net into the sea and drew it up from the sea full of little fish. Among them the wise fisherman discovered a fine large fish. He threw all the little fish back into the sea, and easily chose the large fish. Anyone here with two good ears had better listen!"

GOSPEL OF THOMAS 8 (MILLER)

*In this saying, Jesus is quoting an Aesop fable that goes like this:*

"A fisherman drew in the net which he had cast a short time before and, as luck would have it, it was full of all kinds of delectable fish. But the little ones fled to the bottom of the net and slipped out through its many meshes, whereas the big ones were caught and lay stretched out in the boat."

(FUNK)

*Jesus uses this saying in at least two ways: outwardly when it involves fishing for other people, and inwardly when it means letting down the nets into the depths of the unconscious and seeing what is brought up.*

*The Way of the Tao is within us. Let down your nets for a catch, bring them up, and see what you have found.*

Jesus said, the *Way of the Tao** is like a merchant who had a supply of merchandise and then found a pearl. That merchant was prudent; he sold the merchandise and bought the single pearl for himself. So also with you, seek his treasure that is unfailing, that is enduring, where no moth comes to eat and no worm destroys."

GOSPEL OF THOMAS 76 (MILLER)

*Miller's edition has here "the Father's imperial rule."

## MONDAY

### Intentional Searching and Hidden Surprises

Jesus said, the *Way of the Tao** is like a person who had a treasure hidden in his field but did not know it. And when he died, he left it to his son. The son did not know about it either. He took over the field and sold it. The buyer went plowing, discovered the treasure, and began to lend money at interest to whomever he wished."

GOSPEL OF THOMAS 109 (MILLER)

*Miller's edition has here, and in the quotation that follows, "the Father's imperial rule."

Jesus said, "The *Way of the Tao* is like a shepherd who had a hundred sheep. One of them, the largest, went astray. He left the ninety-nine and looked for the one until he found it. After he had toiled, he said to the sheep, 'I love you more than the ninety-nine.' "

GOSPEL OF THOMAS 107 (MILLER)

## TUESDAY

### *Recognize What Is in Your Sight*

Jesus said, "Know what is in front of your face, and what is hidden from you will be disclosed to you. For there is nothing hidden that will not be revealed."

GOSPEL OF THOMAS 5 (MILLER)

## WEDNESDAY

### *Jesus Teaches About Projections*

Jesus said, "Love your friends like your own soul, protect them like the pupil of your eye."

Jesus said, "You see the speck that is in your friend's eye, but you don't see the beam that is in your own eye. When you take the beam out of your own eye, then you will see clearly to take the speck out of your friend's eye."

Jesus said, "If a blind person leads a blind person, both of them will fall into a hole."

GOSPEL OF THOMAS 25, 26, AND 34 (MILLER)

*In the teaching about "the speck and the beam" Jesus is identifying the process that has come to be known as "projection." The process of projection works like a movie projector and a screen. When I am projecting, I see something in someone else that is actually within me.*

*How do I know when I am projecting? One clue is the particular irritation that flares up quickly, usually without much actual information. For example, when I meet someone for the first time and there is "something about that person I don't like," there is a high degree of probability that I am projecting. There is a way to work with one's projections. First ask, "What is there in this other person that bothers me so much?" Once that characteristic or behavior is identified, gently turn it around and ask, "Am I that way also?" It's important to do this carefully, because when one is projecting, one is likely to deny it quickly.*

*Projections are not always negative. When I am drawn with immediate interest and enthusiasm to something that is especially attractive to me in another person, I am projecting positively. A prime example is "falling in love." Who has not enjoyed this feeling? An important follow-up is to ask oneself, "What do I find so magnetizing about this person?" Then ask, "Is that also part of me?" We may be surprised to discover that what we find delightful in another person is actually a less developed part of ourself! Again, it is important not to deny too quickly.*

*As I learn how to spot my own projections throughout the day, I can begin to see myself and others more clearly.*

## THURSDAY

### Reconciling the Outside and the Inside

Jesus said to them, "When you make the two into one, and when you make the inner like the outer and the outer like the inner, and the upper like the lower, and when you make male and female into a single one, so that the male will not be male nor the female be female, when you make eyes in place of an eye, a hand in place of a hand, a foot in place of a foot, an image in place of an image, then you will enter the *Way of the Tao*."*

GOSPEL OF THOMAS 22:4–7 (MILLER)

*Miller's edition uses "the Father's domain" here.

Jesus said, "If two make peace with each other in a single house, they will say to the mountain, 'Move from here!' and it will move."

GOSPEL OF THOMAS 48 (MILLER)

Jesus said, "When you make the two into one, you will become children of Adam, and when you say, 'Mountain, move from here!' it will move.

GOSPEL OF THOMAS 106 (MILLER)

## FRIDAY

### *Show Us Where You Are*

His disciples said, "Show us the place where you are, for we must seek it."

GOSPEL OF THOMAS 24:1 (MILLER)

*Here are a few of the answers to the question:*

Jesus said, "I took my stand in the midst of the world, and in the flesh I appeared to them."

GOSPEL OF THOMAS 28:1 (MILLER)

Jesus said, "Where there are three deities, they are divine. Where there are two or one, I am with that one."

GOSPEL OF THOMAS 30 (MILLER)

Jesus said, "Often you have desired to hear these words which I am speaking to you, and you have no one else from whom to hear them. There will be days when you will seek me and you will not find me."

GOSPEL OF THOMAS 38 (MILLER)

His disciples said to him, "Twenty-four prophets have spoken in Israel, and they all spoke of you."

He said to them, "You have disregarded the living one who is in your presence, and have spoken of the dead."

GOSPEL OF THOMAS 52 (MILLER)

Jesus said, "Look to the living one as long as you live, otherwise you might die and then try to see the living one, and you will be unable to see."

GOSPEL OF THOMAS 59 (MILLER)

Jesus said, "I am the light that is over all things. I am all: from me all came forth and to me all attained. Split a piece of wood; I am there. Lift up the stone, and you will find me there."

GOSPEL OF THOMAS 77 (MILLER)

Jesus said, "Whoever is near me is near the fire, and whoever is far from me is far from the *Way of the Tao*."*

GOSPEL OF THOMAS 82 (MILLER)

*Miller's edition uses "the Father's domain" here.

Jesus said, "Whoever drinks from my mouth will become like me. I myself shall become that person, and the hidden things will be revealed to him."

GOSPEL OF THOMAS 108 (MILLER)

He [Jesus] said to them, "Anyone here with two ears had better listen! There is light within a person of light, and it shines on the whole world. If it does not shine, it is dark."

GOSPEL OF THOMAS 24:2–3 (MILLER)

## SATURDAY

### *Being Solitary*

Jesus said, "I shall choose you, one out of a thousand, and two out of ten thousand, and they shall stand as a single one."

GOSPEL OF THOMAS 23 (ROBINSON, 3D ED.)

Jesus said, "Congratulations to those who are alone and chosen, for you will find the *Way of the Tao*.* For you have come from it, and you will return there again."

GOSPEL OF THOMAS 49 (MILLER)

*Miller's edition has "the Father's domain" here.

Jesus said, "Many are standing at the door, but it is the solitary who will enter the bridal chamber."

GOSPEL OF THOMAS 75 (ROBINSON, 3D ED.)

# Second Week of Lent

☙

## SUNDAY

*Suffering and Finding Life*

Jesus said, "Blessed is the man who has suffered and found life."

GOSPEL OF THOMAS 58 (ROBINSON, 3D ED.)

## MONDAY

*One Not Born of Woman*

Jesus said, "When you see one who was not born of woman, fall on your faces and worship. That one is your Father."

GOSPEL OF THOMAS 15 (MILLER)

Jesus said, "Those who know all, but are lacking in themselves, are utterly lacking."

GOSPEL OF THOMAS 67 (MILLER)

## TUESDAY

─────────

### *I Shall Give You What No Eye Has Seen*

Jesus said, "I shall give you what no eye has seen and what no ear has heard and what no hand has touched and what has never occurred to the human mind."

**GOSPEL OF THOMAS 17 (ROBINSON, 3D ED.)**

*For the last phrase, the Scholars Version (Miller) translates, "what has not arisen in the human heart." So which is it, mind or heart? From all we see, hear, and know of Jesus and his teachings, wouldn't it be rather safe to say that both are true? Surely he gives us "what has never occurred to the human mind" and "what has not arisen in the human heart."*

Jesus said, "I disclose my mysteries to those who are worthy of my mysteries. Do not let your left hand know what your right hand is doing."

**GOSPEL OF THOMAS 62 (MILLER)**

## WEDNESDAY

─────────

### *Experiencing the Eternal Moment*

The disciples said to Jesus, "Tell us how our end will be."

Jesus said, "Have you discovered, then, the beginning, that you look for the end? For where the beginning is, there will the end be. Blessed is he who will take his place in the beginning; he will know the end and will not experience death."

Jesus said, "Blessed is he who came into being before he came into being. If you become my disciples and listen to my words, these stones will minister to you. For there are five trees for you in Paradise which remain undisturbed summer and winter and whose leaves do not fall. Whoever becomes acquainted with them will not experience death."

GOSPEL OF THOMAS 18 AND 19 (ROBINSON, 3D ED.)

*"Not experience death"—isn't that a rather extravagant claim? Jesus died. Every friend and disciple of Jesus dies sooner or later. So maybe these sayings are not about literal death. Maybe it is a matter of entering into the eternal moment in which all of the past and all of the future are immediately present.*

*Remember, you are highly evolved stardust: The entire history of the planet and of life on earth is being expressed in you right now. When you know that reality, you are experiencing a deep quality of living; death and its power over you drop away.*

## THURSDAY

### *How Is Your Hearing?*

"Anyone here with two good ears had better listen!"

GOSPEL OF THOMAS 8:4 (MILLER)

"Whoever has ears to hear, let him hear."

GOSPEL OF THOMAS 21:5; CF. 24:2, 63:2, 65:2, 96:2
(ROBINSON, 3D ED.)

## FRIDAY

### *Becoming Like a Child*

Jesus said, "The person old in days won't hesitate to ask a little child seven days old about the place of life, and that person will live. For many of the first will be last, and will become a single one."

GOSPEL OF THOMAS 4 (MILLER)

Jesus saw some babies nursing. He said to his disciples, "These nursing babies are like those who enter the *Way of the Tao*."\*

GOSPEL OF THOMAS 22:1 (MILLER)

\*The Scholars Version (Miller) has "the Father's domain" here and in the next quotation.

Jesus said, "From Adam to John the Baptist, among those born of women, no one is so much greater than John the Baptist that his eyes should not be averted. But I have said that whoever among you becomes a child will recognize the *Way of the Tao* and will become greater than John."

GOSPEL OF THOMAS 46 (MILLER)

## SATURDAY

### *Disrobing and Not Being Afraid*

Mary said to Jesus, "What are your disciples like?"
He said, "They are like children living in a field that is not theirs. When the owners of the field come, they will say, 'Give us back our field.'

They take off their clothes in front of them in order to give it back to them."

GOSPEL OF THOMAS 21:1–2 (MILLER)

Jesus said, "Do not fret, from morning to evening and from evening to morning, about what you are going to wear."

His disciples said, "When will you appear to us, and when will we see you?"

Jesus said, "When you strip without being ashamed, and you take your clothes and put them under your feet like little children and trample them, then you will see the son of the living one and you will not be afraid."

GOSPEL OF THOMAS 36 AND 37 (MILLER)

# Third Week of Lent

♨

## Amazing Potential

Jesus said, "Look, the sower went out, took a handful of seeds, and scattered them. Some fell on the road, and the birds came and gathered them. Others fell on rock, and they didn't take root in the soil and didn't produce heads of grain. Others fell on thorns, and they choked the seeds and worms ate them. And others fell on good soil, and it produced a good crop; it yielded sixty per measure and one hundred twenty per measure."

GOSPEL OF THOMAS 9 (MILLER)

The disciples said to Jesus, "Tell us what the *Way of the Tao*\* is like."

He said to them, "It's like a mustard seed. It's the smallest of all seeds, but when it falls on prepared soil, it produces a large plant and becomes a shelter for birds of the sky."

GOSPEL OF THOMAS 20 (MILLER)

\*Miller's edition reads "Heaven's imperial rule" here.

Jesus said, "The *Way of the Tao** is like a man who had good seed. His enemy came by night and sowed weeds among the good seed. The man did not allow them to pull up the weeds; he said to them, 'I am afraid that you will go intending to pull up the weeds and pull up the wheat along with them.' For on the day of the harvest the weeds will be plainly visible, and they will be pulled up and burned."

GOSPEL OF THOMAS 57 (ROBINSON, 3D ED.)

*Robinson's edition uses "the kingdom of the father" here.

Jesus said, "The crop is huge but the workers are few, so beg the harvest boss to dispatch workers to the fields."

GOSPEL OF THOMAS 73 (MILLER)

## MONDAY

### *Come and Dine!*

Jesus said, "A man had received visitors. And when he had prepared the dinner, he sent his servant to invite the guests. He went to the first one and said to him, 'My master invites you.' He said, 'I have claims against some merchants. They are coming to me this evening. I must go and give them my orders. I ask to be excused from the dinner.' He went to another and said to him, 'My master has invited you.' He said to him, 'I have just bought a house and am required for the day. I shall not have any spare time.' He went to another and said to him, 'My master invites you.' He said to him, 'My friend is going to get married, and I am to prepare the banquet. I shall not be able to come. I ask to be excused from the dinner.' He went to another and said to him, 'My master invites you.' He said to him, 'I have just bought a farm, and I am on my way to collect the rent. I shall not be able to come. I ask to be excused.' The servant returned and said to his master, 'Those whom you invited to the dinner have asked to be excused.'

"The master said to his servant, 'Go outside to the streets and bring back those whom you happen to meet, so that they may dine.' "

GOSPEL OF THOMAS 64 (ROBINSON, 3D ED.)

*This story in the Gospel of Thomas is expanded in Luke 14:15–24 and Matthew 22:1–14.*

## TUESDAY

### *You Are What You Eat*

Jesus said, "The *Way of the Tao*\* is like a woman. She took a little yeast, hid it in dough, and made it into large loaves of bread."

GOSPEL OF THOMAS 96 (MILLER)

\*"The Father's imperial rule" in the Scholars Version (Miller).

They saw a Samaritan carrying a lamb on his way to Judea. He [Jesus] said to his disciples, "Why does that person carry the lamb around?"

They said to him, "So that they may kill it and eat it." He said to them, "While it is alive, he will not eat it, but only when he has killed it and it has become a carcass."

They said, "Otherwise he can't do it."

He said to them, "So also with you, seek for yourselves a place for rest, or you might become a carcass and be eaten."

GOSPEL OF THOMAS 60 (ROBINSON, 1977; MILLER)

Jesus said, "Lucky is the lion that the human will eat, so that the lion becomes human. And foul is the human that the lion will eat, and the lion still will become human."

GOSPEL OF THOMAS 7 (MILLER)

## WEDNESDAY

### *When Not to Eat: The Question of Fasting*

His disciples questioned him and said to him, "Do you want us to fast? How shall we pray? Shall we give alms? What diet shall we observe?"

Jesus said, "Do not tell lies, and do not do what you hate, for all things are plain in the sight of heaven. For nothing hidden will not become manifest, and nothing covered will remain without being uncovered."

GOSPEL OF THOMAS 6 (ROBINSON, 3D ED.)

Jesus said to them, "If you fast, you will give rise to sin for yourselves; and if you pray, you will be condemned; and if you give alms, you will do harm to your spirits. When you go into any land and walk about in the districts, if they receive you, eat what they will set before you, and heal the sick among them. For what goes into your mouth will not defile you, but that which issues from your mouth—it is that which will defile you."

GOSPEL OF THOMAS 14 (ROBINSON, 3D ED.)

Jesus said, "If you do not fast as regards the world, you will not find the *Way*. If you do not observe the Sabbath as a Sabbath, you will not see the *Tao*."*

GOSPEL OF THOMAS 27 (ROBINSON, 3D ED.)

*Robinson's English edition uses "the kingdom" and "the father," respectively.

They said to Jesus, "Come, let us pray today and let us fast."

Jesus said, "What is the sin that I have committed, or wherein have I been defeated? But when the bridegroom leaves the bridal chamber, then let them fast and pray."

GOSPEL OF THOMAS 104 (ROBINSON, 3D ED.)

## THURSDAY

### *Losing It*

Jesus said, "The *Way of the Tao*[*] is like a certain woman who was carrying a jar full of meal. While she was walking on the road, still some distance from home, the handle of the jar broke and the meal emptied out behind her on the road. She did not realize it; she had noticed no accident. When she finally reached her house, she set the jar down and found it empty."

GOSPEL OF THOMAS 97 (ROBINSON, 3D ED.)

[*]"Kingdom of the father."

## FRIDAY

### *More Ways of Losing It*

Jesus said, "A grapevine has been planted apart from the Father. Since it is not strong, it will be pulled up by its root and will perish."

GOSPEL OF THOMAS 40 (MILLER)

Jesus said, "Whoever has something in hand will be given more, and whoever has nothing will be deprived of even the little that they have."

GOSPEL OF THOMAS 41 (MILLER)

Jesus said, "Whoever blasphemes against the Father will be forgiven, and whoever blasphemes against the son will be forgiven, but whoever blasphemes against the holy spirit will not be forgiven, either on earth or in heaven."

GOSPEL OF THOMAS 44 (MILLER)

He [Jesus] said, "Lord, there are many around the drinking trough, but there is nothing in the well."

GOSPEL OF THOMAS 74 (MILLER)

"Do not give what is holy to dogs, for they might throw them upon the manure pile. Do not throw pearls to swine."

GOSPEL OF THOMAS 93 (MILLER)

## SATURDAY

### What Is the Condition of Your Heart?

Jesus said, "Grapes are not harvested from thorn trees, nor are figs gathered from thistles, for they yield no fruit. Good persons produce good from what they've stored up; bad persons produce evil from the

THIRD WEEK OF LENT

wickedness they've stored up in their hearts, and say evil things. For from the overflow of the heart they produce evil."

**GOSPEL OF THOMAS 45 (MILLER)**

His disciples said to him, "Is circumcision useful or not?"

He said to them, "If it were useful, their father would produce children already circumcised from their mother. Rather, the true circumcision in spirit has become profitable in every respect."

**GOSPEL OF THOMAS 53 (MILLER)**

Jesus said, "Blessed are the poor, for yours is the *Way of the Tao*."*

**GOSPEL OF THOMAS 54 (ROBINSON, 3D ED.)**

*Robinson's edition uses "kingdom of heaven."

# Fourth Week of Lent

☙

## SUNDAY

---

### Proclaim the Light

Jesus said, "A city being built on a high mountain and fortified cannot fall, nor can it be hidden."

**THOMAS 32 (ROBINSON, 3D ED.)**

Jesus said, "Preach from your housetops that which you will hear in your ear. For no one lights a lamp and puts it under a bushel, nor does he put it in a hidden place, but rather he sets it on a lampstand so that everyone who enters and leaves will see its light."

**THOMAS 33 (ROBINSON, 3D ED.)**

Jesus said, "Images are visible to people, but the light within them is hidden in the image of *the light of the Tao. The Tao* will be disclosed, but the image is hidden by the light."

**GOSPEL OF THOMAS 83 (MILLER)**

## MONDAY

---

### *Be Holistic: Get It Together, Body and Soul*

Jesus said, "I took my stand in the midst of the world, and in the flesh I appeared to them. I found them all drunk, and I did not find any of them thirsty. My soul ached for the children of humanity, because they are blind in their hearts and do not see, for they came into the world empty, and they also seek to depart from the world empty. But meanwhile they are drunk. When they shake off their wine, then they will repent."

GOSPEL OF THOMAS 28 (MILLER)

Jesus said, "How miserable is the body that is dependent on a body, and how miserable is the soul that is dependent on these two."

GOSPEL OF THOMAS 87 (MILLER, CONFLATED WITH ROBINSON, 3D ED.)

Jesus said, "Damn the flesh that depends on the soul. Damn the soul that depends on the flesh."

GOSPEL OF THOMAS 112 (MILLER)

## TUESDAY

---

### *Solve Your Own Problems or Let It All Pass*

A man said to him, "Tell my brothers to divide my father's possessions with me."

He [Jesus] said to the man, "Mister, who made me a divider?"

He turned to the disciples and said to them, "I'm not a divider, am I?"

GOSPEL OF THOMAS 72 (MILLER, CONFLATED WITH ROBINSON, 3D ED.)

Jesus said, "Become passers-by."

GOSPEL OF THOMAS 42 (ROBINSON, 3D ED.)

*In the first saying, someone is asking Jesus to resolve an inheritance problem. Jesus seems to be saying, "You expect me to tell you what to do? Take responsibility and solve your own problems!" In the second, he seems to be suggesting that we practice detachment and let things pass. So when do you take responsibility, and when do you just walk on by? Knowing when to do each may be when you are living in the Way of the Tao.*

## WEDNESDAY

### Give Me What Is Mine!

They showed Jesus a gold coin and said to him, "Caesar's men demand taxes from us."

He said to them, "Give Caesar what belongs to Caesar, give God what belongs to God, and give me what is mine."

GOSPEL OF THOMAS 100 (ROBINSON, 3D ED.)

*One of those verses that has been beaten to death over the years is "Render to Caesar what is Caesar's and to God what is God's." This verse has been seen as support for "separation of church and state" and has been used to tell those who preach sermons to "stay out of politics."*

*But take another look at the verse. Is Jesus making these distinctions? Is he even designating what is Caesar's and what is God's? A trap has been set for Jesus, and he has simply walked away from it, leaving the disciples trying to sort it out.*

*And the Gospel of Thomas adds the zinger "and give me what is mine." Now, go and sort that out! If we see in Jesus a prime example of what it is to be a fully authentic human being, then by discovering first what is "mine" (our true humanity), we will sort out more clearly our allegiances: our first one being to the Tao to whom all belongs. I suspect we could spend the rest of our lives pondering the meaning of these few lines.*

## THURSDAY

### Finding Your Pacing: Movement and Repose

Jesus said, "If they say to you, 'Where have you come from?' say to them, 'We have come from the light, from the place where the light came into being by itself, established itself, and appeared in their image.' If they say to you, 'Is it you?' say, 'We are its children, and we are the chosen of the living *Tao*.'"* If they ask you, 'What is the evidence of the *Tao* within you?' say to them, 'It is motion and rest.' "

GOSPEL OF THOMAS 50 (MILLER)

*"Father."

Jesus said, "Foxes have their dens and birds have their nests, but human beings have no place to lay down and rest."

GOSPEL OF THOMAS 86 (MILLER)

Jesus said, "Come to me, for my yoke is easy and my lordship is gentle, and you will find rest for yourselves."

GOSPEL OF THOMAS 90 (MILLER)

*Living in the Tao means "motion and rest" or as the Robinson edition puts it, "movement and rest." Living in the Tao is living musically, moving and resting in rhythm. The sense of timing in life is what it is all about.*

*Yet "rest" has another meaning, besides just pausing or pacing oneself or lying down and going to sleep. When we discover how to rest in the Tao, we are actually resting all the time—working without striving, laboring without effort.*

*First learn the pacing, then discover the perpetual resting that, as Jesus points out, is easy and gentle. Yet if you strive for that kind of rest, you will not attain it, because that kind of rest is pure gift from the Tao.*

## FRIDAY

### *Hating and Loving Your Father and Mother*

The disciples said to him, "Your brothers and your mother are standing outside."

He [Jesus] said to them, "Those here who do what my Father wants are my brother and my mother. They are the ones who will enter my Father's domain."

**GOSPEL OF THOMAS 99 (MILLER)**

Jesus said, "Whoever does not hate father and mother cannot be my disciple, and whoever does not hate brothers and sisters, and carry the cross as I do, will not be worthy of me."

**GOSPEL OF THOMAS 55 (MILLER)**

"Whoever does not hate father and mother as I do cannot be my disciple, and whoever does not love father and mother as I do cannot be my disciple. For my mother gave me falsehood, but my true mother gave me life."

**GOSPEL OF THOMAS 101 (MILLER, AND ROBINSON, 1977)**

Jesus said, "Whoever knows the father and the mother will be called the child of a whore."

GOSPEL OF THOMAS 105 (MILLER)

## SATURDAY

### A New Set of Values

Jesus said, "If you have money, do not lend it at interest, but give it to one from whom you will not get it back."

GOSPEL OF THOMAS 95 (ROBINSON, 3D ED.)

Jesus said, "A person cannot mount two horses or bend two bows. And a slave cannot serve two masters, otherwise he'll honor one and offend the other.

"Nobody drinks aged wine and immediately wants to drink young wine. Young wine is not poured into old wineskins, or they might break, and aged wine is not poured into a new wineskin, or it might spoil. An old patch is not sewn onto a new garment, since it would create a tear."

GOSPEL OF THOMAS 47 (MILLER)

Jesus said, "I shall destroy this house, and no one will be able to build it."

GOSPEL OF THOMAS 71 (ROBINSON, 3D ED.)

*Sayings like this make no sense to the person who has not yet discovered something of the Way of the Tao. But those who are in the Way read these, smile, and understand.*

# *Fifth Week of Lent*

☙

─────────────

### *Understand the World's Values*

"If the owners of a house know that a thief is coming, they will be on guard before the thief arrives, and will not let the thief break into their house and steal their possessions. As for you, then, be on guard against the world. Prepare yourselves with great strength, so the robbers can't find a way to get to you, for the trouble you expect will come. Let there be among you a person who understands."

GOSPEL OF THOMAS 21:5–8 (MILLER)

Jesus said, "One can't enter a strong person's house and take it by force without tying his hands. Then one can loot his house."

GOSPEL OF THOMAS 35 (MILLER)

Jesus said, "The *Way of the Tao*\* is like a person who wanted to kill someone powerful. While still at home he drew his sword and thrust it into the wall to find out whether his hand would go in. Then he killed the powerful one."

GOSPEL OF THOMAS 98 (MILLER)

*"The Father's imperial rule."

Jesus said, "Congratulations to those who know where the rebels are going to attack. They can get going, collect their imperial resources, and be prepared before the rebels arrive."

GOSPEL OF THOMAS 103 (MILLER)

Jesus said, "Whoever has come to understand the world has found only a corpse, and whoever has found a corpse is superior to the world."

GOSPEL OF THOMAS 56 (ROBINSON, 3D ED.)

Jesus said, "He who has recognized the world has found the body, but he who has found the body is superior to the world."

GOSPEL OF THOMAS 80 (ROBINSON, 3D ED.)

Jesus said, "There was a rich person who had a great deal of money. He said, 'I shall invest my money so that I may sow, reap, plant, and fill my storehouse with produce, that I may lack nothing.' These were the things he was thinking in his heart, but that very night he died. Anyone here with two ears had better listen!"

GOSPEL OF THOMAS 63 (MILLER)

*Jesus understands the world's values—and then stands them on their heads!*

## MONDAY

---

### *Casting Fire upon the Earth!*

Jesus said, "I have cast fire upon the world, and look, I'm guarding it until it blazes."

**GOSPEL OF THOMAS 10 (MILLER)**

Jesus said, "Perhaps people think that I have come to cast peace upon the world. They do not know that I have come to cast conflicts upon the earth: fire, sword, war. For there will be five in a house: there'll be three against two and two against three, father against son and son against father, and they will stand alone."

**GOSPEL OF THOMAS 16 (MILLER)**

*Jesus disturbs the comfortable and comforts the disturbed. The teaching of the Way of the Tao creates division where there was an illusion of peace and brings peace when the opposites are reconciled.*

*The process is intense—something like fire, even the fire Moses knew in the burning bush that was not consumed.*

## TUESDAY

---

### *Heaven and Earth Are Passing Away*

Jesus said, "This heaven will pass away, and the one above it will pass away. The dead are not alive, and the living will not die. During the days when you ate what is dead, you made it come alive. When you are in the light, what will you do? On the day when you were one, you became two. But when you become two, what will you do?"

GOSPEL OF THOMAS 11 (MILLER)

Jesus said, "The heavens and the earth will roll up in your presence, and whoever is living from the living one will not see death." Does not Jesus say, "Those who have found themselves, of them the world is not worthy"?

GOSPEL OF THOMAS 111 (MILLER)

*Sayings like these speak especially clearly when society is in the midst of major shifts and changes. A new age has, in fact, begun in our time. When anyone becomes aware of what is going on and of deep inner changes, the words about "heaven and earth passing away" are understood.*

## WEDNESDAY

### *Resistance to Jesus and His Teachings*

Jesus said, "No prophet is welcome on his home turf; doctors don't cure those who know them."

GOSPEL OF THOMAS 31 (MILLER)

His disciples said to him, "Who are you to say these things to us?"

"You understand who I am from what I say to you. Rather, you have become like the Judeans, for they love the tree but hate its fruit, or they love the fruit but hate the tree."

GOSPEL OF THOMAS 43 (MILLER)

Jesus said, "Show me the stone that the builders rejected: that is the keystone."

GOSPEL OF THOMAS 66 (MILLER)

Jesus said, "Blessed are you when you are hated and persecuted. Wherever you have been persecuted, they will find no place."

GOSPEL OF THOMAS 68 (ROBINSON, 3D ED.)

Jesus said, "Blessed are they who have been persecuted within themselves. It is they who have truly come to know the father. Blessed are the hungry, for the belly of him who desires will be filled."

GOSPEL OF THOMAS 69 (ROBINSON, 3D ED.)

*The more your way of living is in harmony with the Tao, the more at odds you can expect to be with the prevailing attitudes of the times; so when it happens, remember Jesus, who warned you of the risks involved.*

## THURSDAY

### *Great Men and Pharisees Don't Get It*

Jesus said the Pharisees and the scholars have taken the keys of knowledge and have hidden them. They have not entered, nor have they allowed those who want to enter to do so. You, however, be as wise as serpents and as innocent as doves.

GOSPEL OF THOMAS 39 (MILLER, CONFLATED WITH ROBINSON, 3D ED.)

Jesus said, "Damn the Pharisees, for they are like a dog sleeping in the cattle manger, for it neither eats nor lets the cattle eat."

GOSPEL OF THOMAS 102 (AESOP) (MILLER)

Jesus said, "Why do you wash the outside of the cup? Don't you understand that the one who made the inside is also the one who made the outside?"

GOSPEL OF THOMAS 89 (MILLER)

Jesus said, "Why have you come out to the countryside? To see a reed shaken by the wind? And to see a person dressed in soft clothes, like your rulers and your powerful ones? They are dressed in soft clothes, and they cannot understand truth."

GOSPEL OF THOMAS 78 (MILLER)

Jesus said, "Let one who has become wealthy reign, and let one who has power renounce it."

GOSPEL OF THOMAS 81 (MILLER)

Jesus said, "Let one who has found the world, and has become wealthy, renounce the world."

GOSPEL OF THOMAS 110 (MILLER)

## FRIDAY

---

### *The Vineyard*

"There was a good man who owned a vineyard. He leased it to tenant farmers so that they might work it and he might collect the produce from them. He sent his servant so that the tenants might give him the produce of the vineyard. They seized his servant and beat him, all but killing him. The servant went back and told his master. The master said, 'Perhaps he did not recognize them.' He sent another servant. The tenants beat this one as well. Then the owner sent his son and said, 'Perhaps they will show respect to my son.' Because the tenants knew that it was he who was the heir to the vineyard, they seized him and killed him. Let him who has ears hear."

GOSPEL OF THOMAS 65 (ROBINSON, 3D ED.)

The disciples said to Jesus, "We know that you are going to leave us. Who will be our leader?"

Jesus said to them, "No matter where you are, you are to go to James the Just, for whose sake heaven and earth came into being."

GOSPEL OF THOMAS 12 (MILLER)

## SATURDAY

---

### *People Do Not See It*

His disciples said to him, "When will the repose of the dead come about, and when will the new world come?"

He said to them, "What you look forward to has already come, but you do not recognize it."

His disciples said to him, "When will the *Way of the Tao*\* come?"

Jesus said, "It will not come by waiting for it. It will not be a matter of saying 'here it is' or 'there it is.' Rather, the *Way of the Tao* is spread out upon the earth, and *people* do not see it."

GOSPEL OF THOMAS 51, 113 (ROBINSON, 3D ED.)

\*Robinson's edition uses "the kingdom" and the "kingdom of the father" here.

# Holy Week

✧

*This Is the One Who Is Free*

This is the One who is Free!
This is the Physician of all Creation!
This is the One who is rejected by his own people.
This is the One who embodies the Cosmos and manifests Nature.
This is the One who is Eternal and first born from the Depths.
He is called son of the virgin Mary and Joseph the carpenter.
His simplicity we see with our natural eyes, but his greatness we
    receive by faith and see in his works;
His human body we touch with our hands,
and his appearance we see transformed with our own eyes,
but his heavenly form we could not see upon the mount;
who baffles the Authorities and transforms death;
Here is the Truth who does not lie,
Here is the One who pays taxes and for himself and his disciples.
Here is the One whom the Authorities fear when they see him.
Here is the One who confuses those in power.
The Authorities ask, "Who are you and where do you come from?"
They do not know the truth because they are enemies of the Truth.

ACTS OF THOMAS 143
(SEERS VERSION, PARAPHRASED)

*Who is this Jesus who was baptized, experienced his new life in the Spirit, began teaching, and in whose presence people are healed and set free? Who is this Jesus whom the people are planning to kill? Who is this Jesus beginning his final week before his arrest, trial, torture, and crucifixion? This is the One who is Free! Do you truly desire to be free? If so, begin walking alongside this Free Man through this Holy Week.*

## MONDAY

### Jesus Pulled out the Root

Jesus pulled out the root of the whole place, while others did it only partially. As for ourselves, let each one of us dig down after the root of evil which is within one, and let one pluck it out of one's heart from the root. It will be plucked out if we recognize it. But if we are ignorant of it, it takes root in us and produces its fruit in our heart. It masters us. We are its slaves. It takes us captive, to make us do what we do not want; and what we do want we do not do. It is powerful because we have not recognized it. While it exists it is active. Ignorance is the mother of all evil. Ignorance will eventuate death, because those that come from ignorance neither were nor are nor shall be. But those who are in the truth will be perfect when all the truth is revealed. For truth is like ignorance: while it is hidden it rests in itself, but when it is revealed and is recognized, it is praised inasmuch as it is stronger than ignorance and error. It gives freedom. The word said, "If you know the truth, the truth will make you free" [John 8:32]. Ignorance is a slave. Knowledge is freedom. If we know the truth, we shall find the fruits of the truth within us. If we are joined to it, it will bring our fulfillment.

GOSPEL OF PHILIP 83:16–84:13 (ROBINSON, 1977)

## TUESDAY

---

*Conversations with the Disciples*

The Savior said to his disciples, "Already the time has come, brothers, that we should leave behind our labor and stand in the rest; for he who stands in the rest will rest forever. . . .

I will teach you when the time of dissolution will come. . . ."

His disciples said, "Lord who is the one who seeks and who is the one who reveals?"

The Lord said, "The one who seeks is the one who reveals. . . ."

"The one who speaks is also the one who hears,
and the one who sees is also the one who reveals."

Mariam said, "O Lord, behold, when I am bearing the body, for what reason do I weep, and for what reason do I laugh?" [The answer is badly obliterated in the text.]

Judas said, "Tell us, Lord, before the heavens and the earth were, what was it that existed?"

The Lord said, "It was darkness and water and a spirit that was upon a water. But I say to you, as for what you seek after and inquire about, behold it is within you. . . . The true mind came to be within. . . . He who is able, let him deny himself, and repent. And he who knows, let him seek and find and rejoice."

Mariam asked, "Brothers, the things about which you ask . . . where will you keep them?"

EXCERPTS FROM THE DIALOGUE OF THE SAVIOR (ROBINSON, 1977)

## WEDNESDAY

### *A Conversation with Matthew*

Matthew said, "Lord, I wish to see that place of life, that place in which there is no evil, but rather it is the pure light."

The Lord said, "Brother Matthew, you cannot see it, as long as you wear the flesh." Matthew said, "O Lord, even if I cannot see it, let me know it."

The Lord said, "Every one of you who has known himself has seen it; everything that is fitting for him to do, he does it. And he has been doing it in his goodness."

The Lord said, "If one does not understand how the fire came to be, he will burn in it, because he does not know his root. If one does not first understand the water he does not understand anything. For what is the use for him to receive baptism in it? If one does not understand how the body that he wears came to be, he will perish with it.

"And he who does not know the Son, how will he know the Father? And he who will not know the root of all things, they [all things] are hidden from him. He who will not know the root of wickedness is not a stranger to it. He who will not understand how he came will not understand how he will go, and is not a stranger to this world which will perish and which will be humbled."

EXCERPTS FROM THE DIALOGUE OF THE SAVIOR
(ROBINSON, 1977)

## THURSDAY

### *A Conversation with Judas*

Judas said, "Tell me, Lord, what is the beginning of the way?"

The Lord said, "Love and goodness. For if there had been one of these dwelling with the archons, wickedness would never have come to be."

Judas said to him, "Who will rule over us? . . . Behold, the archons dwell in heaven; surely, then, it is they who will rule over us."

The Lord said, "You will rule over them. But when you remove envy from you, then you will clothe yourselves with the light and enter into the bridal chamber."

Judas said, "How will our garments be brought to us?"

The Lord said, "Some will bring them to you and others will receive them, for they are the ones who bring you your garments. Who can reach the place which is the reward? But they gave the garments of life to man, for he knows the way on which he will go. For indeed it is a burden to me as well to reach it."

Judas said to Matthew, "We wish to know with what kind of garments we will be clothed, when we come forth from the corruption of the flesh."

The Lord said, "The archons and the governors have garments that are given to them for a time, which do not abide. As for you, however, since you are sons of the truth, it is not with these temporary garments that you will clothe yourselves. Rather, I say to you that you will be blessed when you strip yourselves."

EXCERPTS FROM THE DIALOGUE OF THE SAVIOR (ROBINSON, 1977)

*Judas wants to know the Way, but his biggest questions are his concerns over power, "Who will rule over us?" People often clothe themselves with garments of power, everything from military uniforms to suits of business executives to the vestments of religious professionals. Jesus teaches Judas and us to remove these garments of power. When we thus strip ourselves, we are blessed. Could this teaching have been too much for Judas to comprehend and accept?*

## THURSDAY EVENING IN THE GARDEN OF GETHSEMANE

### *Questions of Gethsemane*

*All of these and more:*

And who is the one who has bound him?
And who is the one who will loose him?
And what is the light? And what is the darkness?
And who is the one who has created the earth? And who is God?
And who are the angels? And what is the soul? And what is spirit?
And where is the voice? And who is the one who speaks?
And who is the one who hears? Who is the one who gives pain?
And who is the one who suffers?
And who is it who has begotten the corruptible flesh?
And what is the governance? And why are some lame, and some blind, and some rich, and some poor? And why are some powerless, some brigands?
And why is this happening? And why me?

THE TESTIMONY OF TRUTH (ROBINSON, 1977)

## NIGHT BEFORE GOOD FRIDAY

### *Joseph Asks for the Body*

But of the Judeans no one washed his hands, neither Herod nor any one of his judges. Since they were unwilling to wash, Pilate stood up. Then

Herod the king orders the Lord to be taken away, saying to them, "Do what I commanded you to do to him."

Joseph stood there, the friend of Pilate and the Lord, and when he realized that they were about to crucify him, he went to Pilate and asked for the body of the Lord for burial. And Pilate sent to Herod and asked for his body. And Herod replied, "Brother Pilate, even if no one had asked for him, we would have buried him, since the sabbath is drawing near. For it is written in the Law, 'The sun must not set upon one who has been executed.'" And he turned him over to the people on the day before the Unleavened Bread, their feast.

GOSPEL OF PETER 1:1–2:3 (MILLER)

## GOOD FRIDAY MORNING

### *Jesus Is Crucified*

They took the Lord and kept pushing him along as they ran; and they would say, "Let's drag the son of God along, since we have him in our power." And they threw a purple robe around him and sat him upon the judgment seat and said, "Judge justly, king of Israel." And one of them brought a crown of thorns and set it on the head of the Lord. And others standing about would spit in his eyes, and others slapped his face, while others poked him with a rod. Some kept flogging him as they said, "Let's pay proper respect to the son of God."

And they brought two criminals and crucified the Lord between them. But he himself remained silent, as if in no pain. And when they set up the cross, they put an inscription on it, "This is the king of Israel." And they piled his clothing in front of him; then they divided it among themselves, and gambled for it. But one of those criminals reproached them and said, "We're suffering for the evil that we've done, but this fellow, who has become a savior of humanity, what wrong has he done to you?" And they got angry at him and ordered that his legs not be broken so he would die in agony.

GOSPEL OF PETER 3:1–4:5 (MILLER)

## GOOD FRIDAY AT NOON

### *They Set Him on the Ground and the Earth Shook*

It was midday and darkness covered the whole of Judea. They were confused and anxious for fear the sun had set since he was still alive. For it is written that, "The sun must not set upon one who has been executed." And one of them said, "Give him vinegar with something bitter to drink." And they mixed it and gave it to him to drink. And they fulfilled all things and brought to completion the sins on their head. Now many went about with lamps, and, thinking it was night, they laid down. And the Lord cried out, saying, "My power, my power, you have abandoned me." When he said this, he was taken up. And at that moment, the veil of the Jerusalem temple was torn in two.

And they pulled the nails from the Lord's hands and set him on the ground. And the whole earth shook and there was great fear.

GOSPEL OF PETER 5:1–6 (MILLER)

*For comparison:*

*"My God, my God, why, O Lord, have you forsaken me?" (Mark 15:34 and parallels)*

It was on the cross that he said these words, for it was there he was divided.

GOSPEL OF PHILIP 68:27–28 (ROBINSON, 1977)

## GOOD FRIDAY EVENING

---

### Joseph Buries Jesus

Then the sun came out and it was found to be the ninth hour. Now the Judeans rejoiced and gave his body to Joseph so that he might bury it, since Joseph had observed how much good he had done. Joseph took the Lord, washed his body and wound a linen shroud around him, and brought him to his own tomb, called "Joseph's Garden."

Then the Jews and the elders and the priests perceived what evil they had done to themselves, and began to beat their breasts and cry out, "Our sins have brought woes upon us! The judgment and the end of Jerusalem are at hand!" But I began weeping with my friends. And quivering with fear in our hearts, we hid ourselves. After all, we were being sought by them as criminals and as ones wishing to burn down the temple. As a result of all these things, we fasted and sat mourning and weeping night and day until the sabbath.

GOSPEL OF PETER 6:2–7:3 (MILLER)

## HOLY SATURDAY

---

### The Guard at the Tomb

When the scribes and the Pharisees and the priests had gathered together, and when they heard that all the people were moaning and beating their breasts, and saying, "If his death has produced these overwhelming signs, he must have been entirely innocent!" they became frightened and went to Pilate and begged him, "Give us soldiers so that we may guard his tomb for three days, in case his disciples come and steal his body and the people assume that he is risen from the dead and do us harm." So Pilate gave them the centurion Petronius with soldiers

to guard the tomb. And elders and scribes went with them to the tomb.
And all who were there with the centurion and the soldiers helped roll a
large stone against the entrance to the tomb. And they put seven seals on
it. Then they pitched a tent there and kept watch.

GOSPEL OF PETER 8:1–6 (MILLER)

## EASTER EVE

### *Moses and Elijah Come for Jesus and Take Him to Heaven*

Early, at first light on the sabbath, a crowd came from Jerusalem and the
surrounding countryside to see the sealed tomb. But during the night
before the Lord's day dawned, while the soldiers were on guard, two by
two during each watch, a loud noise came from the sky, and they saw the
skies open up and two men come down from there in a burst of light and
approach the tomb. The stone that had been pushed against the entrance
began to roll away by itself and moved away to one side; then the tomb
opened up and both young men went inside.

Now when these soldiers saw this, they roused the centurion from his
sleep, along with the elders. (Remember, they were also there keeping
watch.) While they were explaining what they had seen, again they see
three men leaving the tomb, two supporting the third, and a cross following them. The heads of the two reached up to the sky, while the head
of the third, whom they led by the hand, reached beyond the skies. And
they heard a voice from the skies that said, "Have you preached to those
who sleep?" And an answer was heard from the cross: "Yes!"

These men then consulted with one another about going and report-
ing these things to Pilate. While they were still thinking about it, again
the skies appeared to open and some sort of human being came down
and entered the tomb. When those in the centurion's company saw this,
they rushed out into the night to Pilate, having left the tomb which they

were supposed to be guarding. And as they were recounting everything they had seen, they became deeply disturbed and cried, "Truly, he was a son of God!" Pilate responded by saying, "I am clean of the blood of the son of God; this was all your doing." Then they all crowded around Pilate and began to beg and urge him to order the centurion and the soldiers to tell no one what they saw. "You see," they said, "it is better for us to be guilty of the greatest sin before God than to fall into the hands of the Judean people and be stoned." Pilate then ordered the centurion and the soldiers to say nothing.

GOSPEL OF PETER 9:1–11:7 (MILLER)

*Who are the two men who come for Jesus? These are the same two who appear in the story of the transfiguration (August 6): Moses and Elijah, who represent the Law and the Prophets. These two return for Jesus after he dies and take him with them to heaven. Thus the Gospel of Christ brings together the best of the Law and the Prophets and shows them in a new light.*

# First Week of Easter

*Resurrection Stories*

↔

## SUNDAY (EASTER DAY)

### Mary of Magdala at the Tomb

Early on the Lord's day, Mary of Magdala, a disciple of the Lord, was fearful on account of the Judeans and, since they were enflamed with rage, she did not perform at the tomb of the Lord what women are accustomed to do for their loved ones who die. Nevertheless, she took her friends with her and went to the tomb where he had been laid. And they were afraid that the Judeans might see them and were saying, "Although on the day he was crucified we could not weep and beat our breasts, we should now perform these rites at his tomb. But who will roll away the stone for us, the one placed at the entrance of the tomb, so that we may enter and sit beside him and do what ought to be done?" (remember, it was a huge stone). "We fear that someone might see us. And if we are unable to roll the stone away we should, at least, place at the entrance the memorial we brought for him, and we should weep and beat our breasts until we go home."

And they went and found the tomb open. They went up to it, stooped down, and saw a young man sitting there in the middle of the tomb; he was handsome and wore a splendid robe. He said to them, "Why have you come? Who are you looking for? Surely not the one who was crucified? He is risen and gone. If you don't believe it, stoop down and take a look at the place where he lay, for he is not there. You see, he is risen and gone back to the place he was sent from." Then the women fled in fear.

GOSPEL OF PETER 12:1–13:3 (MILLER)

## MONDAY

### Disciples Grieving and Returning to the Familiar

Now it was the last day of Unleavened Bread, and many began to return to their homes since the feast was over. But we, the twelve disciples of the Lord, continued to weep and mourn, and each one, still grieving on account of what had happened, left for his own home. But I, Simon Peter, and Andrew, my brother, took our fishing nets and went away to the sea. And with us was Levi, the son of Alphaeus.

GOSPEL OF PETER 14:1–3 (MILLER)

## TUESDAY

### "The Seed of True Humanity Exists Within You. Follow It!"

*No complete copy of the Gospel of Mary (written perhaps as early as the late first or early second century) exists. All we have is one battered copy in the Nag Hammadi Library. The first six manuscript pages are missing. At this point in the story, the risen Christ is speaking with his disciples:*

"Every nature, every modelled form, every creature, exists in and with each other. They will dissolve again into their own proper root. For the nature of matter is dissolved into what belongs to its nature. Anyone with two ears capable of hearing should listen!"

Then Peter said to him, "You have been expounding every topic to us; tell us one further thing. What is the sin of the world?"

The Savior replied, "There is no such thing as sin; rather, you yourselves are what produces sin when you act according to the nature of adultery, which is called 'sin.' For this reason, the Good came among you approaching what belongs to every nature. It will set it within its root."

Then . . . he said, "This is why you get sick and die, for you love what deceives you. Anyone with a mind should use it to think!

"Matter gave birth to a passion which has no true image because it derives from what is contrary to nature. Then a disturbing confusion occurred in the whole body. This is why I told you, 'Be content of heart.' And do not conform to the body, but form yourselves in the presence of that other image of nature. Anyone with two ears capable of hearing should listen!"

When the Blessed One had said this, he greeted them all. "Peace be with you!" he said. "Acquire my peace within yourselves!

"Be on your guard so that no one deceives you by saying, 'Look over here!' or 'Look over there!' For the seed of true humanity exists within you. Follow it! Those who search for it, they will find it.

"Go then, preach the gospel of the domain. Do not lay down any rule beyond what I ordained for you, nor promulgate law like the lawgiver, or else it will dominate you."

After he said these things, he left them.

GOSPEL OF MARY 2:2–4:11 (MILLER)

## WEDNESDAY

### *"If They Didn't Spare Him, How Will They Spare Us?"*

But the disciples were distressed and wept greatly. "How are we going to go out into the rest of the world to preach the good news about the domain of the seed of the true humanity?" they said. "If they didn't spare him, how will they spare us?"

Then Mary stood up. She greeted them all and addressed her brothers: "Do not weep and be distressed nor let your hearts be irresolute. For his grace will be with you all and will shelter you. Rather let us praise his greatness, for he has joined us together and made us true human beings."

When Mary said these things, she turned their minds toward the Good, and they began to ask about the words of the Savior.

Peter said to Mary, "Sister, we know that the Savior loved you more than any other woman. Tell us the words of the Savior that you know, but which we haven't heard."

Mary answered, saying, "I will report to you as much as I remember that you don't know." And she began to speak these words to them.

She said, "I saw the Lord in a vision and I said to him, 'Lord, I saw you today in a vision.'

"He answered and said to me, 'Congratulations to you for not wavering at seeing me. For where the mind is, there is the treasure.'

"I said to him, 'Lord, how does a person who sees a vision see it—with the soul or with the spirit?'

"The Savior answered, 'The visionary does not see with the soul or with the spirit, but with the mind which exists between these two—that is what sees the vision.'"

GOSPEL OF MARY 5:1–7:6 (MILLER)

## THURSDAY

### "Who Are You to Disregard Her?"

*Mary is relating how her soul has been interrogated by the seven Powers of Wrath, who finally end their interrogation with this sarcastic question:*

"Where are you coming from, human killer, and where are you going, space-conqueror?"

[Mary's] soul replied, "What binds me has been slain, and what surrounds me has been destroyed, and my desire has been brought to an end, and my ignorance has died. In a world, I was set loose from a world and in a type, from a type which is above, and from the chain of forgetfulness that exists in time. From now on, for the rest of the course of the due measure of the time of the age, I will rest in silence."

When Mary said these things, she fell silent, since it was up to this point that the Savior had spoken to her.

Andrew said, "Brothers, what is your opinion of what has been said? I for one don't believe that the Savior said these things because these opinions seem to be so different from his thought."

After reflecting on these matters, Peter said, "Has the Savior spoken secretly to a woman and not openly so that we would all hear? Surely he did not wish to indicate that she is more worthy than we are?"

Then Mary wept and said to Peter, "Peter, my brother, what are you imagining about this? Do you think that I've made all this up secretly by myself or that I am telling lies about the Savior?"

Levi said to Peter, "Peter, you have a constant inclination to anger and you are always ready to give way to it. And even now you are doing exactly that by questioning the woman as if you're her adversary. If the Savior considered her to be worthy, who are you to disregard her? For he knew her completely and loved her devotedly.

"Instead, we should be ashamed and, once we clothe ourselves with perfect humanity, we should do what we were commanded. We should announce the good news as the Savior ordered, and not be laying down rules or making laws."

After he said these things, Levi left and began to announce the good news.

Gospel of Mary 9:26–10:14 (Miller)

*Jesus the Nazarene lived in a patriarchal, male-dominated society, yet he accepted women and men equally. Likewise, the risen Christ lives and speaks through women and men.*

## FRIDAY

### Joseph of Arimathea's Story

*The rulers of the synagogue and the priests and the Levites said to Joseph,*

"We were very angry because you asked for the body of Jesus, and wrapped it in a clean linen cloth, and placed it in a tomb. And for this reason we secured you in a house with no window, and locked and sealed the door, and guards watched where you were shut up. And on the first day of the week we opened it, and did not find you, and were much troubled, and all the people of God were amazed until yesterday. And now tell us what happened to you."

And Joseph said: "On the day of preparation about the tenth hour you shut me in, and I remained the whole Sabbath. And at midnight as I stood and prayed, the house where you shut me in was raised up by the four corners, and I saw as it were a lightning flash in my eyes. Full of fear I fell to the ground. And someone took me by the hand and raised me up from the place where I had fallen, and something moist like water flowed from my head to my feet, and the smell of fragrant oil reached my nostrils. And he wiped my face and kissed me and said to me: Do not fear, Joseph. Open your eyes and see who it is who speaks with you. I looked up and saw Jesus. Trembling, I thought it was a phantom, and I said the ten commandments. And he said them with me. Now as you well know, a phantom immediately flees if it meets anyone and hears the commandments. And when I saw that he said them with me, I said to him: Rabbi

Elijah! He said: I am not Elijah. And I said to him: Who are you, Lord? He replied: I am Jesus, whose body you asked for from Pilate, whom you clothed in clean linen, on whose face you placed a cloth, and whom you placed in your new cave, and you rolled a great stone to the door of the cave. And I asked him who spoke to me: Show me the place where I laid you. And he took me and showed me the place where I laid him. And the linen cloth lay there, and the cloth that was upon his face. Then I recognized that it was Jesus. And he took me by the hand and placed me in the middle of my house, with the doors shut, and led me to my bed and said to me: Peace be with you! Then he kissed me and said to me: Do not go out of our house for forty days. For see, I go to my brethren in Galilee."

And when the rulers of the synagogue and the priests and the Levites heard these words from Joseph, they became as dead men and fell to the ground and fasted until the ninth hour. And Nicodemus and Joseph comforted Annas and Caiaphas and the priests and Levites, saying: "Get up and stand on your feet, and taste bread and strengthen your souls. For tomorrow is the Sabbath of the Lord."

ACTS OF PILATE XV 5, 6; XVI 1 (HENNECKE AND SCHNEEMELCHER)

## SATURDAY

### A Priest, a Teacher, and a Levite Tell Their Experience

Now Phineës a priest and Adas a teacher and Anagaeus a Levite came from Galilee to Jerusalem, and told the rulers of the synagogue and the priests and the Levites: "We saw Jesus and his disciples sitting upon the mountain which is called Mamilch. And he said to his disciples: *Go into all the world and preach the gospel to the whole creation. He who believes and is baptized will be saved; but he who does not believe will be condemned. And these signs will accompany those who believe: in my name they will cast out demons; they will speak in new tongues; they will pick up* serpents; and if they drink any deadly thing, it will not hurt them; they will lay their hands on the sick, and they will recover [Mark 16:15–18]. And while Jesus was still speaking to his disciples, we saw him taken up into heaven."

ACTS OF PILATE XIV 1 (HENNECKE AND SCHNEEMELCHER)

Whenever a serpent appears in a story, as in the Garden of Eden, questions are being raised and someone has to make a decision. "Handling serpents" means being able to handle the questions and to make our decisions.

# Second Week of Easter

*Teachings from the Risen Christ*

↩

## SUNDAY

### *The Risen Christ Appears as a Pearl Merchant*

A man came out wearing a cloth bound around his waist, and a gold belt girded it. Also a napkin was tied over his chest, extending over his shoulders and covering his head and his hands.

I was staring at the man because he was beautiful in his form and stature. There were four parts of his body that I saw: the soles of his feet and a part of his chest and the palms of his hands and his visage. These things I was able to see. A book cover like those of my books was in his left hand. A staff of styrax wood was in his right hand. His voice was resounding as he slowly spoke, crying out in the city, "Pearls! Pearls!"

I, indeed, thought he was a man of that city. I said to him, "My brother and my friend!" He answered me, then, saying, "Rightly did you say, 'My brother and my friend.' What is it you seek from me?" I said to him, "I ask you about lodging for me and the brothers also, because we are strangers here." He said to me, "For this reason have I myself just said, 'My brother and my friend,' because I also am a fellow stranger like you."

And having said these things, he cried out, "Pearls! Pearls!" The rich men of that city heard his voice. They came out of their hidden storerooms. And some were looking out from the storerooms of their houses.

Others looked out from their upper windows. And they did not see that they could gain anything from him, because there was no pouch on his back nor bundle inside his cloth and napkin. And because of their disdain they did not even acknowledge him. He, for his part, did not reveal himself to them. They returned to their storerooms, saying, "This man is mocking us."

And the poor of that city heard his voice, and they came to the man who sells this pearl. They said, "Please take the trouble to show us the pearl so that we may, then, see it with our own eyes. For we are the poor. And we do not have this price to pay for it. But show us that we might say to our friends that we saw a pearl with our own eyes."

He answered, saying to them, "If it is possible, come to my city, so that I may not only show it before your very eyes, but give it to you for nothing."

ACTS OF PETER AND THE TWELVE APOSTLES 2:11–4:15 (ROBINSON, 3D ED.)

*This story clearly shows that just as Jesus the Nazarene had taught about the "pearl of great value" (Matthew 13:46), the risen Christ continues to offer pearls to those who are ready and willing to ask for and to receive the gift. Those who hold tightly to what they have close themselves off and shut the doors to the greatest value.*

## MONDAY

### The Risen Christ Appears as a Child

[Paul meets a child along the road and says to him,] "By which road shall I go to Jerusalem?" The little child replied, saying, "Say your name so that I may show you the road." The little child knew who Paul was. He wished to make conversation with him through his words in order that he might find an excuse for speaking with him.

The little child spoke, saying, "I know who you are, Paul. You are he who was blessed from his mother's womb. For I have come to you that you may go up to Jerusalem to your fellow apostles. And for this reason you were called. And I am the Spirit who accompanies you. . . .

"Let your mind awaken, Paul, and see that this mountain upon which you are standing is the mountain of Jericho, so that you may know the hidden things in those that are visible. Now it is to the twelve apostles that you shall go, for they are elect spirits, and they will greet you." He raised his eyes and saw them greeting him.

APOCALYPSE OF PAUL 18:3–19:20 (ROBINSON, 3D ED.)

*The story continues as the child points out that Paul is already standing on a high mountain, and from here he launches into each of the heavens, learning what he needs to know at each level until he reaches the tenth heaven. It is the child and the Spirit who guide Paul into this new awareness.*

*This is a continuing understanding of the function of the child in our spiritual life: "And a little child shall lead them" (Isaiah 11:6); "Unless you become as a little child . . ." (Luke 18:17); and "The person old in days won't hesitate to ask a child seven days old about the place of life, and that person will live" (Thomas 4).*

## TUESDAY

### The Risen Christ Appears to John

It happened one day, when John, the brother of James—who are the sons of Zebedee—had come up to the temple, that a Pharisee named Arimanius approached him and said to him, "Where is your master whom you followed?" And he said to him, "He has gone to the place from which he came." The Pharisee said to him, "With deception did this Nazarene deceive you, and he filled your ears with lies, and closed your hearts and turned you from the traditions of your fathers."

When I, John, heard these things I turned away from the temple to a desert place. And I grieved greatly in my heart saying, "How then was the savior appointed, and why was he sent into the world by his Father, and who is his Father who sent him, and of what sort is that aeon to which we shall go?" . . .

Straightway, while I was contemplating these things, behold, the heavens opened and the whole creation which is below heaven shone, and the world was shaken. I was afraid, and behold I saw in the light a youth who stood by me. While I looked at him he became like an old man. And he changed his likeness again becoming like a servant. There was not a plurality before me, but there was a likeness with multiple forms in the light, and the likenesses appeared through each other, and the likenesses had three forms.

He said to me, "John, John, why do you doubt, or why are you afraid? You are not unfamiliar with this image, are you?—that is, do not be timid!—I am the one who is with you always. I am the Father, I am the Mother, I am the Son. I am the undefiled and incorruptible one.

"Now I have come to teach you what is and what was and what will come to pass, that you may know the things which are not revealed and those which are revealed, and to teach you concerning the unwavering race of the perfect Man. Now, therefore, lift up your face, that you may receive the things that I shall teach you today, and may tell them to your fellow spirits who are from the unwavering race of the perfect Man.

THE APOCRYPHON OF JOHN 1:4–25, 30–32, 2:1–25, SECOND CENTURY
(ROBINSON, 3D ED.)

## WEDNESDAY

### *The Risen Christ Appears to Thomas*

The Savior said, "Brother Thomas, while you have time in the world, listen to me, and I will reveal to you the things you have pondered in your mind."

"Now since it has been said that you are my twin and true companion, examine yourself and learn who you are, in what way you exist, and how you will come to be. Since you are called my brother, it is not fitting that you be ignorant of yourself. . . . For he who has not known himself has known nothing, but he who has known himself has at the same time already achieved knowledge about the depth of the All. . . ."

Now Thomas said to the Lord, "Therefore I beg you to tell me what I ask before your ascension, and when I hear from you about the hidden things, then I can speak about them. . . .

"Those who speak about things that are invisible and difficult to explain are like those who shoot their arrows at a target at night. To be sure, they shoot their arrows as anyone would—since they shoot at a target—but it is not visible. Yet when the light comes forth and hides the darkness, then the work of each will appear. And you, your light, enlighten, O Lord."

*Then follows a dialogue between Thomas and Christ. A few gems:*

"Everyone who seeks the truth from true wisdom will make himself wings so as to fly, fleeing the lust that scorches the spirits of men."

*A few warnings:*

"Woe to you, godless ones, who have no hope, who rely on things that will not happen!

"Woe to you who hope in the flesh and in the prison that will perish! How long will you be oblivious? . . .

"Woe to you within the fire that burns in you, for it is insatiable!

"Woe to you because of the wheel that turns in your minds!

"Woe to you within the grip of the burning that is in you, for it will devour your flesh openly and rend your souls secretly."

"You baptized your souls in the water of darkness! You walked by your own whims!"

*Plus a few encouragements:*

"Blessed are you who have prior knowledge of the stumbling blocks and who flee alien things.

"Blessed are you who are reviled and not esteemed on account of the love their Lord has for them.

"Blessed are you who weep and are oppressed by those without hope, for you will be released from every bondage."

"Watch and pray . . . that you come forth from the bondage of the bitterness of this life."

EXCERPTS FROM THE BOOK OF THOMAS THE CONTENDER
(ROBINSON, 3D ED.)

## THURSDAY

### The Risen Christ Appears to Peter

*Christ warns Peter,*

"Some who do not understand mystery speaks of things which they do not understand, but they will boast that the mystery of the truth is theirs alone. . . .

"There shall be others of those who are outside our number who name themselves bishop and also deacons, as if they have received their authority from God. They bend themselves under the judgment of the leaders. These people are dry canals."

APOCALYPSE OF PETER 76:26–34, 79:22–31 (ROBINSON, 3D ED.)

## FRIDAY

*The Risen Christ Converses with James the Just*

*An excerpt from a conversation between the risen Christ and James the Just:*

It is the Lord who spoke with me: "See now the completion of my redemption. I have given you a sign of these things, James, my brother. For not without reason have I called you my brother, although you are not my brother materially. . . ."

James said, "Rabbi, if they arm themselves against you, then is there no blame?

You have come with knowledge,
that you might rebuke their forgetfulness.
You have come with recollection,
that you might rebuke their ignorance. . . .
You walked in mud,
and your garments were not soiled,
and you have not been buried in their filth,
and you have not been caught."

*Another excerpt:*

And the Lord appeared to James. James stopped his prayer and embraced him. He kissed him saying, "Rabbi, I have found you! . . ."

And the Lord said, "Since you are a just man of God, you have embraced me and kissed me."

*Among a number of things that James asks the risen Christ is this question:*

James said, "Another thing I ask of you: who are the seven women who have been your disciples? And behold, all women bless you. I also am amazed how powerless vessels have become strong by a perception which is in them."

*Yet another:*

And he kissed my mouth. He took hold of me saying, "My beloved! Behold, I shall reveal to you these things that neither the heavens nor their archons have known. . . . Behold, I shall reveal to you everything, my beloved."

FIRST APOCALYPSE OF JAMES 24:10–18; 28:5–20; 38:15–23;
SECOND APOCALYPSE OF JAMES 56:15–20, 57:4–5 (ROBINSON, 3D ED.)

*One of the most intimate of the resurrection stories is this one revealing the closeness between James and Jesus. This is a spiritual closeness and intimacy out of which comes new awareness for James, including a new view of women. James recognizes that Jesus is able to put women in touch with what is already within them. Is James beginning to come to an awareness of equality here?*

## SATURDAY

### The Risen Christ with a Large Group

Before the foundation of the world, when the whole multitude of the Assembly came together upon the places of the Ogdoad, when they had taken counsel about a spiritual wedding which is in union, and thus he was perfected in ineffable places by a living word, the undefiled wedding was consummated through the Mesotes of Jesus, who inhabits them all and possesses them, who abides in an undivided love of power.

*At the conclusion of Second Treatise of the Great Seth is written:*

Now these things I have presented to you—I am Jesus Christ, the Son of Man, who is exalted in the heavens—, O perfect and incorruptible ones, because of the incorruptible and perfect mystery and the ineffable one. But they think that we decreed them before the foundation of the world in order that, when we emerge from the places of the world, we may present there the symbols of incorruption from the spiritual union unto knowledge. You do not know it because the fleshly cloud overshadows you. But I alone am a friend of Sophia. I have been in the bosom of the Father from the beginning, in the place of the sons of the truth, and the Greatness. Rest then with me, my fellow spirits and my brothers, for ever.

SECOND TREATISE OF THE GREAT SETH 65:34–66:11; 69:20–70:10
(ROBINSON, 3D ED.)

*The "Ogdoad" is the eightfold originating principle from whom all life comes. From the very beginning, there have been plans for a spiritual wedding, a union that is consummated through Jesus. Who can enter into this union? Who can know the Eternal in an intimate way? Who can enter this union through the risen Christ? Just a few select people, or all those who are open to becoming aware of who they are and who it is who dwells within them? Once you know the risen Christ, then you, too, become a friend of Sophia, the wisdom of life.*

*Resting in her is profoundly simple: It means being in intimate relationship with the one who is as close to us as breathing.*

# Third Week of Easter

*Belonging to a Eucharistic Community*

↔

Sunday

---

*Break Bread on Every Lord's Day*

On every Lord's Day—his special day—come together and break bread and give thanks, first confessing your sins so that your sacrifice may be pure. Anyone at variance with his neighbor must not join you, until they are reconciled, lest your sacrifice be defiled. For it was of this sacrifice that the Lord said, "Always and everywhere offer me a pure sacrifice; for I am a great King, says the Lord, and my name is marveled at by the nations."

*Now about the Eucharist—this is how to give thanks, first in connection with the cup:*

"We thank you, our Father, for the holy vine of David, your child, which you have revealed through Jesus, your child. To you be glory forever.

"As this piece of bread was scattered over the hills and then was brought together and made one, so let your Church be brought together from the ends of the earth into your Kingdom. For yours is the glory and the power through Jesus Christ forever."

*After you have finished your meal, say grace in this way:*

"We thank you, holy Father, for your sacred name which you have lodged in our hearts, and for the knowledge and faith and immortality which you have revealed through Jesus, your child. To you be glory forever.

"Almighty Master, you have created everything for the sake of your name, and have given men food and drink to enjoy that they may thank you. But to us you have given spiritual food and drink and eternal life through Jesus, your child.

"Above all, we thank you that you are mighty. To you be glory forever.

"Remember, Lord, your Church, to save it from all evil and to make it perfect by your love. Make it holy, 'and gather it together from the four winds,' into your Kingdom which you have made ready for it. For yours is the power and the glory forever.

"Let Grace come and let this world pass away."

"Hosanna to the Son of David!"

"If anyone is holy, let him come. If not, let him repent."

"Our Lord come!"

"Amen."

*In the case of prophets, however, you should let them give thanks in their own way.*

THE DIDACHE, SECOND CENTURY (RICHARDSON)

*Living in the Tao involves being in community with others, communicating, and sharing meals, especially the Eucharist. The community that eats together stays together.*

## MONDAY

---

### A Prayer of Thanksgiving

This is the prayer that they spoke: "We give thanks to You! Every soul and heart is lifted up to You, undisturbed name, honored with the name 'God' and praised with the name 'Father,' for to everyone and everything comes the fatherly kindness and affection and love, and any teaching there may be that is sweet and plain, giving us mind, speech, and knowledge: mind, so that we may understand You, speech, so that we may expound You, knowledge so that we may know You. We rejoice, having been illuminated by Your knowledge. We rejoice because You have shown us Yourself. We rejoice because while we were in the body, You have made us divine through Your knowledge.

"The thanksgiving of the one who attains to You is one thing: that we know You. We have known You, intellectual light. Life of life, we have known You. Womb of every creature, we have known You. Womb pregnant with the nature of the Father, we have known You. Eternal permanence of the begetting Father, thus have we worshiped your goodness. There is one petition that we ask: we would be preserved in knowledge. And there is one protection that we desire: that we not stumble in this kind of life."

When they had said these things in the prayer, they embraced each other and they went to eat their holy food, which has no blood in it.

THE PRAYER OF THANKSGIVING, SECOND CENTURY
(ROBINSON, 3D ED.)

## TUESDAY

*Holy Bread and Three Cups: Water, Wine, Milk and Honey*

And when the offering is immediately brought by the deacons to the bishop, and by thanksgiving he shall make the bread into an image* of the body of Christ, and the cup of wine mixed with water according to the likeness of the blood, which is shed for all who believe in him. And milk and honey mixed together for the fulfillment of the promise to the fathers, which spoke of a land flowing with milk and honey; namely Christ's flesh which he gave, by which they who believe are nourished like babes, he making sweet the bitter things of the heart by the gentleness of his word. And the water into an offering in a token of the laver, in order that the inner part of man, which is a living soul, may receive the same as the body.

The bishop shall explain the reason of all these things to those who partake.

The deacons shall bring the offering to the bishop and he, laying his hand upon it, with all the presbytery, shall say as the thanksgiving:

The Lord be with you.

[And all shall say]

*And with your spirit.*

Lift up your hearts

*We lift them up unto the Lord*

It is meet and right.

And then he shall proceed immediately:

We give thanks, O God, through thy beloved Servant Jesus Christ, whom at the end of time You sent to us a Saviour and Redeemer and the Messenger of Your counsel. Who is Your Word, inseparable from You; through whom You make all things and in whom You are well pleased. Whom You sent from heaven into the womb of the Virgin, and who, dwelling within her, was made flesh, and was manifested as Your Son, being born of the Holy Spirit and the Virgin. Who, fulfilling Your will, and winning for himself a holy people, spread out his hands when he came to suffer, that by his death he might set free them who believed on You. Who, when he was betrayed to his willing death, that he might bring to nought death, and break the bonds of the devil, and tread hell under foot, and give light to the righteous, and set up a boundary post, and manifest his resurrection, taking bread and giving thanks to You said,

"Take, eat: this is my body, which is broken for you."

And likewise also the cup, saying,

"This is my blood, which is shed for you.

As often as you perform this, perform my memorial."

Having in memory, therefore, his death and resurrection, we offer to You the bread and the cup, yielding You thanks, because You have counted us worthy to stand before You and to minister to You.

And we pray that You would send Your Holy Spirit upon the offerings of Your holy church; that, gathering them into one, You would grant to all Your saints who partake to be filled with Holy Spirit, that their faith may be confirmed in truth, that we may praise and glorify You. Through Your Servant Jesus Christ, through whom be to You glory and honour, with the Holy Spirit in the holy church, both now and always and world without end. Amen.

And when the bishop breaks the bread and distributes the fragments he shall say:

The heavenly bread in Christ Jesus.

And the recipient shall say, Amen.

And the presbyters—or if there are not enough presbyters, the deacons—shall hold the cups, and shall stand by with reverence and modesty; first he who holds the water, then the milk, thirdly the wine. And the recipients shall taste of each three times, he who gives the cup saying,

In God the Father Almighty;

and the recipient shall say, Amen.

Then: In the Lord Jesus Christ;

and he shall say, Amen.

Then: In the Holy Spirit and the holy church;
And he shall say, Amen.
So it shall be done to each.

And when these things are completed, let each one hasten to do good works, and to please God and to live aright, devoting himself to the church, practising the things he has learned, advancing in the service of God.

APOSTOLIC TRADITION OF HIPPOLYTUS, CA. 217 C.E. (EASTON)

*"Image," in Greek *antitypos*, is an impression answering to a die. Likewise, a type or symbol of Christ.

## WEDNESDAY

### The Eucharist Is Jesus

The eucharist is Jesus. . . .

Before Christ came there was no bread in the world, just as Paradise, the place where Adam was, had many trees to nourish the animals but no wheat to sustain man. Man used to feed like the animals, but when Christ came, the perfect man, he brought bread from heaven in order that man might be nourished with the food of man. . . .

His flesh is the word, and his blood is the Holy Spirit. He who has received these has food and he has drink and clothing. . . .

The cup of prayer contains wine and water, since it is appointed as the type of the blood for which thanks is given. And it is full of the Holy Spirit, and it belongs to the wholly perfect man. When we drink this, we shall receive for ourselves the perfect man. The living water is a body. It is necessary that we put on the living man. Therefore, when he is about to go down into the water, he unclothes himself, in order that he may put on the living man.

GOSPEL OF PHILIP 63:21; 55:6–14; 57:6–9; 75:14–24
(ROBINSON, 3D ED. AND 1977)

## THURSDAY

### *The Priest Is Expected to Be Holy*

The priest is completely holy, down to his very body. For if he has taken the bread, will he consecrate it? Or the cup or anything else that he gets, does he consecrate them? Then how will he not consecrate the body also?

GOSPEL OF PHILIP 77:2–7 (ROBINSON, 3D ED.)

## FRIDAY

### *Spiritual Love Is Wine and Fragrance*

Spiritual love is wine and fragrance. All those who anoint themselves with it take pleasure in it. While those who are anointed are present, those nearby also profit from the fragrance. If those anointed with ointment withdraw from them and leave, then those not anointed, who merely stand nearby, still remain in their bad odor.

The Samaritan gave nothing but wine and oil to the wounded man. It is nothing other than the ointment. It healed the wounds, for "love covers a multitude of sins" [1 Peter 4:8].

GOSPEL OF PHILIP 77:35–78:11 (ROBINSON, 3D ED.)

## SATURDAY

### *Faith, Hope, Love, and Knowledge*

Farming in the world requires the cooperation of four essential elements. A harvest is gathered into the barn only as a result of the natural action of water, earth, wind, and light. God's farming likewise has four elements—faith, hope, love, and knowledge. Faith is our earth, that in which we take root. And hope is the water through which we are nourished. Love is the wind through which we grow. Knowledge is the light through which we ripen. Grace exists in four ways: it is earthborn; it is heavenly; it comes from the highest heaven; and it resides in truth.

GOSPEL OF PHILIP 79:18–33 (ROBINSON, 1977)

*In the famous chapter 13 of his first letter to the Corinthians, Paul writes of "faith, hope, and love." He got three out of four. The missing fourth is "knowledge." This is more than academic learning: It is the deep knowing of the source of life whom we name as the Tao.*

# Fourth Week of Easter

## Tao of Healing

ᘖ

### SUNDAY

---

#### The Risen Christ Appears as Physician

Lithargoel ... had the appearance of a physician, since an unguent box was under his arm, and a young disciple was following him carrying a pouch full of medicine. We did not recognize him.

... He said to Peter, "Peter!" And Peter was frightened, for how did he know that his name was Peter? Peter responded to the Savior, "How do you know me, for you called my name?" Lithargoel answered, "I want to ask you who gave you the name Peter to you?" He said to him, "It was Jesus Christ, the son of the living God. He gave this name to me." He answered, "It is I! Recognize me, Peter." He loosened the garment, which clothed him—the one into which he had changed himself because of us—revealing to us in truth that it was he.

We prostrated ourselves on the ground and worshipped him. We comprised eleven disciples. He stretched forth his hand and caused us to stand. We spoke with him humbly. Our heads were bowed down in unworthiness as we said, "What you wish we will do. But give us power to do what you wish at all times."

ACTS OF PETER AND THE TWELVE APOSTLES 8:15–9:19
(ROBINSON, 3D ED.)

*Jesus the Nazarene brought healing, and so does the risen Christ!*

## MONDAY

*"Heal the Bodies First. . . . Heal the Illnesses of the Heart Also."*

He [the Lord] gave them the pouch of medicine and said, "Heal all the sick of the city who believe in my name." Peter was afraid to reply to him for the second time. He signaled to the one who was beside him, who was John: "You talk this time." John answered and said, "Lord, before you we are afraid to say many words. But it is you who asks us to practice this skill. We have not been taught to be physicians. How then will we know how to heal bodies as you have told us?"

He answered them, "Rightly have you spoken, John, for I know that the physicians of this world heal what belongs to the world. The physicians of souls, however, heal the heart. Heal the bodies first, therefore, so that through the real powers of healing for their bodies, without medicine of the world, they may believe in you, that you have power to heal the illnesses of the heart also."

ACTS OF PETER AND THE TWELVE APOSTLES 10:31–11:26
(ROBINSON, 3D ED.)

## TUESDAY

*Honor Physicians*

Honor physicians for their services,
    for the Lord created them;
for their gift of healing comes from the Most High. . . .
The skill of physicians makes them distinguished,
    and in the presence of the great they are admired.
The Lord created medicines out of the earth,
    and the sensible will not despise them.

Was not water made sweet with a tree
    in order that its power might be known?
And he gave skill to human beings
    that he might be glorified in his marvelous works.
By them the physician heals and takes away pain;
    the pharmacist makes a mixture from them.
God's works will never be finished;
    and from him health spreads over all the earth.
My child, when you are ill, do not delay,
    but pray to the Lord, and he will heal you.
Give up your faults and direct your hands rightly,
    and cleanse your heart from all sin. . . .
Then give the physician his place, for the Lord created him;
    do not let him leave you, for you need him.
There may come a time when recovery lies in the hands of physicians,
    for they too pray to the Lord
that he grant them success in diagnosis
    and in healing, for the sake of preserving life.
He who sins against his Maker,
let such a one come under the care of a physician!

SIRACH 38:1–15 (NEW REVISED STANDARD VERSION)

## WEDNESDAY

---

*Love Causing Distress?*

Blessed is the one who on no occasion caused a soul distress. That person is Jesus Christ. He came to the whole place and did not burden anyone. Therefore, blessed is the one who is like this, because he is a perfect man. This indeed is the Word. Tell us about it, since it is difficult to define. How shall we be able to accomplish such a great thing? How will we give everyone comfort? Above all, it is not proper to cause anyone distress—whether the person is great or small, unbeliever or believer—and then give comfort only to those who take satisfaction in good deeds. Some find it advantageous to give comfort to the one who has fared well. He who does good deeds cannot give comfort to such people because it goes against his will. He is unable to cause distress—not that he intends to do so; rather it is their own wickedness which is responsible for their distress. He who possesses the qualities of the perfect man rejoices in the good. Some, however, are terribly distressed by all this.

GOSPEL OF PHILIP 79:34–80:23 (ROBINSON, 1977)

## THURSDAY

### *The Way of Ascent Is the Way of Descent*

For they all bless these individually and together. And afterwards they shall be silent. And just as they were ordained, they ascend. After the silence, they descend from the third. They bless the second; after these the first. The way of ascent is the way of descent.

THE THREE STELES OF SETH (ROBINSON, 3D ED.)

*Everything that goes up comes back down, right? Yes, according to the law of gravity. But the spiritual life often works the other way around: We go down first before coming up! Following the pattern of Jesus in baptism, first we need to go down into the depths of the unconscious, then we come up into new awareness.*

## FRIDAY

---

### *Anointing with Oil*

If anyone offers oil, he shall give thanks as at the offering of the bread and wine, though not with the same words but in the same general manner, saying, That sanctifying this oil, O God, wherewith You anoint kings, priests and prophets, You would grant health to them who use it and partake of it, do that it may bestow comfort on all who taste it and health on all who use it.

APOSTOLIC TRADITION OF HIPPOLYTUS, CA. 217 C.E. (EASTON)

## SATURDAY

---

### *Thanksgiving over Food*

If anyone offers cheese and olives, let him say thus:

Sanctify this milk that has been united into one mass, and unite us to thy love. Let thy loving kindness ever rest upon this fruit of the olive, which is a type of thy bounty, which thou didst cause to flow from the tree of life for them who hope on thee.

At every blessing shall be said,

Glory be to thee, with the Holy Spirit in the holy church, both now and always and world without end. Amen.

APOSTOLIC TRADITION OF HIPPOLYTUS, CA. 217 C.E. (EASTON)

# Fifth Week of Easter

*Tao of Living in Christ*

↭

## SUNDAY

---

### *The Risen Christ with Twelve Disciples and Seven Women*

After he rose from the dead, his twelve disciples and seven women continued to be his followers and went to Galilee onto the mountain called "Divination and Joy." When they gathered together and were perplexed about the underlying reality of the universe and the plan and the holy providence and the power of the authorities and about everything that the Savior is doing with them in the secret of the holy plan, the Savior appeared, not in his previous form, but in the invisible spirit. And his likeness resembles a great angel of light. But his resemblance I must not describe. No mortal flesh could endure it, but only pure and perfect flesh, like that which he taught us about on the mountain called "Of Olives" in Galilee.

And he said, "Peace be to you! My peace I give to you!" And they all marveled and were afraid.

The Savior laughed and said to them: "What are you thinking about? Why are you perplexed? What are you searching for?"

Philip said, "For the underlying reality and the plan."

THE SOPHIA OF JESUS CHRIST 90:14–92:5,
LATTER HALF OF THE FIRST CENTURY C.E. (ROBINSON, 3D ED.)

## MONDAY

_____

### In Jesus Is Revealed the Christ-Sophia

*Each of the disciples asks a question, concluding with Bartholomew, who asks:*

"How is it that he was designated in the Gospel 'Man' and 'Son of Man'? To which of them is this Son related?" The Holy One said to him:

"I want you to know that First Man is called 'Begetter, Self-perfected Mind.' He is reflected with Great Sophia, his consort, and revealed his first-begotten, androgynous son. His male name is designated 'First Begetter Son of God'; his female name, 'First Begetress Sophia, Mother of the Universe.' Some call her 'Love.' Now First-begotten is called 'Christ.' Since he has authority from his father, he created a multitude of angels without number for retinue from Spirit and Light."

. . . The perfect Savior said: "Son of Man consented with Sophia, his consort, and revealed a great androgynous light. His male name is designated, 'Savior of All things.' His feminine name is designated 'Sophia, All-Begetress.' Some call her 'Trust.'*"

THE SOPHIA OF JESUS CHRIST 103:22–105:2, 106:15–24 (ROBINSON, 3D ED.)

*Pistis in Greek.

## TUESDAY

_____

### Do Not Become a Sausage!

May God dwell in your camp, may his Spirit protect your gates, and may the mind of divinity protect the walls. Let holy reason become a torch in your mind, burning the wood which is the whole of sin. . . .

Live in Christ, and you will acquire a treasure in heaven. Do not become a sausage made of many things which are useless, and do not become a guide in your blind ignorance.

... Cast your anxiety upon God alone. Do not become desirous of gold and silver which are profitless, but clothe yourself with wisdom like a robe, put knowledge on yourself like a crown, and be seated upon a throne of perception.

TEACHINGS OF SILVANUS (ROBINSON, 3D ED.)

## WEDNESDAY

### Return to Your Divine Nature

From now on, then, my son, return to your divine nature. Cast from you these evil deceiving friends! Accept Christ, this true friend, as a good teacher. . . .

Accept Christ, who is able to set you free. . . .

Christ has a single being, and he gives light to every place. This is also the way in which he speaks of our mind, as if it were a lamp which burns and lights up the place. Being in a part of the soul, it gives light to all the parts.

. . . You cannot know God through anyone except Christ who has the image of the Father, for this image reveals the true likeness in correspondence to that which is revealed.

TEACHINGS OF SILVANUS (ROBINSON, 3D ED.)

## THURSDAY

### Do Not Tire of Knocking on the Door of Reason

Consider these things about God: he is in every place; on the other hand, he is in no place. With respect to power, to be sure, he is in every place;

but with respect to divinity, he is in no place. So then it is possible to know God a little. With respect to his power, he fills every place, but in the exaltation of his divinity, nothing contains him. Everything is in God, but God is not in anything. . . .

Do not tire of knocking on the door of reason, and do not cease walking in the way of Christ. Walk in it so that you may receive rest from your labors. If you walk in another way, there is no profit in it. . . .

Accept Christ, the narrow way. . . . The basic choice, which is humility of heart, is the gift of Christ. . . .

Light the light within you. Do not extinguish it.

TEACHINGS OF SILVANUS (ROBINSON, 3D ED.)

## FRIDAY

### *Knock on Yourself as on a Door*

For the Tree of Life is Christ. . . . For he is Wisdom; he is also the Word. He is the Life, the Power, and the Door. He is the Light, the Angel [Messenger], the Good Shepherd. Entrust yourself to this one who became all for your sake.

Knock on yourself as upon a door, and walk upon yourself as on a straight road. For if you walk on the road, it is impossible for you to go astray. And if you knock with this one (Wisdom), you knock on hidden treasuries.

For since Christ is Wisdom, he makes the foolish man wise. . . .

Let Christ alone enter your world, and let him bring to naught all powers which have come upon you. Let him enter the temple which is within you so that he may cast out all the merchants. Let him dwell in the temple which is within you, and may you become for him a priest and a Levite, entering in purity.

Blessed are you, O soul, if you find this one in your temple. Blessed are you still more if you perform his service.

TEACHINGS OF SILVANUS (ROBINSON, 3D ED.)

## SATURDAY

### *If You Do Not Know Yourself, You Will Not Know Anything*

Know who Christ is, and acquire him as a friend, for this is the friend who is faithful. He is also God and Teacher. This one, being God, became man for your sake. It is the one who broke the iron bars of the Underworld and the bronze bolts. It is this one who attacked and cast down every haughty tyrant. It is he who loosened from himself the chains of which he had taken hold. He brought up the poor from the Abyss and the mourners from the Underworld. It is he who humbled the haughty powers; he who put to shame the haughtiness through humility; he who has cast down the strong and the boaster through weakness; he who in his contempt scorned that which is considered an honor so that humility for God's sake might be highly exalted; and he has put on humanity. . . .

For no one who wants to will be able to know God as he actually is, nor Christ, nor the Spirit, nor the chorus of angels, nor even the archangels, as well as the thrones of the spirits, and the exalted lordships, and the Great Mind. If you do not know yourself, you will not be able to know all of these.

Open the door for yourself that you may know the One who is. Knock on yourself that the Word may open for you.

TEACHINGS OF SILVANUS (ROBINSON, 3D ED.)

# Sixth Week of Easter

*Resurrection and Ascension of Christ*

ↅ

―――――――――

*Five Hundred Fifty Days Later*

Now the twelve disciples used to sit all together at the same time, re-membering what the Savior had said to each one of them, whether se-cretly or openly, and setting it down in books. I was writing what went in my book—suddenly, the Savior appeared, after he had departed from us, and while we were watching for him. And so, five hundred fifty days after he rose from the dead, we said to him, "You went away and left us!"

"No," Jesus said, "but I shall go to the place from which I have come. If you wish to come with me, come on!"

They all answered and said, "If you bid us, we'll come."

He said, "Truly, I say to you, no one ever will enter heaven's domain if I bid him, but because you yourselves are full. Let me have James and Peter, so that I may fill them."

And when he called these two, he took them aside, and commanded the rest to carry on with what they had been doing.

. . . "So don't you desire to be filled?

And is your heart drunk?

So don't you desire to be sober?"

SECRET BOOK OF JAMES 2:1–3:1, 3 (MILLER)

## MONDAY

### *"Become Better Than I"*

The Lord said, "If you think about the world, about how long it existed before you and how long it will exist after you, you will discover that your life is but a single day and your sufferings, but a single hour. Accordingly, since what is good will not enter this world, you should scorn death and be concerned about life. Remember my cross and my death, and you will live! . . .

"Become better than I; be like the son of the holy spirit!" . . .

"I first spoke with you parabolically, and you did not understand. Now I am speaking with you openly, and you do not perceive. Nevertheless, for me you were a parable among parables, and the disclosure of openness.

"Be eager to be saved without being urged. Instead, become zealous on your own and, if possible, surpass even me. For that is how the Father will love you.

"Become haters of hypocrisy and evil intent. For intent is what produces hypocrisy, and hypocrisy is far from the truth.

"Don't let heaven's domain wither away. For it is like a date palm shoot whose fruit fell down around it. It put forth buds, and when they blossomed—its productivity was caused to dry up. So it is also with the fruit that came from this singular root: when it was picked, fruit was gathered by many. Truly, this was good. Isn't it possible to produce new growth now? Can't you discover how?"

SECRET BOOK OF JAMES 4:8–11, 5:6, 6:5–12 (MILLER)

## TUESDAY

———————

### *"Become Eager for Instruction!"*

"Become eager for instruction. For the first prerequisite for instruction is faith, the second is love, the third is works; now from these comes life. For instruction is like a grain of wheat. When someone sowed it he had faith in it; and when it sprouted he loved it, because he envisioned many grains in place of one; and when he worked he was sustained, because he prepared it for food, then kept the rest in reserve to be sown. So it is possible for you, too, to receive for yourselves heaven's domain: unless you receive it through knowledge, you will not be able to discover it. . . .

"Pay attention to instruction, understand knowledge, love life. And no one will persecute you, nor will any one oppress you, other than yourselves."

SECRET BOOK OF JAMES 6:16–18, 27 (MILLER)

## WEDNESDAY

———————

### *"Damn You Who Require an Intercessor"*

"Damn you who require an intercessor. Damn you who stand in need of grace. Congratulations to those who have spoken out fearlessly, and have obtained grace for themselves. . . ."

When we heard these things we became distressed. But when he saw that we were distressed, he said, "This is why I say this to you, that you may know yourselves. For *Way of the Tao*\* is like a head of grain which sprouted in a field. And when it ripened, it scattered its fruit and, in turn, filled the field with heads of grain for another year. You also: be eager to reap for yourselves a head of the grain of life, so that you may be filled with the *Way of the Tao*.

"As long as I am with you, pay attention to me and obey me; but when I take leave of you, remember me. Remember me because I was with you, though you did not know me. Congratulations to those who have known me. Damn those who have heard and have not believed. Congratulations to those who have not seen but have had faith.

"Once again do I appeal to you. For I am made known to you building a house of great value to you, since you take shelter in it; likewise, it can support your neighbors' house when theirs is in danger of collapsing. . . .

"Don't let the *Way of the Tao* become desolate among you. Don't be arrogant about the light that enlightens."

SECRET BOOK OF JAMES 7:2–3, 8:1–7, 11–12 (MILLER)

*"Heaven's domain."

*"Damn you who require an intercessor"? This is a shocking statement, particularly as the Scholars Version translates it. So what is the point? Enter into a direct awareness of the Tao, so immediate that no intercessor is needed. And a final warning even more devastating, "Don't let the Way of the Tao become a desert among you." Once you have allowed the free flowing of the Spirit, do not let it dry up and become desolate!*

# THURSDAY (ASCENSION DAY)

### *"Stay in the City Until You Are Invested with Power"*

Jesus said to them, "This is the message I gave you while I was still with you: everything written about me in the Law of Moses and the Prophets and the Psalms is destined to come true."

Then he prepared their minds to understand the scriptures. He said to them, "This is what is written: the Anointed will suffer and rise from the dead on the third day. And all people will be called on to undergo a change of heart for the forgiveness of sins, beginning from Jerusalem. You are witnesses to this. And be prepared: I am sending what my Father promised down on you. Stay here in the City until you are invested with power from, on high." . . .

"This," he said, "is what you have heard from me; for John baptized with water, but you will be baptized with the Holy Spirit not many days from now. . . .

"You will receive power when the Holy Spirit has come upon you; and you will be my witnesses in Jerusalem, in all Judea and Samaria, and to the ends of the earth."

When he had said this, as they were watching, he was lifted up, and a cloud took him out of their sight. While he was going and they were gazing up toward heaven, suddenly two men in white robes stood by them. They said, "Men of Galilee, why do you stand looking up toward heaven? This Jesus, who has been taken up from you into heaven, will come in the same way as you saw him go into heaven."

THE GOSPEL ACCORDING TO LUKE 24:44–49,
ACTS 1:3–11 (MILLER)

*The Gospel of Luke and the Book of Acts are two volumes of the same work. The ascension story is told in the last chapter of Luke and retold in the first chapter of Acts. I have condensed the two into one narrative.*

*These "last words" of the risen Christ before ascending into heaven—"Stay in the city until you are invested with power," "You will be baptized in the holy spirit"—are fulfilled in the story of Pentecost.*

*The "two men in white robes" are the same two, Moses and Elijah, who come to take Christ into heaven (see Holy Saturday reading from the Gospel of Peter) and who are in the transfiguration story (See August 6).*

## FRIDAY

### *A Chariot of Spirit Takes Jesus Away*

"Now I shall ascend to the place from which I have come. But you, when I was eager to go, have rebuffed me; and instead of accompanying me, you have chased me away. Still, pay attention to the glory that awaits me and, having opened your hearts, listen to the hymns that await me up in heaven. For today I must take my place at the right hand of my Father. I have spoken my last word to you; I shall part from you. For a chariot of spirit has lifted me up, and from now on I shall strip myself so that I may clothe myself. So pay attention: congratulations to those who proclaimed the Son before he descended, so that, having come, I might ascend. Congratulations three times over to those who were proclaimed by the Son before they existed, so that you might have a share with them."

When he said this, he went away. So Peter and I knelt down, gave thanks, and sent our hearts up to heaven. We heard with our ears and saw with our eyes the sound of battles and a trumpet's blast and utter turmoil.

And when we passed beyond that place, we sent our minds up further. We saw with our eyes and heard with our ears hymns and angelic praises and angelic rejoicing. Heavenly majesties were singing hymns, and we ourselves were rejoicing.

After this, we desired to send our spirits heavenward to the majesty. And when we went up, we were not permitted to see or hear a thing. For the rest of the disciples called to us and asked us, "What did you hear from the Teacher?" And, "What did he tell you?" and "Where has he gone?"

We answered them, "He has ascended." And, "He has given us a pledge, and promised all of us life, and disclosed to us children who are to come after us, having bid us to love them, since we will be saved for their sake."

And when they heard, they believed the revelation, yet were angry about those who would be born. So, not wishing to give them an occasion to take offense, I sent each one to a different place. And I myself went up to Jerusalem, praying that I might obtain a share with the beloved who are to appear.

SECRET BOOK OF JAMES 9:7–10:9 (MILLER)

## SATURDAY

### Ascension of Enoch

And when Enoch had spoken to his people, the Lord sent the gloom onto the earth, and it became dark and covered the men who were standing and talking with Enoch. And the angels hurried and grasped Enoch and carried him up to the highest heaven, where the Lord received him and made him stand in front of his face for eternity.

Then the darkness departed from the earth, and it became light. And the people looked, but they could not figure out how Enoch had been taken away.

And they glorified God.

And they found a scroll on which was inscribed: THE INVISIBLE GOD.

And they all went to their homes.

2 ENOCH 67:1–3 (CHARLESWORTH)

# Seventh Week of Easter

*Visions, Dreams, and Praying*

⤣

---

### What, Then, Is the Resurrection?

What, then, is the resurrection? It is always the disclosure of those who have risen. For if you remember reading in the Gospel that Elijah appeared and Moses with him, do not think the resurrection is an illusion. It is no illusion, but it is truth! Indeed, it is more fitting to say that the world is an illusion, rather than the resurrection which has come into being through our Lord and Savior, Jesus Christ.

But what am I telling you now? Those who are living shall die. How do they live in an illusion? The rich have become poor, and the kings have been overthrown. Everything is prone to change. The world is an illusion!—lest, indeed, I rail at things to excess!

But the resurrection does not have this aforesaid character, for it is the truth which stands firm. It is the revelation of what is, and the transformation of things, and a transition into newness. For imperishability descends upon the perishable; the light flows down upon the darkness, swallowing it up; and the Pleroma fills up the deficiency. These are the symbols and the images of the resurrection. He it is who makes the good.

TREATISE ON RESURRECTION 48:4–49:8 (ROBINSON, 3D ED.)

## MONDAY

*Interpreting Jacob's Ladder Dream*

Jacob then went to Laban his uncle. He found a place and, laying his head on a stone, he slept there, for the sun had gone down. He had a dream. And behold, a ladder was fixed on the earth, whose top reached to heaven. And the top of the ladder was the face of a man, carved out of fire.

There were twelve steps leading to the top of the ladder, and on each step to the top there were two human faces, on the right and on the left, twenty-four faces [or busts] including their chests. And the face in the middle was higher than all that I saw, the one of fire, including the shoulders and arms, exceedingly terrifying, more than those twenty-four faces.

And while I was looking at it, behold, angels of God ascended and descended on it. And God was standing above its highest face, and he called to me from there, saying, "Jacob, Jacob!" And I said, "Here I am Lord!" And he said to me, "The land on which you are sleeping, to you will I give it, and to your seed after you. And I will multiply your seed, as the stars of heaven and the sand of the sea. And through your seed all the earth and those living on it in the last times of the years of completion shall be blessed. My blessing with which I have blessed you shall flow from you unto the last generation; the East and the West all shall be full of your tribe."

And when I heard this from on high, awe and trembling fell upon me. And I rose up from my dream and, the voice still being in my ears, I said, "How fearful is this place! This is none other than the house of God and this is the gate of heaven."

And I set up the stone which had been my pillow as a pillar, and I poured olive oil on the top of it, and I called the name of that place the House of God.

And I stood and began to sing.

THE LADDER OF JACOB 11:1–12 AND 2:1–4 (CHARLESWORTH)

*The text continues with a psalm, which is included in this volume in the read-*
*ing for December 17, followed by a vision of the archangel Sariel, who gives an*
*interpretation of the dream. The twenty-four faces represent the kings of other*
*nations that Jacob and his posterity must deal with, plus the sojourn in Egypt*
*and the exodus. An additional chapter interprets the angels ascending and de-*
*scending the ladder as the incarnation; see the reading for December 16.*

## TUESDAY

### *"Show Us the Great Vision"*

The Lord said, "When you see him who Is Forever, that is the great vision."

Then all said to him, "Show it to us."

He said to them, "How do you wish to see it? In a vision that will cease? Or in an eternal vision?" And again he said, "Strive to save the one who is able to follow you. Seek him and speak with him, in order that everyone whom you seek may agree with you. For I say to you, truly the living God dwells in you and you dwell in him."

Mary said, "Thus about 'the wickedness of each day,' and 'the laborer being worthy of his food,' and 'the disciple resembling his teacher.'" This word she spoke as a woman who knew the All.

The disciples said to him, "What is the Pleroma and what is the deficiency?"

The Lord said to them, "You are from the Pleroma, and you dwell in the place where the deficiency is. And behold, its light was poured down upon me."

Mary said to him, "Lord, is there then a place that is deprived of the truth?"

The Lord said, "The place where I am not."

Matthew said, "Why do we not put ourselves to rest at once?"

The Lord said, "You will when you lay down these burdens."

Matthew said, "In what way does the little one cleave to the great one?"

The Lord said, "When you leave behind you the things that will not be able to follow you, then you will put yourselves to rest."

Mary said, "What is this mustard seed like? Is it from heaven or from the earth?"

The Lord said, "When the Father established the world for himself, he left behind many things from the Mother of the All. Because of this he speaks and acts."

EXCERPTS FROM THE DIALOGUE OF THE SAVIOR (ROBINSON, 1977)

## WEDNESDAY

### *The Thought of Christ Is Like a Letter*

The thought of Christ is like a letter,
    and his will descends from on high.
And it is sent from a bow like an arrow
    that has been forcibly shot.
And many hands rush to the letter,
    in order to catch it, then take and read it.
But it escapes from their fingers;
    and they are afraid of it and of the seal which is upon it.
Because they are not allowed to loosen its seal;
    for the power which is over the seal is better than they.
But those who see the letter go after it;
    that they might know where it will land,
and who should read it,
    and who should hear it.
But a wheel receives it, and the letter is caught in it.

And with it is a sign, of the *Way of the Tao*\* and of providence.
And everything which is disturbing to the wheel,
   it mows and cuts down.
It restrains a multitude of adversaries; and bridges rivers.
   It crosses over and uproots many peoples, and makes an open Way.
The head goes down to the feet,
   because right to the feet runs the wheel, and whatever comes on it.
The letter is one of command,
   and hence all regions are gathered together.
And there appears at its head, the Head which is revealed,
   even the Son of Truth from the Most High.
And he inherits and possesses everything,
   and then the scheming of the many ceases.
Then all the seducers became headstrong and flee;
   and the persecutors become extinct and are blotted out.
And the letter becomes a large volume,
   which is entirely written by the fingers of God.
And the name of the Father *and the Mother* is upon it;
   and of the Son and of the Holy Spirit, to rule for ever and ever.
   Hallelujah.

**ODES OF SOLOMON (CHARLESWORTH)**

\*"Kingdom."

## THURSDAY

---

### *Prayer of the Apostle Paul*

My redeemer, redeem me, for I am yours: from you have I come forth.
   You are my mind: bring me forth!
   You are my treasure house: open for me!
   You are my fullness: take me to you!
   You are my repose; give me the perfection that cannot be grasped!

I invoke you, the one who is and preexisted, by the name which is called above every name, through Jesus Christ the Lord of Lords, the king of the ages: give me your gifts which you do not regret through the Son of Man, the Spirit, the Paraclete of truth.

Give me authority when I ask you; give healing for my body when I ask you through the Evangelist, and redeem my eternal light-soul and my spirit.

And the First-born of the Pleroma of grace—reveal him to my mind!

Grant what no angel eye has seen, and no archon ear has heard and what has not entered into the human heart, which came to be angelic and came to be after the image of the psychic God when it was formed in the beginning, since I have faith and hope. And place upon me your beloved, elect, and blessed greatness, the First-born, the First-begotten, and the wonderful mystery of your house; for yours is the power and the glory and the praise and the greatness forever and ever. Amen.

PRAYER OF THE APOSTLE PAUL (ROBINSON, 1977)

*The title of this prayer means it is in honor of Paul, but it was written by another person sometime toward the end of the second century or the beginning of the third. This prayer is on the front flyleaf of the first book in the Nag Hammadi Library and thus serves as an introductory prayer to the entire volume and possibly to the entire library. This intense prayer of seeking to know the Eternal One through Jesus Christ is in response to Jesus, who says, "I will give you what no eye has seen, no ear has heard, no hand has touched, and what has never occurred to the human mind" (Gospel of Thomas 17). References to First-born and First-begotten are to Christ. Pleroma means "Fullness." Here is deep desire to know all that is!*

## THURSDAY

### *Sibyl's Releasing the Spirit*

When indeed God stops my most perfectly wise song as I pray many things, he also again places in my breast a delightful utterance of wondrous words. I will speak the following with my whole person in ecstasy. For I do not know what I say, but God bids me utter each thing. . . .

Blessed, heavenly one, who thunders on high, who have the cherubim as your throne, I entreat you to give a little rest to me who have prophesied unfailing truth, for my heart is tired within. But why does my heart shake again?

And why is my heart lashed by a whip, compelled from within to proclaim an oracle to all? But I will utter everything again, as much as God bids me say to people.

SIBYLLINE ORACLES, BOOK 2, LINES 1–5;
BOOK 3, LINES 1–5 (CHARLESWORTH)


## SATURDAY

### *"Sing a Hymn Through Silence"*

*The spiritual life comes in stages. We move through seven spheres of spiritual discipline before we are ready for the higher realms of the eighth and the ninth. In this Discourse on the Eighth and the Ninth, a spiritual guide is in conversation with a seeker. They are simultaneously speaking with each other and praying intensely, and they reach the point of seeing what cannot be adequately described and speaking what can be known only in complete silence. Their prayer goes beyond limited vocabulary into the eternal sound of silence. This transcription of the experience leaves open the final ecstasy of the tenth: complete consummation and bliss.*

*The spiritual guide begins praying:*

"Lord, grant us a wisdom from your power that reaches us, so that we may describe to ourselves the vision of the eighth and the ninth. We have already advanced to the seventh, since we are pious and walk in your law. And your will we fulfill always. For we have walked in your way . . . so that your vision may come. Lord, grant us the truth in the image. Allow us through the spirit to see the form of the image that has no deficiency, and receive the reflection of the pleroma from us through our praise.

"And acknowledge the spirit that is in us. For from you the universe received soul. For from you, the unbegotten one, the begotten one came into being. The birth of the self-begotten one is through you, the birth of all begotten things that exist.

"Receive from us these spiritual sacrifices, which we send to you with all our heart and our soul and all our strength. Save that which is in us and grant us the immortal wisdom."

*In the midst of praying, the guide turns to the seeker and says,*

"Let us embrace each other affectionately, my son. Rejoice over this! For already from the power, which is light, is coming to us. For I see! I see indescribable depths! How shall I tell you, my son? . . . How shall I describe the universe?

"I am Mind and I see another Mind, the one that moves the soul! I see the one that moves me from pure forgetfulness. You give me power! I see myself! I want to speak! Fear restrains me!

"I have found the beginning of the power that is above all powers, the one that has no beginning. I see a fountain bubbling with life.

"I have said, my son, that I am Mind. I have seen! Language is not able to reveal this. For the entire eighth, my son, and the souls that are in it, and the angels, sing a hymn in silence. And I, Mind, understand."

The seeker asks,] "What is the way to sing a hymn through silence?"

[The guide responds,] "Have you become such that you cannot be spoken to?"

"I am silent, my father. I want to sing a hymn to you, while I am silent."

"Then sing it, for I am Mind."

"I understand Mind, Hermes, who cannot be interpreted, because he keeps within himself. And I rejoice, my father, because I see you smiling. And the universe rejoices. Therefore there is no creature that will lack your life. For you are the lord of the citizens in every place. Your providence protects. I call you father, aeon of the aeons, great divine spirit. And by a spirit he gives rain upon everyone. What do you say to me, my father, Hermes?"

"Concerning these things I do not say anything, my son. For it is right before God that we keep silent about what is hidden."

"Trismegistus, let not my soul be deprived of the great divine vision. For everything is possible for you as master of the universe."

"Return to praising, my son, and sing while you are silent. Ask what you want in silence."

When [the seeker] had finished praising he shouted, "Father Trismegistus! What shall I say? We have received this light. And I myself see this same vision in you. And I see the eighth and the souls that are in it and the angels singing a hymn to the ninth and its powers. And I see him who has the power of them all, creating those that are in the spirit."

"It is advantageous from now on that we keep silence in a reverent posture. Do not speak about the vision from now on. It is proper to sing a hymn to the father until the day to quit the body."

"What you sing, my father, I too want to sing."

"I am singing a hymn within myself. While you rest yourself, be active in praise. For you have found what you seek."

"But is it proper, my father, that I praise because I am filled in my heart?"

"What is proper is your praise that you will sing to God so that it might be written in this imperishable book."

"I will offer up the praise in my heart, as I pray to the end of the universe and the beginning of the beginning, to the object of man's quest, the immortal discovery, the begetter of light and truth, the sower of reason, the love of immortal life. No hidden word will be able to speak about you, Lord. Therefore my mind wants to sing a hymn to you daily. I am the instrument of your spirit; Mind is your plectrum. And your counsel plucks me. I see myself! I have received power from you. For your love has reached us."

"Right my son."

"Grace! After these things I give thanks by singing a hymn to you. For I have received life from you, when you make me wise. I praise you. I call your name that is hidden within me: a ō ee ō eee ōōō  iii ōōōō ooooo uuuuuu ōō ōōōōōōōōō ōōōōōōōōō ōō. You are the one who exists with the spirit with the spirit. I sing a hymn to you reverently."

*These sounds may be the experience of praying in the Spirit, commonly known today as praying in tongues. After this experience, the guide says to the seeker,*

"My son, write this book for the temple at Diospolis in hieroglyphic characters, entitling it 'The Eighth Reveals the Ninth.' "

"I will do it, my father, as you command now."

"My son, write the language of the book on steles of turquoise. My son, it is proper to write this book on steles of turquoise, in hieroglyphic characters. For Mind himself has become overseer of these. Therefore I command that this teaching be carved on stone, and that you place it in my sanctuary."

*In addition to turquoise, someone also thought to preserve it in written form on a document that became part of the Nag Hammadi Library so that we, too, might have an example of how one person can assist another into knowing the great mystery of the Spirit.*

THE DISCOURSE ON THE EIGHTH AND NINTH 56:21–61:32
(ROBINSON, 3D ED.)

## THE DAY OF PENTECOST

### *The Friends of Jesus Become His Risen Body*

When the day of Pentecost had come, they were all together in one place. And suddenly from heaven there came a sound like the rush of a violent wind, and it filled the entire house where they were sitting. Divided tongues, as of fire, appeared among them, and a tongue rested on each of them. All of them were filled with the Holy Spirit and began to speak with other languages, as the Spirit gave them ability.

Now there were devout Jews from every nation under heaven living in Jerusalem. And at this sound the crowd gathered and was bewildered, because each one heard them speaking in the native language of each.

Amazed and astonished, they asked, "Are not all these who are speaking Galileans? And how is it that we hear, each of us, in our own native language? Parthians, Medes, Elamites, and residents of Mesopotamia, Judea and Cappodocia, Pontus and Asia, Phrygia and Pamphylia, Egypt and the parts of Libya belonging to Cyrene, and visitors from Rome, both Jews and proselytes, Cretans and Arabs—in our own languages we hear them speaking about God's deeds of power."

All were amazed and perplexed, saying to one another, "What does this mean?" But others sneered and said, "They are filled with new wine."

But Peter, standing with the eleven, raised his voice and addressed them, "Men of Judea and all who live in Jerusalem, let this be known to you, and listen to what I say. Indeed, these are not drunk, as you suppose, for it is only nine o'clock in the morning. No, this is what was spoken through the prophet Joel:

> 'In the last days it will be, God declares,
>     that I will pour out my Spirit upon all flesh,
>         and your sons and your daughters shall prophesy,
>     and your young men shall see visions,
>         and your old men shall dream dreams.
> Even upon my slaves, both men and women,
>     in those days I will pour out my Spirit
>         and they shall prophesy.' "

ACTS 2:1–18 (NEW REVISED STANDARD VERSION)

It is through water and fire that the whole place is purified—the visible by the visible, the hidden by the hidden. There are some things hidden through those visible. There is water in water, there is fire in chrism. . . .

It is from water and fire that the soul and the spirit came into being. It is from water and fire and light that the son of the bridal chamber came into being. The fire is the chrism, the light is the fire. I am not referring to that fire which has no form, but to the other fire whose form is white, which is bright and beautiful and gives beauty.

GOSPEL OF PHILIP 57:19–28 AND 67:2–8 (ROBINSON, 3D ED.)

*After Jesus the Nazarene died, which body rose? Was it the one placed in the tomb, or was it the communal body of his friends, who discovered Christ's presence in one another? Pentecost is the story of Jesus' friends becoming the body of Christ.*

# *Daily Readings Between Pentecost and June 15*

↜

*If you have been following the readings on a daily basis and have just concluded with Pentecost, you may have some extra days before the dated material resumes on June 15.*

*During these days you may wish to use one or two of the CoCreator chants and songs that are at the back of this book. For a complete rationale on the calendar of the natural liturgical year, see the Appendix.*

# *Dated Entries*

JUNE 15 THROUGH OCTOBER 30

# Becoming the Body of Christ

⚓

---

### From His Side Flowed Water and Blood

If we wish to understand the power of Christ's blood, we should go back to the ancient account of its prefiguration in Egypt. *Sacrifice a lamb without blemish,* commanded Moses, *and sprinkle its blood on your doors.* If we were to ask him what that meant, and how the blood of an irrational beast could possibly save men endowed with reason, his answer would be that the saving power lies not in the blood itself, but in the fact that it is a sign of the Lord's blood. In those days, when the destroying angel saw the blood on the doors, he did not dare to enter, so how much less will the devil approach now when he sees, not that figurative blood on the doors, but the true blood on the lips of believers, the doors of the temple of Christ.

If you desire further proof of the power of the blood, remember where it came from, how it ran down from the cross, flowing from the Master's side. The gospel records that when Christ was dead, but still hung on the cross, a soldier came and pierced his side with a lance and immediately there poured out water and blood. Now the water was a symbol of baptism and the blood, of the holy eucharist. The soldier pierced the Lord's side, he breached the walls of the sacred temple, and I have found the treasure and made it my own. So also with the lamb: the Jews sacrificed the victim and I have been saved by it.

*There flowed from his side water and blood.* Beloved, do not pass over this mystery without thought; it has yet another hidden meaning, which I will explain to you. I said that water and blood symbolized baptism and the holy eucharist. From these two sacraments the Church is born: from baptism, *the cleansing water that gives rebirth and renewal through the Holy Spirit,* and from the holy eucharist. Since the symbols of baptism and the eucharist flowed from his side, it was from his side that Christ fashioned the Church, as he had fashioned Eve from the side of Adam. Moses gave a hint of this when he tells the story of the first man and makes him exclaim: *Bone from my bones and flesh from my flesh!* As God then took a rib from Adam's side to fashion a woman, so Christ has given us blood and water from his side to fashion the Church. God took the rib when Adam was in a deep sleep, and in the same way Christ gave us the blood and the water after his own death.

Do you understand, then, how Christ has united his bride to himself and what food he gives us all to eat? By one and the same food we are both brought into being and nourished. As a woman nourishes her child with her own blood and milk, so does Christ unceasingly nourish with his own blood those to whom he himself has given life.

FROM THE CATECHESES BY JOHN CHRYSOSTOM,
BISHOP, FOURTH CENTURY (GALLEY)

## JUNE 16

*Baptism as Practiced in the Early Church—Part 1*

*Preparation on Thursday and Friday*

Those who are set apart for baptism shall be instructed to bathe and free themselves from impurity and wash themselves on Thursday. . . .

Those who are to be baptized shall fast on Friday, and on Saturday the bishop shall assemble them and command them to kneel in prayer. And, laying his hand upon them, he shall exorcise all evil spirits away and never to return; when he has done this he shall breathe in their faces, seal their foreheads, ears and noses, and then raise them up.

They shall spend all that night in vigil, listening to reading and instruction.

Those who are to be baptized shall bring with them no other vessels than the one each will bring for the eucharist; for it is fitting that he who is counted worthy of baptism bring his offering at that time.

APOSTOLIC TRADITION OF HIPPOLYTUS, CA. 217 C.E. (EASTON)

# JUNE 17

*Baptism as Practiced in the Early Church—Part 2*

### Anointing with the Oil of Exorcism

At cockcrow prayer shall be made over the water. The stream shall flow through the baptismal tank or pour into it from above when there is no scarcity of water; but if there is a scarcity, whether constant or sudden, then use whatever water you can find.

They shall remove their clothing. And first baptize the little ones; if they can speak for themselves, they shall do so; if not, their parents or other relatives shall speak for them. Then baptize the men, and last of all the women; they must first loosen their hair and put aside any gold or silver ornaments that they were wearing: let no one take any alien thing down to the water with them.

At the hour set for the baptism the bishop shall give thanks over oil and put it into a vessel: this is called the "oil of thanksgiving." And he shall take other oil and exorcise it: this is called "the oil of exorcism." (The anointing is performed by a presbyter.) A deacon shall bring the oil of exorcism, and shall stand at the presbyter's left hand. Then the presbyter, taking hold of each of those about to be baptized, shall command him to renounce, saying: "I renounce thee, Satan, and all thy servants and all thy works." And when he has renounced all these, the presbyter shall anoint him with the oil of exorcism, saying: "Let all spirits depart from thee."

APOSTOLIC TRADITION OF HIPPOLYTUS (EASTON)

## JUNE 18

*Baptism as Practiced in the Early Church—Part 3*

### Baptismal Covenant

Then, after these things, let him give him over to bishop or presbyter who baptizes, and let the candidates stand in the water, naked, a deacon going with them likewise.

And when he who is being baptized goes down into the water, he who baptizes him, putting his hand on him, shall say thus:

"Do you believe in God, the Father Almighty?" And he who is being baptized shall say: "I believe." Then holding his hand upon his head, he shall baptize him once.

And then he shall say:

"Do you believe in Christ Jesus, the Son of God,
Who was born of the Holy Spirit of the Virgin Mary,
and was crucified under Pontius Pilate, and was dead and buried,
and rose again on the third day, alive from the dead,
and ascended into heaven,
and sat at the right hand of the Father,
and will come to judge the living and the dead?"

And when he says, "I believe," he is baptized again.
And again he shall say:

> "Do you believe in the Holy Spirit, and the holy church,
> and the resurrection of the flesh?"

He who is baptized shall say accordingly, "I believe," and so he is baptized a third time.

APOSTOLIC TRADITION OF HIPPOLYTUS (EASTON)

## JUNE 19

*Baptism as Practiced in the Early Church—Part 4*

*Anointing with the Oil of Thanksgiving and Laying on Hands*

And afterward, when he has come up out of the water, he is anointed by the presbyter with the oil of thanksgiving, the presbyter saying: "I anoint you with holy oil in the name of Jesus Christ." And so each one, after drying himself, is immediately clothed, and then is brought into the church.

Then the bishop, laying his hand upon them, shall pray, saying, "O Lord God, who has made them worthy to obtain the remission of sins through the laver of regeneration of the Holy Spirit, send into them your grace, that they may serve you according to your will; for yours is the glory, to the Father and the Son, with the Holy Spirit in the holy church, both now and world without end. Amen."

Then, pouring the oil of thanksgiving from his hand and putting it on his forehead, he shall say, "I anoint you with oil in the Lord, the Father Almighty and Christ Jesus and the Holy Spirit." And signing them on the forehead he shall say, "The Lord be with you." And he who is signed shall say, "And with your spirit." And so he shall do to each one.

And immediately thereafter they shall join in prayer with all the people, but they shall not pray with the faithful until all these things are completed. And at the close of their prayer they shall give the kiss of peace.

**Apostolic Tradition of Hippolytus, Section 22 (Easton)**

*Then follows the Eucharist. The description is in this book as the reading for the Tuesday in the third week of Easter.*

## JUNE 20

### Death and Resurrection

Jesus revealed himself at the Jordan: it was the fullness of the kingdom of heaven. He who was begotten before everything was begotten anew. He who was once anointed was anointed anew. He who was redeemed in turn redeemed others.

Those who say that the Lord died first and then rose up are in error, for he rose up and then he died. If one does not first attain the resurrection will he not die?

Those who say they will die first and then rise are in error. If they do not first receive the resurrection while they live, when they die they will receive nothing. So also when speaking about Baptism they say, "Baptism is a great thing," because if they receive it they will live.

Some are afraid lest they rise naked. Because of this they wish to rise in the flesh, and they do not know that it is those who wear the flesh who are naked. It is those who unclothe themselves who are not naked. . . .

It is necessary that we put on the living man. Therefore when he is about to go down into the water, he unclothes himself, in order that he may put on the living man. . . .

In this world those who put on garments are better than the garments. In the kingdom of heaven the garments are better than those who have put them on.

One will clothe himself in this light sacramentally in the union. . . .

By perfecting the water of baptism, Jesus emptied it of death. Thus we do go down into the water, but we do not go down into death in order that we may not be poured out into the spirit of the world. When that spirit blows, it brings winter. When the Holy Spirit breathes, the summer comes.

GOSPEL OF PHILIP 70:34–71; 73:2–8; 56:16–19;
75:22–24; 56:27–31; 77:8–15 (ROBINSON, 1977)

## JUNE 21, SUMMER SOLSTICE

### Truth Comes in Types and Images

Truth did not come into the world naked, but it came in types and images. One will not receive truth in any other way. There is a rebirth and an image of rebirth. It is certainly necessary to be born again through the image. Which one?

Resurrection. The image must rise again through the image. The bridal chamber and the image must enter through the image into the truth: this is the restoration.

Not only must those who produce the name of the father and the son and the holy spirit do so, but those who have produced them for you. If one does not acquire them, the name "Christian" will be taken from him. But one receives them in the unction of the power of the cross. This power the apostles called "the right and the left." For this person is no longer a Christian but a Christ.

The Lord did everything in a mystery: a baptism and a chrism and a eucharist and a redemption and a bridal chamber.

GOSPEL OF PHILIP 67:9-30 (ROBINSON, 3D ED.)

*What do we have here in the final verse? Five sacraments? Or five elements of one Mystery? Over time the church has developed sacraments: baptism, confirmation, Eucharist, reconciliation (penance), and marriage. These may, in fact, be part of one continuous process leading to the total union of each person with the Mystery of life whom we name as the Tao.*

## JUNE 22

### *God Is a Dyer*

God is a dyer. As the good dyes, which are called "true," dissolve with the things dyed in them, so it is with those whom God has dyed. Since his dyes are immortal, they are immortal by means of his colors. Now God dips what he dips in water. . . .

The Lord went into the dye works of Levi. He took seventy-two different colors and threw them into the vat. He took them out all white. And he said, "Even so has the Son of Man come as a dyer."

GOSPEL OF PHILIP 61:12-20, 63:25-30 (ROBINSON, 3D ED.)

## JUNE 23

### *Chrism: Anointing with Oil*

The chrism is superior to baptism, for it is from the word "chrism" that we have been called "Christians," certainly not because of the word "baptism." And it is because of the chrism that "the Christ" has his name. For the Father anointed the Son, and the Son anointed the apostles, and the apostles anointed us. He who has been anointed possesses everything. He possesses the resurrection, the light, the cross, the Holy Spirit. The Father gave him this in the bridal chamber; he merely accepted the gift. The Father was in the Son and the Son in the Father. This is the kingdom of heaven.

GOSPEL OF PHILIP 74:13–24 (ROBINSON, 1977)

## JUNE 24, ST. JOHN THE BAPTIST DAY

### Pointless Baptism When Nothing Happens

If one goes down into the water and comes up without having received anything and says, "I am a Christian," he has borrowed the name at interest. But if he receives the Holy Spirit, he has the name as a gift. He who has received a gift does not have to give it back, but of him who has borrowed it at interest, payment is demanded. This is the way it happens to one when one experiences a mystery.

GOSPEL OF PHILIP 64:23–31 (ROBINSON, 1977)

## JUNE 25

### Three Baptisms

There are three men . . . : the spirit-endowed of eternity, and the soul-endowed, and the earthly. Likewise, the three phoenixes in Paradise—the first is immortal; the second lives 1,000 years; as for the third, it is written in the Sacred Book that it is consumed. So too there are three baptisms—the first is spiritual, the second is by fire, the third is by water.

Just as the phoenix appears as a witness concerning the angels, so the crocodiles have become a witness to those going down into the baptism of a true man. . . .

And the worm that has been born out of the phoenix is a human being. . . . It is written [Psalm 91:13 LXX] concerning it, "the just man will blossom like a phoenix." And the phoenix first appears in a living state, and dies, and rises again, being a sign of what has become apparent at the consummation of the age."

ON THE ORIGIN OF THE WORLD (SEERS VERSION)

## JUNE 26

### Anointing and Sealing in the Holy Spirit

*The apostle Thomas takes oil, pours it on their heads, and anoints them saying,*

Come, holy name of Christ which is above every name;
Come, power of the Most High and the perfect compassion;
Come, highest *gift of anointing.*
Come, *compassionate* Mother;
Come, fellowship of the male;
Come, Lady who reveals the hidden mysteries.
Come, Mother of the seven houses, so that your rest might be in the eighth house;
Come, you who are older than the five members—
mind, conception, thought, reflection, reason—

and commune with these youths.

Come, Holy Spirit, cleanse their minds and hearts, and seal them in the name of Father, Son and Holy Spirit.

ACTS OF THOMAS 27 (ATTRIDGE)

## JUNE 27

----

### Calling on Jesus for the Eucharist

Jesus who deemed us worthy to partake of the Eucharist of your sacred body and blood, behold we make bold to approach your Eucharist and to call upon your holy name. Come and partake with us . . .

Come, Perfect Compassion;

Come, Companion of the Masculine;

Come, you who knows the Mysteries of the chosen ones;

Come, Holy Spirit, who shares in all the games of the famous Athlete;

Come, Silence, and reveal the actions of the whole *Tao.*

Come, and manifest all that is secret; make visible all that is hidden.

Come, hidden Mother, Holy Dove, who gives birth to twins;

Come, and reveal yourself in your rhythms; release joy in us and make us one as we rest in you;

Come into union with us as we celebrate this Eucharist in your name.

In this love feast make us one through the sound of your voice.

ACTS OF THOMAS 27 (SEERS VERSION, PARAPHRASED)

## JUNE 28

---

### *Thomas Baptizing Mygdonia*

Mygdonia said to Thomas, "Give me the anointing of Jesus Christ and I shall receive a gift from your hands before you depart this life." . . . With her head bare, she stood in front of the apostle and he took oil, poured it on her head and said, "Holy oil given to us for our wholeness, secret Mystery in which the Cross is revealed to us:

> You are the One who uncovers all secrets;
> You melt down our stubbornness;
> You open up our hidden treasures;
> You shoot forth your Goodness!
> Let your Power come!
> Let it build energy in your servant Mygdonia;
> Through this anointing, heal her and set her free!"

After the anointing with oil, Thomas asked the nurse to unclothe her. There was a spring of water nearby; going into it, the apostle baptized Mygdonia in the Name of the Father, the Son and the Holy Spirit. When she had been baptized and clothed with a linen garment, he broke bread, took the cup of water, and made her a member of the body of Christ and a vessel of the Spirit of God. He said to her, "You have received your anointing and now you contain Eternal Life."

And a Voice from above was heard saying, "Yes, Amen!"

ACTS OF THOMAS 120, 121 (SEERS VERSION)

## June 29

---

*"Wasn't I More Handsome to You Than Jesus Is Now?"*

Carish said to Mygdonia, "If you obey me, I shall no longer have any grief. Remember that day when you first met me. Tell the truth. Wasn't I more handsome to you at that time than Jesus is now?"
    Mygdonia replied,

"That time had its qualities, and this time has its own.
That was a time of beginning; this of ending.
That was a time of temporary life; this is eternal.
That was a time of transitory joy; this of joy that abides forever.
That was a time of day and night; this of day without night.
You knew that past marriage which does not abide; this marriage lasts
    forever.
That intercourse leads to destruction; this to eternal life.
Those members of the bridal party are transitory men and women;
the present ones remain forever.
That marriage stands upon earth in constant turmoil;
this makes love of humanity drop down like dew.
The bridal chamber is removed again; this remains forever.
That bed is covered with spreads; this with love and faith.
You are a groom who departs and is destroyed;
Jesus is the true bridegroom, who remains forever, immortal.
That unveiling festival involves sums of money and clothes that
    grow old;
this involves words that never depart."

ACTS OF THOMAS 124 (ATTRIDGE)

## JUNE 30

*Thomas Attempting to Speak About Baptism*

Thomas went to the home of Siphor and stayed there with him. Siphor said, "I will prepare a room for Thomas where he may teach." He did so and said, "From now on, my wife, daughter, and I will live in trust, freedom, and clarity of intention. I ask to receive the Anointing from you so that we may become vessels of the Eternal Spirit and be included among his lambs and sheep."

Thomas said, "I am afraid to say what I think. I know something, and what I know is impossible to put into words."

He began to speak about baptism, "This baptism is forgiveness of sins. It brings to new birth the Light poured forth in brilliance. It gives birth to the new human being, renews the thinking, and stirs new Spirit in the person's soul. In a three-fold way, it resurrects the new person by providing forgiveness of sins.

Glory to You, secret Energy who unites with us in baptism!
Glory to You, unspoken Power that is in baptism!
Glory to You, Renewer, who baptizes and renews us in your love!"

After saying this, he poured oil on their heads and said,

"Glory to You, Compassionate Love!
Glory to You, Name of Christ!
Glory to You, Power grounded in Christ!"

And he ordered that a basin be brought in and he baptized them in the name of the Father, the Son, and the Holy Spirit.

After they had been baptized and clothed, he set bread on the table, praised it, and said,

"Bread of Life, those who eat remain incorruptible!
Bread that fills hungry souls with your blessing;
You are the one thought worthy to receive a gift
that You may become for us forgiveness of sins,
that those who eat You may become eternal.
We name over you the name of the Mother, of an unspoken
    Mystery, and of hidden authority and power.
We name over you the name of Jesus."

And he said, "Let the power of blessing come and let the bread be consecrated, so that all souls who eat of it may be washed of their sins."
Then he broke the bread and gave it to Siphor, his wife, and daughter.

ACTS OF THOMAS 131–33 (SEERS VERSION)

## JULY 1

### *Knowing Produces Abundance*

The days will come, in which vines shall grow, each having ten thousand branches, and in each branch ten thousand twigs, and in each true twig ten thousand shoots, and in each one of the shoots ten thousand clusters, and on every one of the clusters ten thousand grapes, and every grape when pressed will give five and twenty gallons of wine. And when any one of the saints shall lay hold of a cluster, another shall cry out, "I am a better cluster, take me; bless the Lord through me."

In like manner the Lord declared that a grain of wheat would produce ten thousand ears, and that every ear should have ten thousand grains, and every grain would yield ten pounds of clear, pure, fine flour; and that all other fruit-bearing trees, and seeds and grass, would produce in similar proportions; and that all animals feeding on the productions of the earth, should become peaceful and harmonious among each other and *human beings will be in harmony with them.*"

IRENAEUS, AGAINST HERESIES, BOOK 5, CHAPTER XXXIII, PARAGRAPH 3
(COX; THE PHRASE IN ITALICS IS FROM THE SEERS VERSION)

*Remember the "ten thousand things" in the* Tao Te Ching? *The phrase also appears in Brigid's piece on hospitality (February 1). Here is the same symbol of fullness and abundance.*

## JULY 2

### A Land Flowing with Milk and Honey

*An angel showed Paul a river that watered the whole earth. And Paul asked the angel what it was:*

And he [the angel] said to me: This is the Ocean.

And suddenly I came out of heaven and perceived that it is the light of heaven and perceived that it is the light of heaven which gives light to the whole land there. That land, however, was seven times brighter than silver.

And I said: Sir, what is this place? And he said to me: This is the land of promise. Have you not heard what is written, "Blessed are the meek, for they will inherit the earth"? . . .

And I looked round that land and I saw a river flowing with milk and honey; and at the edge of the river were planted trees full of fruit. And each tree was bearing twelve times twelve fruits in the year, various and different. And I saw the creation of that place and all the work of God. And I saw there palm trees, some of twenty cubits and others of ten cubits. Now that land was seven times brighter than silver. And the trees were full of fruit from root to tree-top.

From the root of each tree up to its heart there were ten thousand branches with tens of thousands of clusters and there were ten thousand clusters on each branch and there were ten thousand dates in each cluster.

And it was the same with the vines. Each vine had ten thousand branches, and each branch had on it ten thousand bunches of grapes, and each bunch had ten thousand grapes.

And there were other trees there, myriads of myriads of them, and their fruit was in the same proportion.

And I said to the angel: Why does each single tree yield thousands of fruits? And the angel answered and said to me: "Because the Lord God of his abundance gives gifts profusely to the worthy, for they, while they were in the world, afflicted themselves of their own will and did everything for his holy name's sake."

APOCALYPSE OF PAUL 21 (HENNECKE AND SCHNEEMELCHER)

## JULY 3

### Four Rivers in the New City of Christ

And the angel . . . said to me: Follow me and I shall lead you into the city of Christ. And he stood by Lake Acherusia and put me in a golden boat and about three thousand angels were singing a hymn before me until I reached the city of Christ. . . .

And in the circuit of the city there were twelve gates of great beauty, and four rivers which encircled it. Now there was a river of honey and a river of milk and a river of wine and a river of oil.

And I said to the angel: What are these rivers which encircle this city? And he said to me: These are the four rivers which flow abundantly for those who are in this land of promise; as for their names: the river of honey is called Phison, and the river of milk Euphrates, and the river of oil Gihon and the river of wine Tigris. . . .

And with the angel leading me I went on, and he brought me to the river of honey; and I saw there Isaiah and Jeremiah and Ezekiel and Amos and Micah and Zechariah, the major and minor prophets, and they greeted me in the city. And I said to the angel: What is this way? And he said to me: This is the way of the prophets. Everyone who has grieved his own soul and on account of God has not done his own will, when he has come forth from the world and been led to the Lord God and has worshipped him, then at God's command he is handed over to Michael who leads him into the city to this place of the prophets; and they greet him as their friend and neighbour because he did the will of God.

Again he led me where the river of milk was; and there I saw in that place all the infants whom king Herod had slain for the name of Christ, and they greeted me. And the angel said to me: All who preserve their innocence and purity, when they come forth from their bodies, are handed over to Michael after they have worshipped the Lord God, and they are brought to the children and they greet them saying, "You are our brothers and friends and associates (members)." Among them they will inherit the promises of God.

Again he took me up and brought me to the north of the city and he led me where the river of wine was, and I saw there Abraham, Isaac and Jacob, Lot and Job and other saints; and they greeted me.

And I asked and said: What is this place, sir? The angel answered and said to me: All those who have given hospitality to strangers, when they come forth from the world, first worship the Lord God and are handed over to Michael and by this route are led into the city, and all the righteous greet them as sons and brothers and say to them, "Because you have kept humanity and hospitality for strangers, come, receive an inheritance in the city of our God." And each righteous person will receive the good gifts of God in the city in accordance with his own behavior.

And again he brought me to the river of oil to the east of the city. And I saw there people who rejoiced and sang psalms, and I said: Who are these, sir? And the angel said to me: These are those who dedicated themselves to God with the whole heart and had no pride in themselves.

For all who rejoice in the Lord God and sing praises to him with the whole heart are brought here into this city. . . .

And I saw in the midst of the city a great and very high altar; and there was standing alongside the altar one whose face shone like the sun and who held in his hands a psaltery and a harp and who sang saying, "Hallelujah!" And his voice filled all the city.

APOCALYPSE OF PAUL 23–29 (HENNECKE AND SCHNEEMELCHER)

# Life of the Country in the Way of the Tao

*A Country in Harmony with the Tao*

When the Tao is present in the universe, the horses haul manure.
When the Tao is absent from the universe, war horses are bred outside
    the city.
There is no greater sin than desire,
no greater curse than discontent,
no greater misfortune than wanting something for oneself.
Therefore he who knows that enough is enough will always have
    enough.

**TAO TE CHING, 46 (FENG AND ENGLISH)**

*For an updating of this passage in contemporary terms:*

> When a country is in harmony with the Tao,
> the factories make trucks and tractors.
> When a country goes counter to the Tao,
> warheads are stockpiled outside the cities.
> There is no greater illusion than fear,

no greater wrong then preparing to defend yourself,
no greater misfortune than having an enemy.
Whoever can see through all fear
will always be safe.

TAO TE CHING, 46 (MITCHELL)

# JULY 5

## *A Great Country and a Little Country*

A great country is like the low lands
    where all the streams unite.

In all things under heaven
    the female overcomes the male by her stillness,
    and because she is still she lies below.

Hence, if the great country will take the low place
    it will win over the little country.
If the little country will take the low place
    it will win over the great country.

Thus, the one gets below and prospers
    and the other remains below and prospers.
All that the great country wants is more people.
All that the little country wants is a place
    for its people to go and be employed.
If each is to get what it wants
    it is necessary for the great country
    to take the low place.

TAO TE CHING, 61 (MCCARROLL)

## JULY 6

### *When Things Are out of Balance*

I do know without any doubt that
I should walk in the way of the Great Tao.
The only fear I have is to go astray from it.
The Great Tao is right and proper,
but people still prefer shortcuts.
When the court is clean and tidy,
the fields may be desolate,
and the granary empty.
When the nobles wear splendid garments,
carrying sharp and shiny swords,
indulging in sumptuous meals,
possessing more wealth than they need,
they are actually heads of all thieves.
Such definitely is not the Tao.

TAO TE CHING, 53 (TAN, 1992)

## JULY 7

### *Weapons Are the Tools of Fear*

Good weapons are instruments of fear;
all creatures hate them.
Therefore followers of Tao never use them.
The wise man prefers the left.
The man of war prefers the right.
Weapons are instruments of fear;
they are not a wise man's tools.

He uses them only when he has no choice.
Peace and quiet are dear to his heart,
and victory no cause for rejoicing.
If you rejoice in victory, then you delight in killing;
if you delight in killing, you cannot fulfill yourself.
On happy occasions precedence is given to the left,
on sad occasions to the right.
In the army the general stands on the left,
the commander in chief on the right.
This means that war is conducted like a funeral.
When many people are being killed,
they should be mourned in heartfelt sorrow.
This is why a victory must be observed like a funeral.

TAO TE CHING, 31 (MITCHELL)

*Compare the last two lines with Talbot McCarroll's translation:*

The army that has killed people
    should be received with sorrow.
Conquerors should be received with the rites of mourning.

TAO TE CHING, 31 (MCCARROLL)

## JULY 8

### *Governing a Big Country Is Like Cooking a Small Fish*

Ruling a country is like cooking a small fish.
Approach the universe with Tao, and evil will have no power.
Not that evil is not powerful,
but its power will not be used to harm others.

Not only will it do no harm to others,
but the sage himself will also be protected.
They do not hurt each other,
and the Virtue in each refreshes both.

TAO TE CHING, 60 (FENG AND ENGLISH)

# JULY 9

## *Ruling with a Light Hand*

When the country is ruled with a light hand, the people are simple.
When the country is ruled with severity, the people are cunning.
Happiness is rooted in misery.
Misery lurks beneath happiness.
Who knows what the future holds?
There is no honesty.
Honesty becomes dishonest.
Goodness becomes witchcraft.
Man's bewitchment lasts for a long time.
Therefore the sage is sharp but not cutting,
pointed but not piercing,
straightforward, but not unrestrained,
brilliant but not blinding.

TAO TE CHING, 58 (FENG AND ENGLISH)

## JULY 10

---

### *Rule a Nation with Justice*

Rule a nation with justice.
Wage war with surprise moves.
Become master of the universe without striving.
How do I know that this is so?
Because of this!
The more laws and restrictions there are, the poorer people become.
The sharper men's weapons, the more trouble in the land.
The more ingenious and clever men are, the more strange things
    happen.
The more rules and regulations, the more thieves and robbers.
Therefore the sage says:
I take no action, people are reformed.
I enjoy peace and people become honest.
I do nothing and people become rich.
I have no desires and people return to the good and simple life.

TAO TE CHING, 57 (FENG AND ENGLISH)

## JULY 11

---

### *Remain Centered in the Tao*

The Tao is forever undefined.
Small though it is in the unformed state, it cannot be grasped.
If kings and lords could harness it,
the ten thousand things would naturally obey.

Heaven and earth would come together
and gentle rain fall.
Men would need no more instruction
   and all things would take their course.

Once the whole is divided, the parts need names.
There are already enough names.
One must know when to stop.
Knowing when to stop averts trouble.
Tao in the world is like a river flowing home to the sea.

TAO TE CHING, 32 (FENG AND ENGLISH)

*Compare this with Mitchell's paraphrase:*

If powerful men and women could remain centered in the Tao,
all things would be in harmony.
The world would become a paradise.
All people would be at peace,
and the law would be written in their hearts.
When you have names and forms, know that they are provisional.
When you have institutions, know where their functions should end.
Knowing when to stop, you can avoid any danger.

All things end in the Tao as rivers flow into the sea.

TAO TE CHING, 32 (MITCHELL)

# Personal Open Space in the Way of the Tao

&

## JULY 12

*Opening Your Heart to the World*

Without going outside
    you can know the ways of the world.
Without looking through the window
    you can see the way of heaven.
The farther you go
    the less you know.
Therefore, the True Person
    arrives without travelling,
    perceives without looking,
    and acts without striving.

TAO TE CHING, 47 (McCARROLL)

*One more time from Stephen Mitchell:*

Without opening your door, you can open your heart to the world.
Without looking out your window, you can see the essence of the Tao.
The more you know, the less you understand.

The Master arrives without leaving, sees the light without looking,
achieves without doing a thing.

TAO TE CHING, 47 (MITCHELL)


## JULY 13

### Adding and Dropping

In the pursuit of knowledge,
every day something is added.
In the practice of the Tao,
every day something is dropped.
Less and less do you need to force things,
until finally you arrive at non-action.
When nothing is done,
nothing is left undone.
True mastery can be gained
by letting things go their own way.
It can't be gained by interfering.

TAO TE CHING, 48 (MITCHELL)


## JULY 14

### The Primal Virtue

Carrying body and soul and embracing the one, can you avoid
    separation?
Attending fully and becoming supple, can you be as a newborn babe?

Washing and cleansing the primal vision, can you be without stain?
Loving all men and ruling the country, can you be without cleverness?
Opening and closing the gates of heaven, can you play the role of
    woman?
Understanding and being open to all things, are you able to do nothing?
Giving birth and nourishing, bearing yet not possessing,
working yet not taking credit, leading yet not dominating,
this is the primal virtue.

TAO TE CHING, 10 (FENG AND ENGLISH)

## JULY 15

### The Value of Nothing

Thirty spokes connect to the wheel's hub;
    yet, it is the center hole
    that makes it useful.
Clay is shaped into a vessel;
    yet, it is the emptiness within
    that makes it useful.
Doors and windows are cut for a room;
    yet, it is the space where there is nothing
    that makes it useful.
Therefore, though advantage comes from what is,
    usefulness comes from what is not.

TAO TE CHING, 11 (McCARROLL)

## JULY 16

### *Being Very Open*

The five colors blind the eye.
The five tones deafen the ear.
The five flavors dull the taste.
Racing and hunting *drive the heart wild*.
Precious things lead one astray.
Therefore the sage is guided by what he feels
and not by what he sees.
He lets go of that and chooses this.

TAO TE CHING, 12 (FENG AND ENGLISH)

## JULY 17

### *If You Want to Become Whole*

Yield and overcome;
bend and be straight.
Empty out and be full;
wear out and be renewed.
Have little and gain;
have much and be confused.
Therefore, the True Person embraces the one
and becomes a model for all.
Do not look only at yourself,
and you will see much.
Do not justify yourself,
and you will be distinguished,
Do not brag, and you will have merit.

Do not be prideful,
and your work will endure.
It is because you do not strive
that no one under heaven can strive with you.
The saying of the Old Ones,
"Yield and Overcome,"
is not an empty phrase.
True wholeness is achieved by blending with life.

TAO TE CHING, 22 (FENG AND ENGLISH)

## JULY 18

### *Being Planted in the Tao*

Being planted in the Tao
What is well rooted cannot be pulled up.
What is firmly grasped will not slip loose.
It will be honored from generation to generation.
When cultivated in your person, Virtue will be real.
When cultivated in your household, Virtue will be plentiful.
When cultivated in your village, Virtue will endure.
When cultivated in your country, Virtue will abound.
When cultivated in your world, Virtue will be universal.
Hence, through yourself, look at Self.
Through your household, look at Household.
Through your community, look at Community.
Through your country, look at Country.
Through your world, look at World.
How do I know that the world is like this?
Because of what is within me.

TAO TE CHING, 54 (FENG AND ENGLISH)

# Authentic Relationships in the Way of the Tao

ॐ

## JULY 19

---

### Open and Honest Communicating

Do not hide one thought in your heart while you say another.
Do not change in your place like a many-footed creature which clings to
    rock.
Be straightforward with all. Speak what comes from your soul.
Do not boast of wisdom or strength or wealth.
There is One, God, at once wise, powerful, and rich.
Do not wear out your heart with passing evils,
for that which has happened can no longer be undone.
Be not precipitous to the hand.
Bridle wild anger, for often one who struck a blow unintentionally
    committed murder.
Let your passions be normal, neither great nor excessive. . . .
Anger is a propensity, but wrath goes to excess. . . .
Eat, drink, and discourse in moderation.

SIBYLLINE ORACLES, BOOK 2, LINES 121–40
(CHARLESWORTH)

## JULY 20

*Communicating Freely*

My son, do not utter everything that comes into your mind, for there are eyes and ears everywhere. But keep watch over your mouth, lest it bring you to grief! Above all else, guard your mouth; and as for what you have heard, be discreet!

For a word is a bird, and he who releases it is a fool. Choose the sayings you shall utter, then speak them to your [brother] to help him. For the treachery of the mouth is more dangerous than the treachery of battle.

AHIQAR, LINES 97–99 (CHARLESWORTH)

## JULY 21

*Question Your Friend*

Question your friend, he may have done nothing at all;
and if he has done anything, he will not do it again.
Question your neighbor, he may have said nothing at all;
and if he has said anything, he will not say it again.
Question your friend, for slander is very common,
Do not believe everything you hear.
Question your neighbor before you threaten him,
and let the law of the Most High take its course.
People sometimes make a slip, without meaning what they say;
and which of us has never sinned by speech?

SIRACH 19:13–17 (NEW JERUSALEM BIBLE, ADAPTED)

## JULY 22

---

### *To Talk Little Is Natural*

To talk little is natural.
High winds do not last all morning.
Heavy rains do not last all day.
Why is this?
Heaven and earth!
If heaven and earth cannot make things eternal, how is it possible
    for man?
He who follows the Tao is at one with the Tao.
He who is virtuous experiences Virtue.
He who loses the way feels lost.
When you are at one with the Tao, the Tao welcomes you.
When you are at one with Virtue, the Virtue is always there.
When you are at one with loss, the loss is experienced willingly.
He who does not trust enough will not be trusted.

                     TAO TE CHING, 23 (FENG AND ENGLISH)

## JULY 23

---

### *When to Be Silent*

There is the rebuke that is untimely,
    and there is the person who is wise enough to keep silent.
How much better it is to rebuke than to fume!
And the one who admits his fault will be kept from failure.
Like a eunuch lusting to violate a girl
    is the person who does right under compulsion.

Some people keep silent and are thought to be wise.
  while others are detested for being talkative.
Some people keep silent because they have nothing to say,
  while others keep silent because they know when to speak.
The wise remain silent until the right moment,
  but a boasting fool misses the right moment. ....
A slip on the pavement is better than a slip of the tongue. ....
A proverb from a fool's lips will be rejected,
  for he does not tell it at the proper time.

SIRACH 20:1–7, 18, 20 (NEW REVISED STANDARD VERSION)

Speak when it is not proper to be silent, but speak concerning the things
  you know only when it is fitting. ....
When it is proper to act, do not use a word. ....
While it is a skill to speak, it is also a skill to be silent. ....
It is better for you to be defeated while speaking the truth, than to be
  victorious through deceit. ....
It is better for you to be silent about the word of God than to speak
  recklessly.

SENTENCES OF SEXTUS (ROBINSON, 3D ED.)

## JULY 24

### On Being a True Friend

Prick an eye and you will draw a tear,
prick a heart and you reveal its feelings.
Throw stones at birds and you scare them away,
reproach a friend and you destroy a friendship.

If you have drawn a sword on a friend,
do not despair; there is a way back.
If you have opened your mouth against a friend,
do not worry; there is hope for reconciliation.
But insult, arrogance, betrayal of secrets, and the stab in the back—
in these cases any friend is lost.
Win your neighbor's confidence when he is poor, . . .
stand by him in times of trouble. . . .
Be not be ashamed to shelter a friend. . . .
There are three things my soul delights in,
and which are delightful to God and to all people:
concord between brothers, friendship between neighbors,
and a wife and husband who live happily together.

SIRACH 22:19–25; 25:1–2 (NEW JERUSALEM BIBLE, ADAPTED)

# Ways of Living in the Way of the Tao

⟡

---

*Beatitudes*

Happy is the person who reverences the name of the Lord,
    and who serves in front of his face always,
    and who organizes his gifts with fear, offerings of life,
    and who in this life lives and dies correctly!
Happy is he who carries out righteous judgment,
    not for the sake of payment, but for justice,
    not expecting anything whatever as a result;
    and the result will be that judgment without favoritism will follow
      for him.
Happy is he who clothes the naked with his garment,
    and to the hungry gives bread!
Happy is he who judges righteous judgment for orphan and widow,
    and who helps anyone who has been treated unjustly!
Happy is he who turns aside from the secular path of this vain world,
    and walks in the right paths, and who lives that life which is without
      end!
Happy is he who sows right seed, for he shall harvest sevenfold!
Happy is he in whom is the truth,
    so that he may speak truth to his neighbor!

Happy is he who has compassion on his lips and gentleness in his heart!
Happy is he who understands all the works of the Lord, performed by
    the Lord, and glorifies him!

2 ENOCH 42:6–14 (CHARLESWORTH)


## JULY 26

### *Walking*

Walk my children,
in long-suffering,
in meekness [honesty],
in affliction,
in distress,
in faithfulness,
in truth,
in hope,
in weakness,
in derision,
in assaults,
in temptation,
in deprivation,
in nakedness,
having love for one another, until you go out from
    this age of suffering,
so that you may be inheritors of the never-ending age.

2 ENOCH 66:6 (CHARLESWORTH)

## JULY 27

### *Great Commandments*

He who does harm to a human soul creates harm for his own soul,
and there is for him no healing of his flesh, nor any forgiveness for
  eternity.
He who carries out the murder of a human soul causes the death of his
  own soul,
and murders his own body, and there is no healing for him for eternity.
He who lies in wait for a person with any kind of trap,
he himself will be entangled in it; and there is no healing for him for
  eternity.
He who lies in wait for a person in judgment, his retribution will not be
  slackened in the great judgement for eternity.
He who acts perversely, or says anything against any soul,
righteousness will not be created for him for eternity.

2 ENOCH 60:1–5 (CHARLESWORTH)

## JULY 28

### *Responding to Human Need*

Give to the poor at once and do not tell them to come tomorrow.
With perspiring hand give a portion of corn to one who is in need.
Whoever gives alms knows he is lending to God.
Mercy saves from death when judgment comes.
God wants not sacrifice but mercy instead of sacrifice.
Therefore clothe the naked. Give the hungry a share of your bread.

Receive the homeless into your house and lead the blind.
Pity the shipwrecked, for the voyage is uncertain.
Give a hand to one who has fallen. Save a solitary man.
All have a common lot, the wheel of life, unstable prosperity.
If you have wealth, stretch out your hand to the poor.
The things which God gave you, give of them to one in need.
Every life of men is common, but falls out unequally.

SIBYLLINE ORACLES, BOOK 2, LINES 78–90 (CHARLESWORTH)

## JULY 29

### *Let the Tao Be a Bridge over Troubled Waters*

Raging rivers are like the power of the *Tao*\* they bring headlong those who despise them. For they are more swift than lightning, even more rapid. But those who cross them in faith shall not be disturbed. And those who walk on them faultlessly shall not be shaken because the sign on them is the Lord, and the sign is the Way for those who cross in the name of the Lord.

Therefore, put on the name of the Most High and know the *Tao,* and you shall cross without danger. The Lord bridges the waters by the Word, who walks and crosses them on foot.

On this side and on that the waves are lifted up, but the *Way of the Tao* makes walking secure. And the Way has been appointed for those who cross over after the Lord and for those who adhere to the path of faith and adore the name of the *Tao.*

ODES OF SOLOMON 39 (CHARLESWORTH)

\*Here and subsequently where I've used Tao, the original reads "the Lord."

## JULY 30

―――――――――――

*Proverbs: A Few One-Liners*

It is better to entertain your guests with a simple meal quickly than extensive festivity drawn out beyond the right time.

PSEUDO-PHOCYLIDES, LINES 81 AND 82 (CHARLESWORTH)


Persuade a senseless brother not to be senseless; if he is mad, protect him. . . .
The love of man is the beginning of godliness. . . .
It is better for man to be without anything than to have many things while not giving to the needy. . . .
What is right to do, do it willingly. What is not right to do, don't do it in any way.

SENTENCES OF SEXTUS (ROBINSON, 3D ED.)


Nobody knows what will be after tomorrow or after an hour.
Accommodate yourself to circumstances, do not blow against the wind.
Nip the evil in the bud, and heal the wound.
Do not apply your hand violently to tender children.
Work hard so you can live from your own means.
Love your friends to death, for faithfulness is a good thing.
May you live out your life well to the threshold of old age.

PSEUDO-PHOCYLIDES, LINES 116, 121, 143, 150,
153, 218, 230 (CHARLESWORTH)

# JULY 31

---

### *Proverbs: A Few More One-Liners*

There are two hateful things, and in both of them the stomach is involved: starvation, the stomach is swollen; satiety, the stomach is at the bursting point.

Blessed is the man who has mastered his stomach and his lust, he is one on whom one can rely at all times.

Do not laugh at old age, for that is where you shall arrive and remain.

Old age has its infirmities, and man has to accept them.

Sleep carries us into Sheol, dreams unite us with the dead.

There exists nothing better than silence.

Rest is a great blessing.

THE SENTENCES OF SYRIAC MENANDER, PART 2, LINES 59–62, 65–66, 11, 102–3, 68–69, 293, 311, 430 (CHARLESWORTH)

# Knowing the Mystery

☙

*Going to the Root*

Most things in the world, as long as their inner parts are hidden, stand upright and live. If they are revealed they die, as is illustrated by the visible man: as long as the intestines of a man are hidden, the man is alive; when his intestines are exposed and come out of him, the man will die. So also with the tree: while its root is hidden it sprouts and grows. If its root is exposed, the tree dries up.

So it is with every birth that is in the world, not only with the revealed but with the hidden. For so long as the root of wickedness is hidden, it is strong. But when it is recognized it is dissolved. When it is revealed it perishes. That is why the word says, "Already the ax is laid at the root of the trees" [Matthew 3:10]. It will not merely cut—what is cut sprouts again—but the ax penetrates deeply until it brings up the root. Jesus pulled out the root of the whole place, while others did it only partially.

As for ourselves, let each one of us dig after the root of evil which is within one, and let one pluck it out of one's heart from the root. It will be plucked out if we recognize it. But if we are ignorant of it, it takes root in us and produces its fruit in our heart. It masters us. We are its slaves. It takes us captive, to make us do what we do not want; and what we do want we do not do. It is powerful because we have not recognized it.

While it exists it is active. Ignorance is the mother of all evil. Ignorance will result in death, because those that come from ignorance neither were nor are nor shall be.

But those who are in the truth will be perfect when all the truth is revealed. For truth is like ignorance: while it is hidden it rests in itself, but when it is revealed and is recognized, it is praised inasmuch as it is stronger than ignorance and error. It gives freedom. The word said, "If you know the truth, the truth will make you free" [John 8:32]. Ignorance is a slave. Knowledge is freedom. If we know the truth, we shall find the fruits of the truth within us. If we are joined to it, it will bring our fulfillment.

GOSPEL OF PHILIP 82:30–84:13 (ROBINSON, 3D ED.)

*August 1 is midway between the summer solstice on June 21 and the fall equinox on September 21 (the other midpoints are November 1, February 1, and May 1). The Celtic calendar observes Lugh with attention particularly to Yang energy, balance to the Yin energy of February 1 with Brigid.*

*Lugh means "shining one," a warrior, sorcerer, and master of all crafts and skills who knows how to go to the root and heart of things. The raven is his symbol.*

## AUGUST 2

### Strength of Inner Mysteries

At the present time we have the manifest things of creation. We say, "The strong who are held in high regard are great people. And the weak who are despised are the obscure." Contrast the manifest things of truth: they are weak and despised, while the hidden things are strong and held in high regard. The mysteries of truth are revealed, though in type and image. The bridal chamber, however, remains hidden. It is the holy in the holy. . . .

If anyone becomes a son of the bridal chamber, he will receive the light. . . . This is the way it is: it is revealed to him alone, not hidden in the darkness and the night, but hidden in a perfect day and a holy light.

GOSPEL OF PHILIP 84:14–23, 86:4, 15 (ROBINSON, 3D ED.)

## AUGUST 3

### The Holy of Holies Is the Bridal Chamber

There were three buildings specifically for sacrifice in Jerusalem. The one facing west was called "the Holy." Another facing south was called the "Holy of the Holy." The third facing east was called "the Holy of the Holies," the place where only the high priest enters. Baptism is "the Holy" building. Redemption is "the Holy of the Holy." "The Holy of the Holies" is the bridal chamber. . . . Its veil was rent from top to bottom. For it was fitting for some from below to go upward. . . .

It was rent from top to bottom. Those above opened to us who are below, in order that we may go into the secret of the truth. This is what is held in high regard, since it is strong! But we shall go in there by means of lowly types and forms of weakness. They are indeed lowly when compared with the perfect glory. There is glory which surpasses glory. There is power which surpasses power. Therefore the perfect things have opened to us, together with the hidden things of truth. The holies of the holies were revealed, and the bridal chamber invited us in. . . .

Christ came to repair the separation that was from the beginning and again unite the two, and to give life to those who died as a result of the separation and unite them. But the woman is united to the man in the bridal chamber. Indeed those who have been united in the bridal chamber will no longer be separated.

GOSPEL OF PHILIP 69:15 AND 85:10–21, AND 70:13–17
(ROBINSON, 1977)

## AUGUST 4

### *The Soul's Baptism*

Wise men of old gave the soul a feminine name. Indeed she is female in her nature as well. She even has her womb. . . .

As long as the soul keeps running about everywhere copulating with whomever she meets and defiling herself, she exists in suffering her just desserts. But when she perceives the straits she is in and weeps before the Father and *sighs deeply*, and repents, then the Father will have mercy on her and he will make her womb turn from the external domain and will turn it again inward, so that the soul will regain her proper character. . . .

So when the womb of the soul, by the will of the Father, turns itself inward, it is baptized and is immediately cleansed of the external pollution which was pressed upon it, just as garments, when dirty, are put into the water and turned about until their dirt is removed and they become clean. And so the cleansing of the soul is to regain the newness of her former nature and to turn herself back again. That is her baptism.

THE EXEGESIS ON THE SOUL (ROBINSON, 3D ED.)

## AUGUST 5

---

### *Knowing God in the Bridal Chamber*

The soul cleanses herself in the bridal chamber; she fills it with perfume; she sits in waiting for the true bridegroom. . . .

When the bridegroom, according to the Father's will, comes down to her into the bridal chamber, she is prepared. . . . This marriage brings them back together again and the soul is joined to her true love, her real master. . . .

She recognizes him, and she rejoices once more, weeping before him as she remembers the disgrace of her former widowhood. And she adorns herself still more so that he might be pleased to stay with her. . . .

And when she has intercourse with him, she gets from him the seed that is the life-giving Spirit, so that by him she bears good children and rears them. For this is the great, perfect marvel of birth. And so this marriage is made perfect by the will of the Father.

THE EXEGESIS ON THE SOUL (ROBINSON, 3D ED.,
RECAST IN PRESENT TENSE)

## AUGUST 6

---

### *Transfiguration*

About eight days after these sayings, Jesus happened to take Peter and John and James along with him and climbed up the mountain to pray. And it so happened as he was praying that his face took on a strange appearance, and his clothing became dazzling white. The next thing you know, two figures were talking with him, Moses and Elijah, who appeared in glory and were discussing his departure, which he was destined to carry out in Jerusalem.

Now Peter and those who were with him were half asleep at the time. But they came wide awake when they saw his glory and the two men standing next to him. And it so happened as the men were leaving him that Peter said to Jesus, "Master, it's a good thing we're here. In fact, why not set up three tents, one for you, one for Moses, and one for Elijah!" (He didn't know what he was saying.)

While he was still speaking, a cloud moved in and cast a shadow over them. And their fear increased as they entered the cloud. And out of the cloud a voice spoke: "This is my son, my chosen one. Listen to him!" When the voice had spoken, Jesus was perceived to be alone. And they were speechless and told no one back then anything of what they had seen.

On the following day, when they came down from the mountain, a huge crowd happened to meet him. . . .

GOSPEL OF LUKE 9:28–37 (MILLER)

*Traditionally August 6 is observed as celebration of the transfiguration. On this same day in 1945 the atomic bomb was dropped on the people of Hiroshima, Japan. Denial of the mystery results in genocide.*

*"Trinity" is the name given to the first atomic bomb explosion that was set off fifty miles northwest of Alamogordo, New Mexico, on July 16, 1945.*

*Ironically and symbolically, this explosion destroys forever the conventional theological concept of the Trinity. It demonstrates what happens when we are governed by an inadequate concept of God that does not include the Yin, the feminine, Sophia, Wisdom. In my opinion, the conventional concept of the Trinity is outmoded, counterproductive to life on earth, and needs to be replaced with a new, yet primordial, Trinity as follows:*

*The Tao of Yin and Yang,*
*the Tao incarnating in Jesus and*
*the Spirit of the Tao who is seeking full expression in us and all that is*
*—these are the three expressions of the One Tao.*

## AUGUST 7

---

### *New Transfiguration*

Transfiguration not only transcends appearance and materials, it also transcends space and time. And so after some one thousand and nine hundred years Jesus went up to Mount Everest in the Himalayas. There before the people of Asia living on both sides of the mountains Jesus transfigured once more. His face shined as the sun, and his raiment was white as the snow. And, behold, there appeared unto them Lao Tzu and Gandhi talking with Jesus. (They spoke of his resurrection which he had accomplished at Jerusalem.)

And the people of Asia living on both sides of the mountains said unto Jesus, "Lord, it is good for us to be here: and let us make three tabernacles; one for thee, and one for Lao Tzu, and one for Gandhi."

And there was a cloud that overshadowed them: and a voice came out of the cloud, saying, "This is my Beloved Son. Blessed are those who have heard him and have practiced his teachings." And suddenly, the eyes of their hearts opened. They saw that Jesus was with them also and that all peoples were the children of God.

Jesus said: "And they shall come from the East, and from the West, and from the North, and from the South, and shall sit down with Abraham, and Isaac, and Jacob, in the kingdom of God."

THE VISION OF THE NEW TRANSFIGURATION (TAN, 1982)

*The vision of the transfiguration is updated to become more inclusive and appropriate to a whole-earth consciousness.*

## AUGUST 8

### *The Soul Experiences Regeneration*

Now it is fitting that the soul regenerate herself and become again as she formerly was. The soul then moves of her own accord. And she received the divine nature from the Father for her rejuvenation, so that she might be restored to the place where originally she had been. This is the resurrection that is from the dead. This is the ransom from captivity. This is the upward journey of ascent to heaven. . . .

Thus it is by being born again that the soul will be saved. And this is due not to rote phrases or to professional skills or to book learning. Rather it is grace, it is gift. For such is this heavenly thing. . . .

It is therefore fitting to pray to the Father and to call on him with all our soul—not externally with the lips but with the spirit, which is inward, which came forth from the depth—sighing; repenting for the life we lived; confessing our sins; perceiving the empty deception we were in, and the empty zeal; weeping over how we were in darkness and in the wave. . . .

Therefore it is fitting to pray to God night and day, spreading out our hands towards him as do people sailing in the middle of the sea: they pray to God with all their hearts without hypocrisy. . . . God examines the inward parts and searches the bottom of the heart.

THE EXEGESIS ON THE SOUL (ROBINSON, 3D ED.)

## AUGUST 9

### *The Sweetness, the Silence, and the Union*

Just as one is drawn by a pleasant aroma to search for the thing from which the aroma arises, since the aroma of the Father surpasses these ordinary ones [, . . . ] his sweetness leaves the aeons in ineffable pleasure and it gives them the idea of mingling with him who wants them to know him in a united way and to assist one another in the spirit which is sown within them. . . .

Baptism is called "silence" because of the quiet and the tranquility. It is also called "bridal chamber" because of the agreement and the indivisible state of those who know they have known him. . . .

For the end will receive a unitary existence just as the beginning is unitary, where there is no male nor female, nor slave and free, nor circumcision and uncircumcision, neither angel nor man, but Christ is all in all.

THE TRIPARTITE TRACTATE 72:5–19; 128:30–35; 132:20–27
(ROBINSON, 3D ED.)

## AUGUST 10

### The Soul Resting in God

But the rational soul who also wearied herself in seeking—she learned about God. She labored with inquiring, enduring distress in the body, wearing out her feet after the evangelists, learning about the Inscrutable One. She found her rising. She came to rest in him who is at rest. She reclined in the bride-chamber. She ate of the banquet for which she had hungered. She partook of the immortal food. She found what she had sought after. She received rest from her labors, while the light that shines forth upon her does not sink. To it belongs the glory and the power and the revelation for ever and ever. Amen.

THE AUTHORITATIVE TEACHING (ROBINSON, 3D ED.)

## AUGUST 11

---

### *How to Live After the Bridal Chamber Experience*

You have come into being inside the bridal chamber, and you have been illuminated in mind. My son [daughter], do not swim in any kind of water, and do not allow yourself to be defiled by strange kinds of knowledge. . . . For it is fitting for you to be in agreement with the intelligence of these two: with the intelligence of the snake and with the innocence of the dove.

Remember the words of Jesus, "Be wise as serpents and innocent as doves" [Matthew 10:16, Kings James Version]. In the bridal chamber experience we become that way.

THE TEACHINGS OF SILVANUS (ROBINSON, 1977)

## AUGUST 12

---

### *Resting in the One Who Encircles All Spaces*

You are in the one who encircles all spaces while there is none that encircles him.

In time unity will perfect the spaces.

Rest in him who is at rest not striving nor being involved in the search for truth. For you are now in the truth.

You are set at rest in the Spirit. Heed your root.

This is the place of the blessed. This is your place.

Say then from the heart that you are the perfect day and in you dwells the light that does not fail.

Speak of the truth with those who search for it and of knowledge to those who have committed sin in their error.

Make firm the foot of those who have stumbled and stretch out your hands to those who are ill. Feed those who are hungry and give repose to those who are weary, and raise up those who wish to rise, and awaken those who are asleep. For you are the understanding that is drawn forth.

EXCERPTS FROM THE GOSPEL OF TRUTH, MID-SECOND CENTURY
(ROBINSON, 3D ED.)

## AUGUST 13

*I Love Wisdom and Am Determined to Take Her to Live with Me*

I loved Wisdom and sought her from my youth;
I desired to take her for my bride
and became enamored of her beauty. . . .
She is an initiate in the knowledge of God,
and an associate in his works.
If riches are a desirable possession in life,
what is richer than Wisdom, the active cause of all things? . . .
If anyone longs for wide experience,
she knows the things of old, and infers the things to come;
she understands turns of speech and the solutions of riddles;
she has foreknowledge of signs and wonders
and of the outcome of seasons and times.
Therefore I determined to take her to live with me,
knowing that she would give me good counsel
and encouragement in cares and grief. . . .
When I enter my house, I shall find rest with her;
for companionship with her has no bitterness,
and life with her has no pain, but gladness and joy.

EXCERPTS FROM WISDOM OF SOLOMON 8
(NEW REVISED STANDARD VERSION)

## AUGUST 14

### *A Cup of Milk Was Offered to Me*

A cup of milk was offered to me,
>and I drank it in the sweetness of the Lord's kindness.

The Son is the cup, and the Mother is she who was milked;
>and the Holy Spirit is the One who milked her;

Because her breasts were full,
>and it was undesirable that her milk should be released without
>>purpose.

The Holy Spirit opened her bosom,
>and mixed the milk of the two breasts of the Mother.

Then she gave the mixture to the generation without their knowing,
>and those who have received it are in the perfection of the right
>>hand.

The womb of the Virgin took it,
>and she received conception and gave birth.

So the Virgin became a mother with great mercies.
>And she labored and bore the Son without pain.

And she did not seek a midwife,
>because She caused her to give life.

She bore as a strong man with desire,
>and she bore according to the manifestation, and possessed with
>>great power.

And she loved with salvation, and guarded with kindness,
>and declared with greatness. Hallelujah.

**ODES OF SOLOMON 19 (CHARLESWORTH, ADAPTED)**

# Knowing the Great Mother

❧

---

*"Hail, Queen of Heaven and Earth"*

I say, "Hail" to the Holy One who appears in the heavens!
I say, "Hail" to the Holy Priestess of Heaven!
I say, "Hail" to Inanna, Queen of Heaven *and Earth!*
Holy Torch! You fill the sky with light!
You brighten the day at dawn!
I say, "Hail!" to Inanna, Great Lady of Heaven!
Awesome Lady of *God above and below!* Crowned with great horns,
You fill the heavens and earth with light!
I say, "Hail!" to Inanna, First Daughter of the Moon!
Mighty, majestic, and radiant,
You shine brilliantly in the evening,
You brighten the day at dawn,
You stand in the heavens like the sun and the moon,
Your wonders are known both above and below,
To the greatness of the holy priestess of heaven *and earth,*
To you, Inanna, I sing!

QUEEN OF HEAVEN AND EARTH, THIRD MILLENNIUM B.C.E
(WOLKSTEIN AND KRAMER, ADAPTED)

*Inanna means "Queen of Heaven." She is also known in all the natural mysteries of the earth, including birth, death, rebirth, and fertility in animals and human beings.*

## AUGUST 16

### The Lady Who Ascends into the Heavens

My Lady, the Amazement of the Land
The Brave One who appears in the heavens—
All the lands fear her.
In the pure places of the steppe,
On the high roofs of the dwellings,
On the platforms of the city,
They make offering to her:
Piles of incense like sweet-smelling cedar.
Fine sheep, fat sheep, long-haired sheep,
Butter, cheeses, dates, fruits of all kinds.
They purify the earth for My Lady.
They celebrate her in song.
They fill the table of the land with first fruits.
They pour dark beer for her.
They pour light beer for her.
Dark beer, emmer beer,
Emmer beer for My Lady.
The *vats* make a bubbling noise for her.
They prepare *bread* in date syrup for her.
Flour, flour in honey, beer at dawn.
They pour wine and honey for her at sunrise.
The *Holy Ones and the People* go to her with food and drink.
They feed the Queen of Heaven and Earth in the pure clean place.

My Lady looks in sweet wonder from heaven.
The People parade before the holy Queen of Heaven and Earth.
The Lady Who Ascends into the Heavens is radiant.
I sing your praises, Queen of Heaven and Earth.
The Lady Who Ascends into the Heavens is radiant on the horizon.

QUEEN OF HEAVEN AND EARTH (WOLKSTEIN AND KRAMER, ADAPTED)

## AUGUST 17

### *The Apostles Ask Mary, "How Did You Conceive?"*

Now the apostles were in the place Chritir with Mary. And Bartholomew came to Peter and Andrew and John, and said to them: Let us ask Mary, her who is highly favoured, how she conceived the incomprehensible or how she carried him who cannot be carried or how she bore so much greatness. But they hesitated to ask her. . . .

But Mary answered: Do not ask me concerning this mystery. If I begin to tell you, fire will come out of my mouth and consume the whole earth. But they asked her still more urgently. And since she did not want to deny the apostles a hearing, she said: Let us stand up in prayer. . . .

Then Mary stood up before them, and spread out her hands to heaven and began to pray thus: O God exceeding great and all-wise, king of the ages, indescribable, ineffable, who creates the breadths of the heavens by your word and arranges the vault of heaven in harmony, who gives form to disorderly matter and brings together that which was separated, who parts the gloom of the darkness from the light, who makes the waters to flow from the same source, before whom the beings of the air tremble and the creatures of the earth fear, who gives to the earth its place and does not wish it to perish, in bestowing upon it abundant rain and caring for the nourishment of all things, the eternal Word (Logos) of the Father.

The seven heavens could scarcely contain You, but You are pleased to be contained in me without causing me pain, You are the perfect Word (Logos) of the Father, through whom everything is created. Glorify Your exceedingly great Name, and allow me to speak before Your holy apostles.

And when she had ended the prayer, she began to say to them: Let us sit down on the ground. Come, Peter, chief of the apostles, sit on my right hand and put your left hand under my shoulder. And you, Andrew, do the same on my left hand. And you, chaste John, hold my breast. And you, Bartholomew, place your knees on my shoulders and press close my back so that, when I begin to speak, my limbs are not loosed.

And when they had done that, she began: When I lived in the temple of God and received my food from the hand of an angel, one day there appeared to me one in the form of an angel; but his face was indescribable and in his hand he had neither bread nor cup, as had the angel who came to me before. And immediately the veil of the temple was rent and there was a violent earthquake, and I fell to the earth, for I could not bear the sight of him. But he took me with his hand and raised me up. And I looked toward heaven; and there came a cloud of dew on my face and sprinkled me from head to foot, and he wiped me with his robe.

Then he said to me: Hail, you who are highly favoured, the chosen vessel. And then he struck the right side of his garment and there came forth an exceedingly large loaf, and he placed it upon the altar of the temple, and first ate of it himself and then gave to me also. And again he struck his garment, on the left side, and I looked and saw a cup full of wine. And he placed it upon the altar of the temple, and drank from it first himself and gave it also to me. And I looked and saw that the bread did not diminish and the cup was full as before.

Then he said: Three years more, and I will send my word and you shall conceive my son, and through him the whole world shall be saved. But you will bring salvation to the world. Peace be with you, favoured one, and my peace shall be with you forever. And when he had said this, he vanished from my eyes and the temple was as before.

As she was saying this, fire came from her mouth, and the world was on the point of being burned up. Then came Jesus quickly and said to Mary: Say no more, or today my whole creation will come to an end. And the apostles were seized with fear lest God should be angry with them.

GOSPEL OF BARTHOLOMEW II, THIRD CENTURY
(HENNECKE AND SCHNEEMELCHER, ADAPTED)

O womb more spacious than a city!
O womb wider than the span of heaven!
O womb that contained him whom the seven heavens do not contain.
You contained him without pain and held in your bosom him who
    changed his being into the smallest of things. . . .
O womb that became more spacious than the whole creation.

GOSPEL OF BARTHOLOMEW IV 17 (HENNECKE AND SCHNEEMELCHER)

# Tao of Holy Union

↩

## AUGUST 18

### Praying in the Bedroom

*In this story Sarah's parents are hoping that she and Tobias will marry, so they retire to their bedroom and leave the couple alone in another bedroom.*

When the parents had gone out and shut the door of the room, Tobias got out of bed and said to Sarah, "Sister, get up, and let us pray and implore our Lord that he grant us mercy and safety." So she got up, and they began to pray and implore that they might be kept safe. Tobias began by saying,

> "Blessed are you, O God of our ancestors,
>     and blessed is your name in all generations forever.
> Let the heavens and the whole creation bless you forever.
> You made Adam, and for him you made his wife Eve
>     as a helper and support.
> From the two of them the human race has sprung.
> You said, 'It is not good that the man should be alone;
>     let us make a helper for him like himself.'
> I now am taking this kinswoman of mine,

not because of lust,
but with sincerity.
Grant that she and I may find mercy
and that we may grow old together."

And they both said, "Amen, Amen." Then they went to sleep for the night.

[The next day Tobias and Sarah and their families began making preparations for a wedding celebration that lasted fourteen days.]

TOBIT 8:1, 4–9 (NEW REVISED STANDARD VERSION)

## AUGUST 19

### *Preparing for the Sacred Marriage Rite*

The people of Sumer assemble in the palace,
The house which guides the land.
The king builds a throne for the queen of the palace.
He sits beside her on the throne.
In order to care for the life of all the lands,
The exact first day of the month is closely examined,
And on the day of the disappearance of the moon,
On the day of the sleeping of the moon,
The [orders] are perfectly carried out
So that the New Year's Day, the day of rites,
May be properly determined,
And a sleeping place be set up for Inanna.
The people cleanse the rushes with sweet-smelling cedar oil,
They arrange the rushes for the bed.
They spread a bridal sheet over the bed.

A bridal sheet to rejoice the heart,
A bridal sheet to sweeten the loins,
A bridal sheet for Inanna and Dumuzi.
The queen bathes her holy loins,
Inanna bathes for the holy loins of Dumuzi,
She washes herself with soap.
She sprinkles sweet-smelling cedar oil on the ground.

THE SACRED MARRIAGE RITE (WOLKSTEIN AND KRAMER)

## AUGUST 20

### *Rejoicing in the Sacred Union*

Inanna spread the bridal sheet across the bed.
She called to the king: "The bed is ready!"
She called to her bridegroom: "The bed is waiting!"
He put his hand in her hand.
He put his hand to her heart.
Sweet is the sleep of hand-to-hand.
Sweeter still the sleep of heart-to-heart.
Inanna spoke,
"I bathed for the wild bull,
I bathed for the shepherd Dumuzi,
I perfumed my sides with ointment,
I coated my mouth with sweet-smelling amber,
I painted my eyes with kohl.
He shaped my loins with his fair hands,
The shepherd Dumuzi filled my lap with cream and milk,
He stroked my pubic hair,
He watered my womb.
He laid his hands on my holy vulva,

He smoothed my black boat with cream,
He quickened my narrow boat with milk,
He caressed me on the bed.
Now I will caress my high priest on the bed,
I will caress the faithful shepherd Dumuzi,
I will caress his loins, the shepherdship of the land,
I will decree a sweet fate for him." . . .
The king goes with lifted head to the holy loins,
Dumuzi goes with lifted head to the holy loins of Inanna.
He lies down beside her in the bed.
Tenderly he caresses her, murmuring words of love:
"O my holy jewel! O my wondrous Inanna!"
After he enters her holy vulva, causing the queen to rejoice,
After he enters her holy vulva, causing Inanna to rejoice,
Inanna holds him to her and murmurs:
"O Dumuzi, you are truly my love." . . .
Inanna spoke:
"My beloved, the delight of my eyes, met me.
We rejoiced together.
He took his pleasure of me.
He brought me into his house.
He laid me down on the fragrant honey bed.
My sweet love, lying by my heart,
Tongue playing, one by one,
My fair Dumuzi did so fifty times.
Now, my sweet love is sated.
Now he says:
'Set me free, my sister, set me free.
You will be a little daughter to my father.
Come, my beloved sister, I would go to the palace.
Set me free.' "

THE JOY OF SUMER (WOLKSTEIN AND KRAMER)

## AUGUST 21

### *Sharing the Joy of Love with All*

The king bids the people enter the great hall.
The people bring food offerings and bowls.
They burn juniper resin, performing laving rites,
And pile up sweet-smelling incense.
The king embraces his beloved bride,
Dumuzi embraces Inanna.
Inanna, seated on the royal throne, shines like daylight.
The king, like the sun, shines radiantly by her side.
He arranges abundance, lushness, and plenty before her.
He assembles the people of Sumer.
The musicians play for the queen:
They play the loud instrument which drowns out the southern storm,
They play the sweet *algar*-instrument, the ornament of the palace,
They play the stringed instrument which brings joy to all people,
They play songs for Inanna to rejoice the heart.
The king reaches out his hand for food and drink,
Dumuzi reaches out his hand for food and drink.
The palace is festive. The king is joyous.
In the pure clean place they celebrate Inanna in song.
She is the ornament of the assembly, the joy of Sumer!
The people spend the day in plenty.
The king stands before the assembly in great joy.
He hails Inanna with the praises of the gods and the assembly:
"Holy Priestess! Created with the heavens and earth,
Inanna, First Daughter of the Moon, Lady of the Evening!
I sing your praises!"

**THE JOY OF SUMER (WOLKSTEIN AND KRAMER)**

## AUGUST 22

*The Mystery of Sexual Intercourse*

And if you wish to see the reality of the mystery, then you should see the wonderful representation of the intercourse that takes place between male and female. For when the semen reaches the climax, it leaps forth. In that moment the female receives the strength of the male; the male for his part receives the strength of the female, while the semen does this.

Therefore the mystery of intercourse is performed in secret, in order that the two sexes might not disgrace themselves in front of many who do not experience that reality. For each of them (the sexes) contributes its (own part in) begetting. For if it happens in the presence of those who do not understand the reality, it is laughable and unbelievable. And, moreover, they are holy mysteries, of both words and deeds because not only are they not heard but also they are not seen.

ASCLEPIUS (ROBINSON, 3D ED.)

# Tao of Childhood

↬

## AUGUST 23

### Children Resemble Their Parents

The children a woman bears resemble the man who loves her. If her husband loves her, then they resemble her husband. If it is an adulterer, then they resemble the adulterer. Frequently, if a woman sleeps with her husband out of necessity, while her heart is with the adulterer with whom she usually has intercourse, the child she will bear is born resembling the adulterer.

Now you who live together with the Son of God, love not the world, but love the Lord, in order that those you will bring forth may not resemble the world, but may resemble the Lord.

GOSPEL OF PHILIP 78:12–24 (ROBINSON, 3D ED.)

## AUGUST 24

### Child Jesus and Clay Pigeons

I, Thomas the Israelite, make this proclamation to all of you, gentile brothers, to make known the wondrous youthful deeds of our Lord

Jesus Christ that he performed after being born in our land. It begins as follows.

When this child Jesus was five years old, he was playing at the ford of a wadi. He was gathering the flowing waters into pools and instantly purifying them; he accomplished all this simply by his word of command.

He made soft mud and out of it fashioned twelve sparrows. It was the sabbath when he did this. There were many other children playing with him.

A certain Jew, when he saw what Jesus was doing while playing on the sabbath, went off quickly and told his father, Joseph: "See here, your child is at the wadi, and he took mud and fashioned twelve sparrows. He has violated the sabbath!"

Joseph went to the place. He had a look and cried out, "Why are you doing what is not permitted on the sabbath?"

Jesus clapped his hands and called to the sparrows: "Off you go!" The sparrows flew away chirping.

When the Jews heard this they were amazed. They went off and reported to their leading men what they had seen Jesus do.

INFANCY GOSPEL OF THOMAS 1 AND 2, SECOND CENTURY (MILLER)

*Delightful stories about Jesus like this one developed from the question, "I wonder what he was like as a boy?" Notice that this story occurs on the sabbath, when no one is allowed to work. Even as a child, Jesus is seen as challenging the conventional rules and expectations!*

## AUGUST 25

### Child Jesus Learning His Alphabet

A teacher by the name of Zacchaeus . . . approached Joseph and said to him, "You have a clever child and he has his wits about him. Come, hand him over to me so he can learn his alphabet. Along with his letters, I'll teach him all other subjects, as well as how to address his elders and to honor them as his ancestors and parents deserve. I'll also teach him to love children his own age."

He recited for him, clearly and carefully, all the letters of the alphabet from alpha to omega.

Jesus looked at the instructor Zacchaeus and said to him, "You don't really know the alpha; how are you going to teach others the beta? You phony, if you know it, teach the alpha first, and then we'll trust you about the beta." He then left his teacher speechless on the subject of the first letter, since he was unable to say anything in response.

While many people were listening, the child said to Zacchaeus, "Listen, teacher, to the arrangement of the first letter and pay attention to how it has straight lines and a crossbar bisecting the other lines that you see drawn together in common, with the upper part of the letter going on and reaching a cap. There you have the lines of the alpha, triple but uniform, commanding and subordinate, of equal measure."

When Zacchaeus the teacher heard the child giving so many profound allegorical interpretations of the first letter, he was amazed at the child's explanation and teaching.

INFANCY GOSPEL OF THOMAS 6:1–7:1 (MILLER)

## AUGUST 26

### Child Jesus Says, "I Never Pushed Him"

A few days later, Jesus was playing on the roof of a house. One of the children who were playing with him on the roof fell off and died. When the other children saw what had happened, they ran away and Jesus was left alone.

The parents of the dead child came and accused Jesus of having pushed him. Jesus said, "I never pushed him." But they threatened him anyway.

Jesus jumped down from the roof and stood beside the body of the child and called out at the top of his voice: "Zeno,"—for that was his name—"get up and tell me whether I pushed you."

He stood up at once and said, "No, sir, you did not push me down, but you did raise me up."

When the child's parents saw this they were amazed, praised God for the sign that had occurred, and they worshiped Jesus.

INFANCY GOSPEL OF THOMAS 9 (MILLER)

## AUGUST 27

### *Jesus Working with His Father*

Now Jesus' father was a carpenter and at that time made plows and yokes. He received an order from a certain rich man to make a couch. When one of the boards, called the cross-beam, was shorter than the other, they didn't know what to do.

Then the child Jesus said to his father, Joseph, "Set the two planks down and line them up at the midpoints."

Joseph did as the child instructed him. Jesus stood on one side and took hold of the shorter plank, stretched it out, and made it the same length as the other.

His father Joseph saw it and was amazed. He hugged and kissed the child and said, "God has blessed me in giving me this son."

INFANCY GOSPEL OF THOMAS 13 (MILLER)

## AUGUST 28

### *Jesus Makes His Bar Mitzvah*

When he was twelve years old his parents went to Jerusalem, as was their custom, for the Passover festival, along with their traveling companions. After Passover they returned home. As they returned, the child Jesus went back to Jerusalem, but his parents thought he was in the caravan. When they had gone a day's journey, they sought him among their relatives. When they didn't find him, they were upset and returned to the city to look for him.

Three days later they found him in the temple, seated among the teachers, listening to them and asking questions. Everyone paid attention to him and all were amazed how, though a child, he was able to silence the elders and teachers of the people, interpreting the main points of the Law and the enigmatic sayings of the prophets.

His mother Mary approached. "Why did you do this to us, child," she said to him. "Look how we have been searching for you in our grief."

"Why are you looking for me?" Jesus answered. "Don't you know that I must be in my Father's house?"

The scholars and Pharisees said, "Are you the mother of this child?"

"I am," Mary responded.

They said to her, "You of all women are to be congratulated, because God has blessed the fruit of your womb. For we have never seen nor heard of such glory or such virtue and wisdom."

Jesus got up, followed his mother, and was obedient to his parents. His mother remembered all these events. Jesus grew in wisdom and age and grace. To him be glory for ever and ever. Amen.

INFANCY GOSPEL OF THOMAS 19 (MILLER)

# Tao of Finance

❧

## AUGUST 29

*Borrowing and Lending*

The merciful lend to their neighbors;
    by holding out a helping hand they keep the commandments.
Lend to your neighbor in his time of need;
    repay your neighbor when a loan falls due.
Keep your promise and be honest with him,
    and on every occasion you will find what you need.
Many regard a loan as a windfall,
    and cause trouble to those who help them.
One kisses another's hands until he gets a loan,
    and is deferential in speaking of his neighbor's money;
but at the time for repayment he delays,
    and pays back with empty promises,
    and finds fault with the time.
If he can pay, his creditor will hardly get back half,
    and will regard that as a windfall.
If he cannot pay, the borrower has robbed the other of his money,
    and he has needlessly made him an enemy;
he will repay him with curses and reproaches,
    and instead of glory will repay him with dishonor.

Many refuse to lend, not because of meanness,
  but from fear of being defrauded needlessly.

SIRACH 29:1–7 (NEW REVISED STANDARD VERSION)

## AUGUST 30

---

### *Helping the Poor*

Nevertheless, be patient with someone in humble circumstances,
  and do not keep him waiting for your alms.
Help the poor for the commandment's sake,
  and in their need do not send them away empty-handed.
Lose your silver for the sake of a brother or a friend,
  and do not let it rust under a stone and be lost.
Lay up your treasure according to the commandments of the Most
  High,
  and it will profit you more than gold.
Store up almsgiving in your treasury,
  and it will rescue you from every disaster.

SIRACH 29:8–12 (NEW REVISED STANDARD VERSION)

## AUGUST 31

---

### *Make Christ a Partner in Your Possessions*

You save your money which, when saved, does not save you. You heap up
an inheritance which burdens you with its weight; and you do not remember what God replied to the rich farmer who boasted with foolish

elation over the abundance of his luxuriant harvest: "You fool! This very night shall your life be required of you. To whom will this piled-up wealth of yours go?"

Why do you keep a lonely vigil over your riches? Why do you increase your burdens by increasing your wealth? Why do you want to become so rich when you will only have to become that much poorer before God? Divide your returns with the Lord your God. Share your gains with Christ. Make Christ a partner in your earthly possessions, so that he may also make you co-heir of his heavenly kingdom.

CYPRIAN, TREATISE ON WORKS AND ALMSGIVING 12–14 (WRIGHT)

Often when Socrates looked at the multitude of wares exposed for sale, he would say to himself, "How many things I can do without!"

DIOGENES LAERTIUS, LIVES OF
THE EMINENT PHILOSOPHERS 2.25 (ROBBINS)

# Tao of Working

↩

---

### An Ass Turning a Millstone

An ass which turns a millstone did a hundred miles walking. When it was loosed it found that it was still at the same place. There are men who make many journeys, but make no progress towards any destination. When evening came upon them, they saw neither city nor village, neither human artifact nor natural phenomenon, power nor angel. In vain have the wretches labored.

GOSPEL OF PHILIP 63:12–21 (ROBINSON, 3D ED.)

---

### Do You Think You Can Take over the Universe and Improve It?

Do you think you can take over the universe and improve it?
I do not believe it can be done.
The universe is sacred.
You can not improve it.

If you try to change it, you will ruin it.
If you try to hold it, you will lose it.
So sometimes things are ahead and sometimes they are behind;
Sometimes breathing is hard, sometimes it comes easily;
Sometimes there is strength and sometimes there is weakness;
Sometimes one is up and sometimes down.
Therefore the sage avoids extremes, excesses, and complacency.

TAO TE CHING, 29 (FENG AND ENGLISH)

*The last portion is translated this way by Wee Chong Tan:*

Therefore, all things are in a state of flux,
whether already in progress or about to commence,
whether in process of fermenting or in active respiration,
whether in strength or in decay,
whether in repair or in destruction.
That is why the Saint avoids all extremes, excesses, and luxuries.

TAO TE CHING, 29B (TAN, 1992)

## SEPTEMBER 3

### *Be Content with What You Have*

Fame or self: Which matters more?
Self or wealth: Which is more precious?
Gain or loss: Which is more painful?
He who is attached to things will suffer much.
He who saves will suffer heavy loss.
A contented man is never disappointed.

He who knows when to stop
   does not find himself in trouble.
He will stay forever safe.

TAO TE CHING, 44 (FENG AND ENGLISH)

## SEPTEMBER 4

*The Highest Good Is Like Water*

The highest good is like water.
Water gives life to the ten thousand things and does not strive.
It flows in places men reject and so is like the Tao.
In dwelling, be close to the land.
In meditation, go deep in the heart.
In dealing with others, be gentle and kind.
In speech, be true.
In ruling, be just.
In business, be competent.
In action, watch the timing.
No fight; no blame.

TAO TE CHING, 8 (FENG AND ENGLISH)

## SEPTEMBER 5

*Do Your Work, Then Step Back*

Fill your bowl to the brim
and it will spill.
Keep sharpening your knife

and it will blunt.
Chase after money and security
and your heart will never unclench.
Care about people's approval
and you will be their prisoner.
Do your work, then step back.
The only path to serenity.

TAO TE CHING, 9 (MITCHELL)

Do you have the patience to wait
till your mud settles and the water is clear?
Can you remain unmoving
till the right action arises by itself?

TAO TE CHING, 15 (MITCHELL)

## SEPTEMBER 6

*Do Your Job, Then Let Go*

He who stands on tiptoe is not steady.
He who strides cannot maintain the pace.
He who makes a show is not enlightened.
He who is self-righteous is not respected.
He who boasts achieves nothing.
He who brags will not endure.

TAO TE CHING, 24, PART 1 (FENG AND ENGLISH)

He who has power over others can't empower himself.
He who clings to work will create nothing that endures.
If you want to accord with the Tao,
just do your job, then let go.

TAO TE CHING, 24, PART 2 (MITCHELL)

## SEPTEMBER 7

*In Harmony with the Tao*

The best athlete wants his opponent at his best.
The best general enters the mind of his enemy.
The best businessman serves the communal good.
The best leader follows the will of the people.
All of them embody the virtue of non-competition.
Not that they don't love to compete, but they do it in the spirit of play.
In this they are like children and in harmony with the Tao.

TAO TE CHING, 68 (MITCHELL)

## SEPTEMBER 8

*Broken Contracts*

After a bitter quarrel, some resentment must remain.
What can one do about it?
Therefore the sage keeps his half of the bargain
But does not exact his due.

A man of Virtue performs his part,
but a man without Virtue requires others to fulfill their obligations.
The Tao of heaven is impartial.
It stays with good men all the time.

TAO TE CHING, 79 (FENG AND ENGLISH)

## SEPTEMBER 9

### *How to Handle Problems*

Act without action.
Do without ado.
Taste without tasting.
Whether it is big or small, many or few, repay hatred with virtue.
Prepare for the difficult while it is still easy.
Deal with the big while it is still small.
Difficult undertakings have always started with what is easy
and great undertakings have always started with what is small.
Therefore the sage never strives for the great,
and thereby the great is achieved.
He who makes rash promises surely lacks faith.
He who takes things too easily will surely encounter much difficulty.
For this reason, even the sage regards things as difficult.
And therefore he encounters no difficulty.

TAO TE CHING, 63 (CHAN)

## SEPTEMBER 10

*Let Things Take Their Course*

What remains still is easy to hold.
What is not yet manifest is easy to plan for.
What is brittle is easy to crack.
What is minute is easy to scatter.
Deal with things before they appear.
Put things in order before disorder arises.
A tree as big as a man's embrace grows from a tiny shoot.
A tower of nine stories begins with a heap of earth.
The journey of a thousand *miles* starts from where one stands.
He who takes action fails.
He who grasps things loses them.
For this reason, the sage takes no action and therefore does not fail.
He grasps nothing and therefore he does not lose anything.
People in their handling of affairs often fail when they are about to
    succeed.
If one remains as careful at the end as he was at the beginning,
there will be no failure.
Therefore the sage desires to have no desire,
He does not value rare treasures.
He learns to be unlearned and returns to what the multitude has missed
    (Tao).
Thus he supports all things in their natural state,
but does not take any action.

TAO TE CHING, 64 (CHAN)

## SEPTEMBER 11

---

*Let Your Workings Remain a Mystery*

If you want to shrink something,
you must first allow it to expand.
If you want to get rid of something,
you must first allow it to flourish.
If you want to take something,
you must first allow it to be given.
This is called the subtle perception
of the way things are.
The soft overcomes the hard.
The slow overcomes the fast.
Let your workings remain a mystery.

TAO TE CHING, 36 (MITCHELL)

## SEPTEMBER 12

---

*A Good Traveler Has No Fixed Plans*

A good traveler has no fixed plans and is not intent upon arriving.
A good artist lets his intuition lead him wherever it wants.
A good scientist has freed himself of concepts and keeps his mind open
    to what is.
Thus the Master is available to all people and doesn't reject anyone.
He is ready to use all situations and doesn't waste anything.

TAO TE CHING, 27, PART 1 (MITCHELL)

He is always good in saving things and consequently nothing is rejected.
This is called "following the light" (of Nature)
Therefore the good man is the teacher of the bad,
And the bad is the material from which the good may learn.
He who does not value the teacher,
Or greatly care for the material,
Is greatly deluded although he may be learned.
Such is the essential mystery.

TAO TE CHING, 27, PART 2 (CHAN)

## SEPTEMBER 13

*Possessions and Knowing Yourself*

Is it not necessary for all those who possess everything to know themselves? Some indeed, if they do not know themselves, will not enjoy what they possess. But those who have come to know themselves will enjoy their possessions.

GOSPEL OF PHILIP 76:18–22 (ROBINSON, 3D ED.)

# Tao of Leading

↵

*Trusting People*

When the Master governs, the people
are hardly aware that he exists.
Next best is a leader who is loved.
Next, one who is feared.
Next, one who is despised.
If you don't trust the people,
you make them untrustworthy.
The Master doesn't talk, he acts.
When his work is done,
the people say, "Amazing: we did it, all by ourselves!"

TAO TE CHING, 17 (MITCHELL)

*Work with the Mind of the People*

The sage has no fixed (personal) ideas.
He regards the people's ideas as his own.

I treat those who are good with goodness,
And I also treat those who are not good with goodness.
Thus goodness is attained.
I am honest to those who are honest,
And I am also honest to those who are not honest.
Thus honesty is attained.
The sage, in the government of his empire, has no subjective viewpoint.
His mind forms a harmonious whole with that of his people.

TAO TE CHING, 49 (CHAN)


## SEPTEMBER 16

### Put Self-Interest Behind

How does the sea become the king of all the rivers?
Because it prefers to lie below all rivers,
That's how it becomes the king of all rivers.
Therefore, in order to be above the people,
One must be humble in speech with the people.
In order to lead the people,
One must be willing to put self-interest behind.
That's why the Saint is located above the people,
and the people do not feel oppressed;
in front of the people,
and the people do not feel hindered.
Hence the world is happy to promote such a leader,
without getting disgusted.
Because the Saint does not contend with anyone,
therefore the world is unable to contend with such a one.

TAO TE CHING, 66 (TAN, 1992)

## SEPTEMBER 17

---

### *Stay in the Center*

He who knows others is wise;
He who knows himself is enlightened.
He who conquers others has physical strength.
He who conquers himself is strong.
He who is contented is rich.
He who acts with vigor has will.
He who does not lose his place (with Tao) will endure.
He who dies but does not really perish enjoys long life.

TAO TE CHING, 33 (CHAN)

## SEPTEMBER 18

---

### *I Have Three Treasures*

Everyone under heaven says that my Tao is great and beyond compare.
Because it is great, it seems different.
If it were not different, it would have vanished long ago.
I have three treasures that I hold and keep.
The first is *Tzu;*\*
The second is economy;
The third is daring not to be ahead of others.
From *Tzu* comes courage;
From economy comes generosity;
From humility comes leadership.
Nowadays men shun *Tzu*, but try to be brave;
They abandon economy, but try to be generous.
They do not believe in humility, but always try to be first.

This is certain death.
*Tzu* brings victory in battle and strength in defense.
It is the means by which heaven saves and guards.

TAO TE CHING, 67 (FENG AND ENGLISH)

*Compare a version of the last portion by Stephen Mitchell:*

> I have just three things to teach:
> simplicity, patience, compassion.
> These three are your greatest treasures.
> Simple in actions and in thoughts,
> you return to the source of being.
> Patient with both friends and enemies,
> in accord with the way things are.
> Compassionate toward yourself,
> you reconcile all beings in the world.

TAO TE CHING, 67 (MITCHELL)

*Tzu is translated as "deep love" by Wing-Tsit Chan, "mercy" by Gia-Fu Feng and Jane English, and "gentleness" by Talbot McCarroll. An alternative reading for "economy" is "simplicity." An alternative reading for "not being ahead" is "humility."

## SEPTEMBER 19

### *Success Is as Dangerous as Failure*

Success is as dangerous as failure. Hope is as hollow as fear.
What does it mean that success is as dangerous as failure?
Whether you go up the ladder or down it, your position is shaky.
When you stand with your two feet on the ground,

you will always keep your balance.
What does it mean that hope is as hollow as fear?
Hope and fear are both phantoms that arise from thinking of the self.
When we don't see the self as self, what do we have to fear?
See the world as your self,
Have faith in the way things are.
Love the world as your self;
then you can care for all things.

TAO TE CHING, 13 (MITCHELL)

## SEPTEMBER 20

### *Don't Try to Force Issues*

Whenever you advise a ruler in the way of the Tao,
Counsel him not to use force to conquer the universe.
For this would only cause resistance.
Thorn bushes spring up wherever the army has passed.
Lean years follow in the wake of a great war.
Just do what needs to be done.
Never take advantage of power.
Achieve results, but never glory in them.
Achieve results, but never boast.
Achieve results, but never be proud.
Achieve results, because this is the natural way.
Achieve results, but not through violence.
Force is followed by loss of strength.
This is not the way of the Tao.
That which goes against the Tao comes to an early end.

TAO TE CHING, 30 (FENG AND ENGLISH)

# The Way of the Tao
# and Vocation

⦿

---

## My Work Is the Psalm of the Lord

As the work of the plowman is the plowshare, and the work of the
   helmsman is the steering of the ship,
   so also my work is the psalm of the Lord in his praises.
My art and my service are in his praises, because his love has nourished
   my heart,
   and his fruits he poured unto my lips.
For my love is the Lord;
   hence I shall sing unto him.
For I am strengthened in his praises,
   and I have faith in him.
I shall open my mouth, and his spirit will speak through me
   the praise of the Lord and his beauty,
The work of his hands,
   and the service of his fingers;
For the multitude of his mercies,
   and the strength of his word.
For the word of the Lord investigates that which is invisible,
   and perceives his thought.

It is he who spread out the earth,
  and placed the waters in the sea.
He expanded the heaven,
  and set the stars.
And he set the creation and aroused it,
  then he rested from his works.
And created things run according to their courses, and work their
  works,
  and they are not able to cease and be idle.
The reservoir of light is the sun,
  and the reservoir of darkness is the night.
For he made the sun for the day so that it will be light;
  but night brings darkness over the face of the earth.
And by their acceptance one from another
  they complete the beauty of God.
And there is nothing outside of the Lord,
  because he was before anything came to be.
And the worlds are by his word,
  and by the thought of his heart.
Praise and honor be his name.
  Hallelujah.

**ODES OF SOLOMON 16 (CHARLESWORTH)**

## SEPTEMBER 22

### *Good Administration in the Church*

The church as a city built on a hill must have an order pleasing to God
and good administration. Above all the bishop as the authoritative leading spokesman must be heard. The elders have to attend to the carrying

through of his orders. The deacons should walk about, looking after the bodies and souls of the brethren, and report to the bishop. All the rest of the brethren should be ready even to suffer wrong. But if they desire an inquiry into a wrong that has been done to them, then they should be reconciled in the presence of the elders, and the elders should submit the agreement to the bishop. . . .

If you love your brethren, take nothing of what is theirs, but rather give them of what you possess; for you should feed the hungry, give drink to the thirsty, clothe the naked, visit the sick, do your best to help those in prison, receive strangers willingly into your dwellings and hate no one.

How you have to manifest your devotion, that, if you are sufficiently wise, your own intelligence should show you. Above all, if indeed I need to say it, you must assemble very frequently, where possibly hourly, but by all means on the appointed days of the assembly. When you do that, you find yourselves within the walls of a place of refuge. For perdition begins in eccentric ways. Therefore let no one keep himself away from the community out of a petty attitude of mind towards a brother. For if one of you abandons the community, then he will be counted in the number of those who scatter the church of Christ. . . .

Moreover, hear your bishop and do not become weary in showing him all honour; for you must show that, by showing it to him, it is carried over to Christ and from Christ to God; and to him who shows it, it is requited manifold.

Hold then the chair of Christ in honour, for you are also bidden to honour the chair of Moses, although its occupants may have to be reckoned sinners. Therewith I have perhaps said enough to you.

THE PSEUDO-CLEMENTINES, THIRD CENTURY, FROM SYRIA
(HENNECKE AND SCHNEEMELCHER)

## SEPTEMBER 23

### *The Offering of a Priest*

I am a priest of the Lord, and to him I serve as a priest;
And to him I offer the offering of his thought.
For his thought is not like the world, nor like the flesh,
nor like them who serve according to the flesh.
The offering of the Lord is righteousness, and purity of heart and lips.
Offer your inward being faultlessly; and do not let your compassion
     oppress compassion; and do not you yourself oppress anyone.
But put on the grace of the Lord generously, and come into his Paradise,
and make for yourself a crown from his tree.
Then put it on your head and be refreshed, and recline upon his
     serenity.
For his glory will go before you; and you will receive of his kindness and
     of his grace; and you will be anointed in truth with the praise of his
     holiness.
Praise and honor to his name. Hallelujah.

ODES OF SOLOMON 20 (CHARLESWORTH)

## SEPTEMBER 24

### *The Scholar*

The one who concentrates his mind and his meditation
     on the Law of the Most High researches into the wisdom of the
Ancients,
     he occupies his time with the prophecies.
     He preserves the sayings of the famous and penetrates the subtleties
of parables.

He seeks out the hidden meaning of proverbs and is at home with the unknown meaning of parables. . . .

He travels in foreign countries, he has experienced human good and human evil.

At dawn and with all his heart he turns to the Lord his Creator. . . .

He opens his mouth in prayer and asks pardon for his sins.

If the Lord is willing, he will be filled with the spirit of understanding;
he will pour forth words of wisdom of his own
and give thanks to the Lord in prayer.

The Lord will direct his counsel and his knowledge,
as he meditates on his mysteries.

He will show the wisdom of what he has learned,
and will glory in the Law of the Lord's covenant.

Many will praise his understanding; and it will never be forgotten.

His memory will not disappear, and his name will live through all generations. . . .

If he lives long, his name will be more glorious than a thousand others;
and if he dies without recognition, that will satisfy him just as well.

ECCLESIASTICUS (SIRACH) 39:1–11 (NEW REVISED STANDARD VERSION
AND THE NEW JERUSALEM BIBLE, CONFLATED)


## SEPTEMBER 25

### Joseph Becomes Aware of Mary's Pregnancy

*The annunciation is observed on March 25, nine months before Christmas on December 25. When the woman is about six months along, the partner finally notices that something is different.*

Mary was in her sixth month when one day Joseph came home from his building, entered his house, and found her pregnant. And so he struck himself in the face, threw himself to the ground on sackcloth, and began to cry bitterly: "What sort of face should I present to the Lord God? What prayer should I say on her behalf since I received her as a virgin from the temple of the Lord God and did not protect her? Who has deceived me? Who has done this evil deed in my house and defiled her? The story of Adam has been repeated in my home, hasn't it? For just as Adam was praying when the serpent came and found Eve alone, deceived her, and defiled her, so the same thing has happened to me, too."

So Joseph got up from the sackcloth and summoned Mary and said to her, "God has looked after you; so why have you done this? Have you forgotten the Lord your God? Why have you brought shame on yourself, you who were raised in the Holy of Holies and were fed by a heavenly messenger?"

But she began to cry bitter tears: "I am innocent. I've had no sex with any man."

And Joseph said to her, "Then where did the child you're carrying come from?"

And she replied, "As the Lord my God lives, I don't know where it came from."

And Joseph became very frightened and no longer spoke with her as he pondered what he was going to do with her. And Joseph said, "If I hide her sin, I'll end up going against the law of the Lord. And if I disclose her condition to the people of Israel, I'm afraid that the child inside her might be heaven-sent and I'll end up handing innocent blood over to a death sentence. So what should I do with her? Should I divorce her quietly?"

But when night came a messenger of the Lord suddenly appeared to him in a dream: "Don't be afraid of this child" it said, "because it is of the holy spirit. She will have a son and you will name him Jesus, for he alone will save his people from their sins." And Joseph got up from his sleep and praised the God of Israel who had given him this favor. And so he began protecting the child.

INFANCY GOSPEL OF JAMES 13:1–14:8 (MILLER)

*Symbolically this story illustrates the process when someone has already been touched by the Holy Spirit. New life is growing within that person toward a new birth. Part way through the process, others may become aware that changes are occurring within the person.*

*How important it is to be sensitive to and conscious of one another's spiritual processes.*

## SEPTEMBER 26

### The Authorities Question Joseph and Mary

Annas the scholar came to Joseph and said to him, "Joseph, why haven't you attended our assembly?"

And he replied to him, "Because I was worn out from the trip and rested my first day home."

Then Annas turned and saw that Mary was pregnant. He left and ran to the high priest and told him, "Joseph, the man whom you yourself endorse, has seriously broken the law."

And the high priest asked, "In what way?"

"He has defiled the virgin he received from the temple of the Lord," he replied, "and had his way with her and has not disclosed his action to the people of Israel."

And the high priest asked him, "Has Joseph really done this?"

And he replied, "Send temple assistants and you'll find the virgin pregnant."

And so the temple assistants went and found her just as Annas had reported and brought her along with Joseph to the court.

"Mary, why have you done this?" the high priest asked her, "Why have you humiliated yourself? Have you forgotten the Lord your God, you who were raised in the Holy of Holies and were fed by heavenly messengers? You heard their hymns and danced for them; why have you done this?"

And she wept bitterly: "As the Lord lives, I stand innocent before him and I've not had sex with any man."

And the high priest said, "Joseph, why have you done this?"

And Joseph said, "As the Lord lives, I am innocent where she is concerned."

And the high priest said, "Don't perjure yourself, but tell the truth. You've had your way with her and haven't disclosed this action to the people of Israel. And you haven't humbled yourself under God's mighty hand, so that your offspring might be blessed."

But Joseph was silent.

INFANCY GOSPEL OF JAMES 15:1–18 (MILLER)

## SEPTEMBER 27

### The Water Test

Then the high priest said, "Return the virgin you received from the temple of the Lord."

And Joseph burst into tears. . . .

And the high priest said, "I'm going to give you the drink test, and the Lord will make you see your sin."

And the high priest took the water and made Joseph drink it and sent him into the wilderness. Joseph returned unharmed. And he made the child drink it, too, and sent her into the wilderness. She also came back unharmed.

And everybody was surprised because their sin had not been revealed. And so the high priest said, "If the Lord God has not exposed your sin, then neither do I condemn you." And he dismissed them. Joseph took Mary and returned home celebrating and praising the God of Israel.

INFANCY GOSPEL OF JAMES 16:1–8 (MILLER)

## SEPTEMBER 28

*Celebration of All Famous People*

Let us now sing the praises of the famous,
our ancestors in their successive generations.
The Lord apportioned to them great glory, his majesty from the
    beginning.
Some wielded authority as rulers and were renowned for their strength.
Others were intelligent advisers and spoke prophetic sayings.
Others directed the people by their advice,
by their understanding of the popular mind;
they were wise in their instruction.
Others composed musical tunes, or put verses in writing;
rich people endowed with resources living peacefully in their homes.
All these were honored by their contemporaries
and were the glory of their day.
Some of them left a name behind them, so that their praises are still
    sung.
While others have left no memory and disappeared as though they had
    never existed. . . .
  But here is a list of illustrious people whose good works have not been
      forgotten. . . .
  The peoples will proclaim their wisdom, the assembly will celebrate
      their praises.

ECCLESIASTICUS (SIRACH) 44:1–15 (NEW JERUSALEM BIBLE AND
THE NEW REVISED STANDARD VERSION, CONFLATED)

# The Way of the Tao and Conflict with the Social Order

⋍

*Sadducees, Pharisees, Zealots, and Essenes*

The Judean community to which Jesus belonged comprised various political and social sectors, and these can be viewed in four main groups:

Two groups, the Sadducees and the Pharisees, worked within the prevailing system, which meant cooperating with the officials of the Roman Empire. By cooperating they were allowed to continue their temple worship and religious practices largely unhindered. The Sadducees were the conservatives of the time, and the Pharisees were the liberals.

Two other groups, the Zealots and the Essenes, lived outside the system. The Zealots were the revolutionaries of the time. They based themselves in a fortress at Masada, a high bluff overlooking the Dead Sea.

The Essenes were the radicals. They dropped out of society and formed their own separate community centered in renewing the old teachings and committed to intense devotion and practice.

Although it cannot be absolutely proved, there is evidence that John the Baptizer may have come up through the Essene community. Likewise, Jesus, baptized by John, may have been influenced by the Essenes.

The early followers of the Way were outside the system, persecuted by both the religious leadership and the Roman Empire. They remained outside the system until Constantine had his vision of the cross with the words, In Hoc

Signe Vinces, *meaning "In this sign you shall conquer." From that point on, Christianity became the religion of the state.*

*Christians switched roles rather quickly—from being persecuted to being the persecutors. History records the results of this bloody union.*

*The Way of the Tao that Jesus proclaims is self-renewing and is continually resurrected in new forms when there is radical devotion. The Cathars, Francis of Assisi, Martin Luther, John Wesley, George Fox, Phineas F. Bresee, Teilhard de Chardin, Matthew Fox, and a host of others give evidence of the self-renewing force of the Way.*

*There are four main ways of relating oneself and one's faith to the social order: conservative, liberal, revolutionary, and radical. I find I contain some of each attitude, all in the Tao. How about you?*

*In what ways are you conservative, holding on to what you know is of value?*

*In what ways are you liberal, seeking to apply the values you hold dear?*

*In what ways are you revolutionary, wanting to scrap the system and begin again?*

*Where are you radical, seeking to go as deep as possible to the essential roots?*

## SEPTEMBER 30

### Perpetua's Refusal to Sacrifice to Emperors

*The followers of the Way were initially a group within Judaism, but tensions were great and by the end of the first century they had become separate communities. They were also very much at odds with the existing social and governing system of the time and found themselves in conflict with the social order. The readings for the next seven days provide examples.*

While we were at dinner, we were suddenly taken away to be heard, and we arrived at the town hall. At once the rumor spread through the neighborhood of the public place, and an immense number of people were gathered together. We mounted the platform. The rest were interrogated and confessed. Then they came to me, and my father immediately appeared with my boy, and withdrew me from the step, and said in a supplicating tone, "Have pity on your baby."

And Hilarianus the procurator, who had just received the power of life and death in the place of the proconsul Minucius Timianius, who was deceased, said, "Spare the grey hairs of your father, spare the infancy of your boy, offer sacrifice for the well-being of the emperors."

And I replied, "I will not do so."

Hilarianus said, "Are you a Christian?"

And I replied, "I am a Christian."

And as my father stood there to cast me down from the faith, he was ordered by Hilarianus to be thrown down, and was beaten by rods. And my father's misfortune grieved me as if I myself had been beaten, I so grieved for his wretched old age. The procurator then delivers judgment on all of us, and condemns us to the wild beasts, and we went down cheerfully to the dungeon.

Then, because my child had been used to receive suck from me, and to stay with me in the prison, I send Pomponius the deacon to my father to ask for the infant, but my father would not give it to him. And even as God willed it, the child no longer desired the breast, nor did my breast cause me uneasiness, lest I should be tormented by care for my baby and by the pain of my breasts at once.

TERTULLIAN, THE PASSION OF PERPETUA AND FELICITAS,
CHAPTER II, PARAGRAPH 2, 202 C.E. (COX)

## OCTOBER 1

### James Is Stoned and Clubbed to Death

Control of the Church passed to the apostles, together with the Lord's brother, James, whom everyone from the Lord's time till our own has called the Righteous. . . .

The Scribes and Pharisees made James stand on the Sanctuary parapet and shouted to him, "Righteous one, whose word we are all obliged to accept, the people are going astray after Jesus who was crucified; so tell us what is meant by 'the door of Jesus.' " He replied as loudly as he could, "Why do you question me about the Son of Man? I tell you, He is sitting in heaven at the right hand of the Great Power, and He will come on the clouds of heaven." Many were convinced, and gloried in James's testimony, crying: "Hosanna to the Son of David!" Then again the Scribes and Pharisees said to each other: "We made a bad mistake in affording such testimony to Jesus. We had better go up and throw him down, so that they will be frightened and not believe him."

So they went up and threw down the Righteous one. Then they said to each other, "Let us stone James the Righteous," and began to stone him, as in spite of his fall he was still alive. But he turned and knelt, uttering the words, "I beseech you, Lord God and Father, forgive them; they do not know what they are doing." While they pelted him with stones, one of the descendants of Rechab the son of Rachabim—the priestly family to which Jeremiah the Prophet bore witness, called out: "Stop! what are you doing? The Righteous one is praying for you." Then one of them, a fuller, took the club which he used to beat out the clothes, and brought it down on the head of the Righteous one. Such was his martyrdom. He was buried on the spot, by the Sanctuary, and his headstone is still there by the Sanctuary. He has proved a true witness to Jews and Gentiles alike that Jesus is the Christ.

EUSEBIUS, ECCLESIASTICAL HISTORY 2, 23,
SECOND CENTURY (WRIGHT)

## OCTOBER 2

___

*Andrew Embraces the Cross*

*Andrew arrived at the place where he was to be crucified. When he saw the cross set in the sand at the seashore, he went to the cross and spoke to it with a strong voice as though it were alive:*

"Greetings, O cross! May you rejoice! Even though you have been weary for a long time, planted and waiting for me. Now you can rest. I am coming to you whom I recognize. I recognize your mystery and why you were planted.

"You are set up in the cosmos to establish the unstable. One part of you stretches up to heaven so that you may point out the heavenly *Tao*,* the Source of everything. Another part of you stretches out to the right and to the left so that you may draw the cosmos to unity. Another part of you is planted in the earth, rooted in the depths, that you may connect heaven and earth.

O Cross, tool of wholeness!
O Cross, symbol of Christ's victory over enemies!
O Cross, planted in earth and bearing fruit in heaven!
Well done, O Cross, who restrains the error of the world!
Well done, vision of violence who overcomes violence!
Well done, O Cross, that you have clothed yourself with the Lord,
produced the thief as your fruit, called the apostle to repentance,
and did not disqualify us from being received.

"So then, cross, pure, radiant, and full of life and light, receive me, the one who for so long has been weary. . . .

"How long shall I say these things before I am embraced by the cross, that in the cross I may be made to live and through the cross may go out of this life into the common death?

"Approach, you ministers of my joy. Fulfill the intention and bind the lamb to the suffering, the mortal to the Creator, the soul to its Savior."

**ACTS OF ANDREW, SECOND CENTURY (SEERS VERSION, CONDENSED)**

*Greek: Logos.

## OCTOBER 3

### Peter Is Crucified Upside Down

*Just before his crucifixion, Peter said,*

"I ask you, public executioners, to crucify me head downward, and not otherwise. I shall explain the reason to those who hear."

When they had flung him up in the manner he had requested, he began to speak again, "You for whom it is fitting to hear, pay special attention to what I am about to tell you now as I am hanging. Understand the mystery of all nature and what the beginning of all things was. For the first human being, whose race I bear in appearance, fell head downward and thereby displayed a process of generation that had not existed before; for it was dead because it had no movement. When this one, who also cast his own beginning onto the earth, was pulled down, he established the whole cosmic order, since he was suspended as an image in which he displayed the things on the right as on the left and those on the left as on the right. He interchanged all the signs of their nature, so that he considered beautiful the things that are not beautiful, and good the things that are in reality bad.

"Concerning these things, the Lord said in a mystery, 'Unless you make the things on the right as the things on the left and the things on the left as the things on the right and the things above as the things below, and the things behind as the things in front, you will not recognize the kingdom.'

"This understanding I now bring before you, and the manner in which you see me hanging is a representation of that human being who first departed into the realm of generation. Now, my beloved ones, both you who now hear and you who will soon hear, you ought to desist from your former error and return. For it is fitting to mount the cross of Christ, who is the word stretched out, the one and only, concerning whom the Spirit said, 'What is the Christ, but the word, the sound of God?' Thus, the word is the upright on which I am crucified. The sound is the crosspiece, human nature. But the nail that attaches the crosspiece on the upright tree near the middle is human conversion and repentance.

"Because you have revealed these things and made them known to me, O Word of Life, now called tree by me, I thank you. Not with these lips which are nailed up, nor by the tongue through which truth and falsehood proceed, by which the spirit within me encounters you as it loves you, speaks with you, and sees you. You are perceptible only to the spirit; you who are father to me; you who are mother to me; you who are brother to me; you, friend; you, servant; you, steward. You are the all, and the all is in you. You are what is, and there is nothing else that is except you alone.

"Now brothers and sisters, when you too take refuge in this one and learn that you exist in him alone, you shall obtain these things concerning which he says to you, 'Things which neither the eye has seen nor the ear heard nor has it entered the human heart.'

"We ask now about the things that you promised to give us, immaculate Jesus. We praise you and we thank you. We who are still weak human beings glorify you, and we confess that you alone are God and no other, to whom be glory both now and to the end of all the ages, Amen!"

The multitude standing by pronounced the "Amen" with a great resounding noise. Together with that "Amen," Peter gave his spirit over to the Lord. When Marcellus saw that blessed Peter had breathed his last, he took him down from the cross with his own hands, without receiving authorization from anyone, which was not allowed. He washed him in milk and wine, and pounding together seven pounds of mastic, and fifty of myrrh and aloes and other herbs, he embalmed his remains. He filled a stone sarcophagus with Attic honey of the greatest value and placed it in his own tomb.

Peter came to Marcellus at night and said, "Marcellus, have you not hear the saying of the Lord, 'Leave the dead to be buried by their own dead?'" When Marcellus answered, "Yes," Peter said to him, "These things that you have provided for the dead, you have lost; for you, even while you remain alive, care for the dead as though you were dead." When Marcellus awoke, he reported Peter's appearance to the brothers and sisters. He remained with those who had been strengthened in faith in Christ by Peter. He himself was further strengthened until Paul's arrival in Rome.

ACTS OF PETER 36–40 (ATTRIDGE)

## OCTOBER 4

*Thecla Follows Paul and the Way He Teaches*

Thecla said to Paul, "I shall cut my hair short and follow you wherever you go." He said, "The times are shameless, and you are attractive. I am afraid temptation may come and you may not be able to resist, but rather give in."

Thecla replied, "Just anoint me with Christ and I will stand any test."

"Be patient, Thecla, and you shall receive the water of baptism."

As they entered Antioch, Paul and Thecla met a Syrian named Alexander who was influential in Antioch and moved in the ruling class. Seeing Thecla, he fell in love with her and tried to influence Paul with money and gifts. But Paul said, "I don't know the woman that you mention, nor is she mine."

Alexander was very strong and embraced her right on the street. She would not put up with it, but cried out for Paul's help. "Don't force a complete stranger! And don't try to force a servant of God! In Iconium I am well known even though I have been run out of the city because I was unwilling to marry Thamyris!" She grabbed Alexander, tore his cloak, pulled the crown off his head, and made him look ridiculous.

Even though Alexander thought he still loved her, he felt embarrassed at what had happened to him in public, so he took her to the governor. When she admitted having done these things, the governor condemned her to the wild beasts. Alexander was arranging the "games."

The women were irate and shouted before the judgment seat, "An evil judgment! A godless decision!"

Thecla asked the governor that she not be molested until it was time for her to fight the beasts. A wealthy woman named Tryphaena, whose daughter had died, protected Thecla, who comforted her in her grief.

ACTS OF PAUL 25–27 (SEERS VERSION)

## OCTOBER 5

### Thecla Is Thrown to the Wild Beasts

When the "games" began and the beasts came in, the executioners roped her to a fierce lioness. Queen Tryphaena followed along behind her. The lioness started licking Thecla's feet and the crowd was astonished. . . .

A bear came after her, but the lioness charged the bear and tore it apart. Alexander's trained lion was set loose and the lioness fought the lion and died along with him. The women were screaming even more when the lioness who was helping her had died.

Then the executioners sent in many more wild beasts. Thecla stood up, raised her hands and prayed. When she finished praying, she turned toward a large pit full of water and seals. "Now is the time for my bath!"

When the women and all the crowd heard this, they cried, "Don't throw yourself into the water." Even the governor wept when the seals were about to eat such a beauty.

But Thecla threw herself into the water saying, "In the name of Jesus Christ I baptize myself on my last day!" The seals, seeing a flash of lightning, floated dead on the water.

A cloud of fire encircled Thecla so that beasts could not touch her nor could she be seen naked. Women kept screaming and some threw petals, others nard, others cassia, others amomum creating a cloud of perfumes. . . .

Alexander said to the governor, "I have some very ferocious bulls, let's tie her to them." The governor gave his consent, saying, "Do whatever you want."

They tied her by the feet between the bulls and ran red hot irons under their genitals so their violent movements would kill her. But when the bulls leaped forward, the flames burned through the ropes and Thecla was freed!

Queen Tryphaena fainted and the governor was afraid that she was dead. Alexander fell at the feet of the governor and begged for mercy, "If Caesar hear this, he may destroy the city along with us since his relative, Queen Tryphaena, has died!"

The governor summoned Thecla from the midst of the beasts and said to her, "Who are you? What is it about you that not one of the beasts touched you?"

She answered, "I am a servant of the living God. I put my trust in the one who is the Source of wholeness and Eternal Life. To those tossed in storms, he is a refuge, to the oppressed, relief, to the despairing, shelter. In a word, whoever does not trust in the Eternal will not live, but die for ever."

When the governor heard this, he commanded that clothing be brought in and he said, "Put on these clothes."

But she replied, "The one who clothed me when I was naked among the beasts shall clothe me with wholeness on the day of judgment." And taking the clothes, she put them on.

Immediately the governor sent around a decree, "I release to you Thecla, the trusting servant of God."

All the women cried out with one voice and gave praise saying, "One is God who has delivered Thecla!"

ACTS OF PAUL 33–38 (SEERS VERSION, CONDENSED)

## OCTOBER 6

### *Thecla Teaches by Sharing Her Experience*

Thecla longed to be with Paul and inquired in every direction to find him. Word came back that he was in Myra. Taking other young men and women with her, she dressed herself like a man and went to Myra, where she found Paul speaking the word of God and she went to him. He was astonished when he saw her and the crowd with her.

"I have taken the bath, Paul; for the one who works with you for the gospel has also worked with me for my baptism."

Taking her by the hand, Paul took her to the house of Hermias and heard from her everything that had happened. Paul was amazed and those who listened were strengthened in their faith and prayed for Tryphaena.

Thecla stood up and said to Paul, "I am going to Iconium." And Paul said, "Go and teach the word of God!"

When Thecla arrived in Iconium she entered the house of Onesiphorus and threw herself down on the floor where Paul had sat teaching the word of God before. She prayed, "My God and God of this house where the Light shines on me, Christ Jesus the Son of God, my helper in prison, my helper before governors, my helper in the fire, my helper among the beasts. You are God and to you be glory forever. Amen!"

ACTS OF PAUL 39–42 (SEERS VERSION, CONDENSED)

## OCTOBER 7

### Paul Is Beheaded

*Caesar had commanded that Paul be beheaded. When Paul was brought before Caesar, he said,*

"Caesar, it is not for just a little while that I live for my king. Even if you behead me, I shall do this! When I am raised up, I shall show myself to you, that I have not really died but am alive to my lord Christ Jesus, who is coming to judge the world." . . .

Paul stood facing the east, and raising his hands he prayed a long time; in prayer he communed with his forefathers in Hebrew, then, saying no more, stretched forth his throat. When his executioner cut off his head, milk spurted onto the soldier's clothing. The soldier and all those standing nearby were amazed when they saw this and glorified God who had given Paul such glory. They left to report to Caesar all that had happened.

When Nero had heard he marvelled greatly and was at a loss. Then when Paul arrived at the ninth hour, many philosophers, as well as the centurion, were standing with Caesar. Standing before him, Paul said, "Caesar, behold Paul, God's soldier—I did not die, but am alive to my God! But there shall be many bad things and great punishment for you, you wretch, and soon, on account of the blood of the righteous people that you have unjustly shed!" After saying this, Paul left him. But Nero was greatly distressed when he heard this and ordered that the prisoners be freed, both Patroclus and those around Barsabbas.

As Paul had arranged, Longus and Cestus the centurion went at dawn and approached Paul's tomb with fear. They saw two men standing there praying, with Paul in their midst, and so they were astonished when they saw the marvel. Titus and Luke, afflicted by a human fear when they saw Longus and Cestus coming to them, turned in flight, but running after them they said, "We are not pursuing you for death, as you suppose, blessed people of God, but for life—so that you might give it as Paul promised us, the one we saw standing and praying in your midst long ago." When Titus and Luke heard this from them, they gave them the seal of anointing in the Lord with great gladness, glorifying the God and Father of our Lord Jesus Christ, to whom be the glory for ever and ever. Amen.

ACTS OF PAUL (ATTRIDGE)

# Belonging to a Community of the Tao

ॐ

## OCTOBER 8

### *Truth Is Sprung out of the Earth*

Truth is sprung out of the earth, for the *Tao** was made flesh . . .

Let us have peace with God, the *Tao,* for justice and peace have kissed each other, through our Lord Jesus Christ, for Truth is sprung out of the earth. Through Christ we have gained access to this grace in which we stand, and we glory in our hope of sharing the glory of God.

Truth is sprung out of the earth—flesh born of Mary. And justice looked down from heaven, for no one can receive anything, unless it be given him from heaven. . . .

Christ is our peace, who has made both one, that we might be people of good will, bound together by the sweet bonds of unity.

Let us, then, rejoice in this grace, that our glory may be the testimony of our conscience, and we may glory, not in ourselves, but in the Lord *Tao.*

FROM A SERMON BY SAINT AUGUSTINE, FOURTH CENTURY
(BROTHER KENNETH)

---

*The "Word," here and below.

## OCTOBER 9

*You Are the Temple of the Tao*

"Unless the Lord *Tao* builds the house, those who build it labour in vain." "Do you not know that you are the Temple of the *Tao* and that the Spirit of the *Tao* dwells in you?" This is the house and this is the temple of the *Tao*, full of the precepts and of the energies of the *Tao*, and capable of receiving the divine indwelling by holiness of heart. . . .

This house, therefore, must be built by the agency of the *Tao*, for one which is constructed by human efforts does not endure, nor does it stand firm when reared by the teachings of this age, nor will it be kept safe by the care of vain toil and of our anxiety.

It must be constructed in another way, it must be guarded in another way; it must not have its beginnings upon slippery and shifting sand, but its foundations must be laid firmly upon the prophets and apostles.

It must be increased with living stones, and held together by the cornerstone. It must be built up by an increase of mutual connections until it reaches to "mature humanity, to the measure of the stature of the fullness of Christ." It must be adorned by the beauty and ornament of spiritual graces.

So this house which is built by the *Tao*, that is by the teachings of the *Way*, will not collapse. This house will grow and expand into several houses as the divine buildings of the faithful make for the adornment and increase of the blessed community in each one of us. . . .

"Lo, I am with you always, to the close of the age." This is the eternal protection of this blessed and holy community which is formed by the coming together of many into one and which is in each individual one of us. . . .

The building already begun has not reached perfection, but through its building the completion of its perfection is being achieved.

FROM THE COMMENTARY OF SAINT HILARY ON PSALM 126,
EARLY FOURTH CENTURY (BROTHER KENNETH)

## OCTOBER 10

---

### *Assembling with the Community*

On the day called Sunday, all who live in cities or in the country gather together to one place, and the memoirs of the apostles or the writings of the prophets are read, as long as time permits; then, when the reader has ceased, the presider verbally instructs and exhorts to the imitation of these good things. Then we all rise together and pray. Having ended the prayers, we greet one another with a kiss. Bread and wine and water are brought, and the presider in like manner offers prayers and thanksgiving according to his ability, and the people assent, saying Amen; and there is a distribution to each, and a participation of that over which thanks have been given, and to those who are absent a portion is sent by the deacons. And they who are well to do, and willing, give what each thinks fit; and what is collected is deposited with the presider, who succours the orphans and widows, and those who, through sickness or any other cause, are in want, and those who are in bonds, and the stranger sojourning among us, and in a word takes care of all who are in need.

Sunday is the day on which we all hold our common assembly, because it is the first day on which God, having wrought a change in the darkness and matter, made the world; and Jesus Christ our Saviour on the same day rose from the dead.

FIRST APOLOGY OF JUSTIN, CHAPTER 67,
EARLY SECOND CENTURY (COX)

## OCTOBER 11

---

*Being Open to the Word of the Tao*

Let us be for ever pondering on Wisdom in our hearts and speaking of her with our lips. . . . For that is what scripture enjoins on us: "let your concern be only with such things as these when you sit in your house and walk by the way, and when you lie down, and when you rise." Let the Lord Jesus Christ then be the sole object of your discourse, for *Christ is Wisdom and the Word, the Tao.*

Scripture also commands, "Open your mouth to receive God's word." You manifest Christ when you constantly repeat Christ's sayings and meditate on Christ's words. . . .

When you sit in your house, meditate and speak always of the things of God. "House" we can take to mean the Church or our own interior house where we may speak within ourselves. Choose your words when you speak so that you avoid sin and do not fall through empty chatter. When you are seated speak to yourself as one who is a judge. When you are "by the way" speak lest you be idle. You speak "by the way" if you speak in Christ, for Christ is the Way. Speak to yourself "by the Way" and you speak to Christ. . . .

Hear how you should speak as you go to sleep, "I will not give sleep to my eyes or slumber to my eyelids, until I find a place for the Lord, a dwelling place for the mighty one of Jacob."

In your rising or resurrection speak of Christ that you may carry out what you are commanded to do. Hear how Christ wakens you. Your soul says, "The voice of my brother sounds at the gate," and Christ says, "Open to me, my sister, my spouse." And hear how you are to awaken to Christ. The soul says, "I have adjured you, O daughters of Jerusalem, to waken and re-awaken love." Love is Christ.

SAINT AMBROSE (BROTHER KENNETH)

## OCTOBER 12

---

### *Who Can Grasp the Wealth of Your Words?*

Lord, who can grasp all the wealth of just one of your words? What we understand is much less than what we leave behind, like thirsty people who drink from a fountain. For your word, Lord, has many shades of meaning just as those who study it have many different points of view. The Lord has coloured his words with many hues so that each person who studies it can see in it what he loves. He has hidden many treasures in his word so that each of us is enriched as we meditate on it.

The word of God is a tree of life that from all its parts offers you fruits that are blessed. It is like the rock opened in the desert that from all its parts gave forth a spiritual drink. As the Apostle says, "All ate the same supernatural food and all drank the same supernatural drink."

Anyone who comes into contact with some share of its treasure should not think that the only thing contained in the word is what he himself has found. He should realize that he has only been able to find that one thing from among many others.

SAINT EPHRAEM ON THE DIATESSARON, FOURTH CENTURY
(BROTHER KENNETH)

## OCTOBER 13

---

### *Love Toward the Tao Cannot Be Taught*

Love toward God, *the Tao,* cannot be taught. . . . We possess the power to love implanted in us at the moment we were created. The proof of this is not external, but anyone can learn it from himself and within himself. For by nature we desire beautiful things though we differ as to what is supremely beautiful; and without being taught we have affection towards those near and dear to us, and we spontaneously show goodwill to all our benefactors.

Now what is more marvellous than the divine beauty? What thought has more charm than the magnificence of God, the *Tao?* What yearning of the soul is so keen and intolerable as that which comes from God, the *Tao,* upon the soul which is cleansed from all evil and cries with true affection, "I am wounded with love"? Ineffable wholly and inexplicable are the flashes of divine beauty.

SAINT BASIL THE GREAT, FOURTH CENTURY (BROTHER KENNETH)

## OCTOBER 14

### *Stretching Ourselves out to the Tao*

What have we been promised? "We shall be like him, for we shall see him as he is." The tongue has said all it can, the rest must come from the thoughtful heart. . . .

The whole life . . . is a holy desire. What you desire you cannot see yet. But the desire gives you the capacity, so that when it does happen that you see, you may be fulfilled.

Suppose you want to fill some sort of bag, and you know the bulk of what you will be given, you stretch the bag or sack or the skin or whatever it is. You know how big the object that you want to put in and you see that the bag is narrow so you increase its capacity by stretching it. In the same way by delaying the fulfillment of desire God stretches it, by making us desire he expands the soul, and by this expansion he increases its capacity. . . .

You are to be filled with good, pour out the bad. Consider that God wants to fill you up with honey, but if you are already full of vinegar where will you put the honey? What was in the vessel must be emptied out; the vessel must be washed out and made clean and scoured, hard work though it may be, so that it be made fit for something else, whatever it may be.

Let us say honey, or gold, or wine, whatever we say it cannot be named and whatever we want to say is in fact called "God," *the Tao.* And when we say "God" or the *Tao,* what have we said? That one syllable contains all that we hope for. . . . Let us stretch ourselves out toward the *Tao* so that the *Tao* may fill us.

FROM THE TREATISE OF SAINT AUGUSTINE ON THE FIRST LETTER OF JOHN
(BROTHER KENNETH)

## OCTOBER 15

### Singing to the Tao a New Song

"Praise the Lord with the lyre, make melody to God with the harp of ten strings! Sing to the *Tao* a new song!". . . We are a new humanity, we have a new alliance with the *Tao;* so let our song be new; a new song is not for the old person. Only the new humanity can learn it, humanity made new out of the ancient stuff; whose new alliance is the *Way of the Tao.* All our heart yearns for it as we sing the new song, not with our voices but our lives. . . .

This is the Way of singing God gives you; do not search for words. You cannot express in words the sentiments which please God: so, praise the *Tao* with your jubilant singing. . . .

You ask, what is singing in jubilation? It means to realize that words are not enough to express what we are singing in our hearts. At the harvest, in the vineyard, whenever men must labour hard, they begin with songs whose words express their joy. But when their joy brims over and words are not enough, they abandon even this coherence and give themselves up to the sheer sound of singing.

What is this jubilation, this exultant song? It is the melody that means our hearts are bursting with feelings words cannot express. And to whom does this jubilation most belong? Surely to God who is unutterable. And does not unutterable mean what cannot be uttered? If words will not come and you may not remain silent, what else can you do but let the melody soar? What else, when the rejoicing heart has no words and the immensity of your joys will not be imprisoned in speech? What else but "sing out with jubilation"?

FROM THE DISCOURSES OF SAINT AUGUSTINE ON THE PSALMS
(BROTHER KENNETH)

## OCTOBER 16

### *Responding to the Varied Ways of the Spirit*

Those who by God's gracious gift have been born anew by the Holy Spirit, possessing Christ within themselves to illuminate and recreate them, are guided in the many and varied ways of the Spirit, as grace works in their hearts invisibly and in peace of soul.

Sometimes, they are, as it were, in grief and lamentation for the human race, and pouring out prayers for the whole race of Adam, they give way to tears and grief, burning with the love of the Spirit for mankind.

At another time they are inflamed by the Spirit with such joy and love that, were it possible, they would take all humankind, good and bad alike, into their hearts....

Then again, they are thrust down below all men in the humility of the Spirit so that they look on themselves as the most abject and least of all.

At other times they are sustained by the Spirit in a joy beyond words.

Sometimes they are like some strong man, who, clad in the full panoply of royal armor and going down to battle, fights strongly against his enemies and overcomes them. In the same way, the spiritual man takes up the heavenly arms of the Spirit, attacks the enemy, does battle and brings him into submission beneath his feet.

At another time the soul rests in a most profound, untroubled silence and peace, and has its being only in the joys of the Spirit, in matters that neither tongue nor lips can express.

Again at other times it is like any other human being.

In so many varied ways grace has its effect in these people and guides each soul by different means.

A FOURTH-CENTURY SPIRITUAL WRITER (BROTHER KENNETH)

## OCTOBER 17

### *Being Like Sheep, Serpents, and Doves*

So long as we continue to behave as sheep, we are victorious. Even if ten thousand wolves surround us, we conquer and are victorious. But the moment we become wolves, we are conquered, for we lose the help of the shepherd. He is the shepherd of sheep, not of wolves. If he leaves you and goes away, it is because you do not allow him to show his power.

These are his words: Do not be troubled that I send you out in the midst of wolves and tell you to be like sheep and like doves. I could have done just the opposite, and not have allowed you to suffer any hurt. I could have prevented you from being the victims of wolves and made you fiercer than lions. But I chose a better way. My Way makes you more glorious and proclaims my power. These were his words to Paul: "My grace is sufficient for you, for my power is made perfect in weakness." That is why I made you. When he says: "I send you out as sheep," he implies: "Do not despair, for I know very well that in this way you will be invincible against all your enemies."

Next he wants them to make some contribution of their own, so that everything will not seem to come from grace. He does not want it thought that their crown was not earned, and so he says, "So be as wise as serpents and innocent as doves." What power, he asks, does our wisdom have in such perils? How can we have wisdom at all when we are deluged by such billows? However wise the sheep may be when in the midst of wolves, and the wolves are as numerous as they are, what more will wisdom be able to achieve? However innocent the dove may be, what advantage will its innocence be when it is beset by so many hawks? So long as you are talking about irrational beasts, of course, the answer is none, but when you are dealing with people like you, the answer is, the greatest possible advantage.

But let us see what sort of wisdom he then demands. He calls it the wisdom "of a serpent." The serpent abandons everything, even if its body has to be cut off, and does not resist much, provided only it can save its head. In the same way, he says, abandon everything except your *trust,* even if it means giving up your wealth, your body, your life itself. Your *trust* is your head and your roots. If you preserve that, you will get everything back again with greater glory. . . .

A man should have the wisdom of the serpent, so as not to receive mortal wounds. He should have the innocence of a dove, so as not to take vengeance on those who do him injury, nor bear a grudge against those who plot against him. Wisdom is no use by itself unless there is innocence as well.

No one should think these demands are impossible to fulfill. More than anyone else he knows the nature of things. Violence he knows is not overcome by violence, but by forbearance.

FROM THE HOMILIES OF SAINT JOHN CHRYSOSTOM ON
MATTHEW'S GOSPEL (BROTHER KENNETH)

## OCTOBER 18

---

### *Looking After the Poor*

Would you honor the body of Christ? Do not despise his nakedness; do not honor him here in church clothed in silk vestments and then pass him by unclothed and frozen outside. Remember that he who said, "This is my body," and made good his words, also said, "You saw me hungry and gave me no food," and, "in so far as you did it not to one of these, you did it not to me." In the first sense the body of Christ does not need clothing but worship from a pure heart. In the second sense it does need clothing and all the care we can give it.

We must learn to be discerning and to honor Christ in the way in which he wants to be honored. It is only right that honor given to any-one should take the form most acceptable to the recipient not to the giver. Peter thought he was honoring the Lord when he tried to stop him from washing his feet, but this was far from being genuine homage. So give God the honor he asks for, that is give your money generously to the poor. God has no need of golden vessels but of golden hearts.

I am not saying you should not give golden altar vessels and so on, but I am insisting that nothing can take the place of almsgiving. The Lord will not refuse the first kind of gift but he prefers the second, and quite naturally, because in the first case only the donor benefits, in the second case the poor get the benefit. The gift of a chalice may be ostenta-tious; almsgiving is pure benevolence.

What is the use of loading Christ's table with gold cups while he himself is starving? Feed the hungry and then if you have any money left over, spend it on the altar table. Will you make a cup of gold and withhold a cup of water? What use is it to adorn the altar with cloth of gold hangings and deny Christ a coat for his back! What would that profit you?

Tell me: if you saw someone starving and refused to give him any food but instead spent your money on adorning the altar with gold, would he thank you? Would he not rather be outraged? Or if you saw someone in rags and stiff with cold and then did not give him clothing but set up gold columns in his honor, would he not say he was made a fool of and insulted?

Consider that Christ is that tramp who comes in need of a night's lodging. You turn him away and then start laying rugs on the floor, draping the walls, hanging lamps on silver chains on the columns. Meanwhile the tramp is locked up in prison and you never give him a glance.

Well again I am not condemning munificence in these matters. Make your house beautiful by all means but also look after the poor, or rather look after the poor first.

FROM THE HOMILIES OF SAINT JOHN CHRYSOSTOM (BROTHER KENNETH)

## OCTOBER 19

### Mary Magdalene Anoints Jesus

Six days before the Passover Jesus came to Bethany, the home of Lazarus, whom he had raised from the dead. There they gave a dinner for him. Martha served, and Lazarus was one of those at the table with him. Mary [Magdalene] came with an alabaster jar of very costly ointment of nard, and she broke open the jar and poured the ointment on his head. She anointed Jesus' feet, and wiped them with her hair. The house was filled with the fragrance of the perfume.

But some were there who said to one another in anger, "Why was the ointment wasted in this way? For this ointment could have been sold for more than three hundred denarii, and the money given to the poor." And they scolded her.

But Jesus said, "Let her alone; why do you trouble her? She has performed a good service for me. For you always have the poor with you, and you can show kindness to them whenever you wish; but you will not always have me. She has done what she could; she has anointed my body beforehand for its burial. Truly, I tell you, wherever the good news is proclaimed in the whole world, what she has done will be told in remembrance of her."

THE GOSPEL ACCORDING TO JOHN 12:1–3 AND THE GOSPEL ACCORDING TO MARK 14:3–9 (NEW REVISED STANDARD VERSION)

## OCTOBER 20

*Jesus Washes the Disciples' Feet*

Now before the festival of the Passover, Jesus knew that his hour had come to depart from this world and go to the Father. Having loved his own who were in the world, he loved them to the end.

The devil had already put it into the heart of Judas son of Simon Iscariot to betray him. And during supper Jesus, knowing that the Father had given all things into his hands, and that he had come from God and was going to God, got up from the table, took off his outer robe, and tied a towel around himself. Then he poured water into a basin and began to wash the disciples' feet and to wipe them with the towel that was tied around him. He came to Simon Peter, who said to him, "Lord, are you going to wash my feet?" Jesus answered, "You do not know now what I am doing, but later you will understand." Peter said to him, "You will never wash my feet." Jesus answered, "Unless I wash you, you have no share with me." Simon Peter said to him, "Lord, not my feet only but also my hands and my head." Jesus said to him, "One who has bathed does not need to wash, except for the feet, but is entirely clean. And you are clean, though not all of you." For he knew who was to betray him; for this reason he said, "Not all of you are clean."

After he had washed their feet, had put on his robe, and had returned to the table, he said to them, "Do you know what I have done to you?

You call me Teacher and Lord—and you are right, for that is what I am. So if I, your Lord and Teacher, have washed your feet, you also ought to wash one another's feet. For I have set you an example, that you should do as I have done to you."

THE GOSPEL ACCORDING TO JOHN 13:1–15
(NEW REVISED STANDARD VERSION)

*Mary Magdalene washes Jesus' feet, and one week later he, in turn, washes his disciples' feet. Love passes from Mary the Magdalene to Jesus the Nazarene, to the disciples, and on to us. It is time for us to pass it on.*

# Ways of Grieving

⊷

### On the Death of a Beloved Child

I looked around, and on my right I saw a woman; she was mourning and weeping with a loud voice, and was deeply grieved at heart; her clothes were torn, and there were ashes on her head. Then I dismissed the thoughts with which I was engaged, and turned to her and said to her, "Why are you weeping, and why are you grieved at heart?"

She said to me, "Let me alone, my lord, so that I may weep for myself and continue to mourn, for I am deeply embittered in spirit and deeply distressed."

I said to her, "What has happened to you? Tell me."

And she said to me, "Your servant was barren and had no child, though I lived with my husband for thirty years. Every hour and every day during those thirty years I prayed to the Most High, night and day. And after thirty years God heard your servant, and looked upon my low estate, and considered my distress, and gave me a son. I rejoiced greatly over him, I and my husband and all my neighbors; and we gave great glory to the Mighty One. And I brought him up with much care. So when he grew up and I came to take a wife for him, I set a day for the marriage feast.

"But it happened that when my son entered his wedding chamber, he fell down and died. So all of us put out our lamps, and all my neighbors attempted to console me; I remained quiet until the evening of the second day. But when all of them had stopped consoling me, encouraging me to be quiet, I got up in the night and fled, and I came to this field, as you see. And now I intend not to return to the town, but to stay here; I will neither eat nor drink, but will mourn and fast continually until I die."

Then I broke off the reflections with which I was still engaged, and answered her in anger and said, "You most foolish of women, do you not see our mourning, and what has happened to us? For Zion, the mother of us all, is in deep grief and great distress. It is most appropriate to mourn now, because we are all mourning, and to be sorrowful, because we are all sorrowing; you are sorrowing for one son, but we, the whole world, for our mother.

"Now ask the earth, and she will tell you that it is she who ought to mourn the more. From the beginning all have been born of her, and others will come; and, lo, almost all go to perdition, and a multitude of them will come to doom. Who then ought to mourn the more, she who lost so great a multitude, or you who are grieving for one alone?

"But if you say to me, 'My lamentation is not like the earth's, for I have lost the fruit of my womb, which I brought forth in pain and bore in sorrow; but it is with the earth according to the way of the earth—the multitude that is now in it goes as it came'; then I say to you, 'Just as you brought forth in sorrow, so the earth also has from the beginning given her fruit, that is, humankind, to him who made her.'

". . . Therefore shake off your great sadness and lay aside your many sorrows, so that the Mighty One may be merciful to you again, and the Most High may give you rest, a respite from your troubles."

2 ESDRAS 9:38–10:14, 24 (NEW REVISED STANDARD VERSION)

## October 22

---

### *Shed Tears over the Dead*

My child, shed tears over the dead,
lament for the dead to show your sorrow,
then bury the the body with due ceremony
and do not fail to honor the grave.
Weep bitterly, beat your breast,
observe the mourning the dead deserves,
for a day or two, *for seven or for forty,*
and then be comforted in your sorrow;
for a grief can lead to death,
a grief-stricken heart loses all energy.
In affliction sorrow persists,
a life of grief is hard to bear.
Do not abandon your heart to grief,
drive it away, think of the future.
Do not forget, there is no coming back;
you cannot help the dead, and you will harm yourself.
"Remember my doom, since it will be yours too;
  I yesterday, you today!"
Once the dead are laid to rest, let their memory rest,
do not fret for them, once their spirit departs.

ECCLESIASTICUS 38:16–23 (ITALICIZED SECTION ADDED;
SEE ECCLESIASTICUS 22:12, GENESIS 50:4)
NEW JERUSALEM BIBLE

# Ways of Aging and Dying

❧

*The Afterbirth of the Body Is Old Age*

The afterbirth of the body is old age, and you exist in corruption. You have absence as a gain. For you will not give up what is better if you depart. That which is worse has diminution, but there is grace for it.

THE TREATISE ON THE RESURRECTION 47:17–24 (ROBINSON, 3D ED.)

*You Have a Short Time to Live*

*Speaking to the soul:*

> Drink your fill of understanding, O my soul,
> and drink wisdom, O my heart.
> For not of your own will did you come into the world,
> and against your will you depart,
> for you have been given only a short time to live.

*Speaking to the Lord:*

> Hear, O Lord, the prayer of your servant,
> and give ear to the petition of your creature;
> attend to my words.
> For as long as I live I will speak,
> and as long as I have understanding I will answer.

2 ESDRAS 8:4–5, 24–25 (NEW REVISED STANDARD VERSION)

## OCTOBER 25

*Practice Emptying*

> Empty yourself of everything.
> Let the mind rest at peace.

TAO TE CHING, 16, FIRST TWO LINES (FENG AND ENGLISH)

All things come into being, and I see thereby their return.
All things flourish, but each one returns to its root.
This return to its root means tranquility.
It is called returning to its destiny.
To return to destiny is called the eternal (Tao).
To know the eternal is called enlightenment.
Not to know the eternal is to act blindly to result in disaster.
He who knows the eternal is all-embracing.
Being all-embracing he is impartial.
Being impartial, he is kingly (universal).
Being kingly, he is one with Nature.
Being one with Nature, he is in accord with Tao.

TAO TE CHING, 16, BEGINNING WITH THE THIRD LINE (CHAN)

Immersed in the wonder of the Tao, you can deal with whatever life
   brings you,
and when death comes, you are ready.

TAO TE CHING, 16, LAST TWO LINES (MITCHELL)

## OCTOBER 26

### *Being Ready for Death*

The Master gives himself up to whatever the moment brings.
He knows that he is going to die, and he has nothing left to hold on to:
no illusions in his mind, no resistance in his body.
He doesn't think about his actions; they flow from the core of his being.
He holds nothing back from life; therefore he is ready for death,
as a person is ready for sleep after a good day's work.

TAO TE CHING, 50 (MITCHELL)

If you realize that all things change, there is nothing you will try to hold
   on to.
If you aren't afraid of dying, there is nothing you can't achieve.

TAO TE CHING, 74 (MITCHELL)

## OCTOBER 27

### *Death of Methusalam*

And Methusalam summoned Nir, the son of Lamek, Noe's younger
brother, and he invested him with the vestments of priesthood in front

of the face of all the people, and made them stand at the head of the altar of the Lord.

And he taught him everything that he would have to do among the people.

[And Methusalam spoke to the people:] "Here is Nir. He will be in front of your face from the present day as a prince and a leader."

And the people said to Methusalam, "Let it be so for us in accordance with your word. And you be the voice of the Lord, just as he said to you."

And when Methusalam had spoken to the people in front of the altar, his spirit was convulsed, and, having knelt on his knees, he stretched out his hands to heaven, and prayed to the Lord. And, as he was praying to him, his spirit went out in accordance with the will of the Lord.

And Nir and all the people hurried and constructed a sepulcher for Methusalam in the place Akhuzan, very thoughtfully adorned with all holy things, with lamps.

2 ENOCH 60:1–5 (CHARLESWORTH)

## OCTOBER 28

### *Joyous Questioning*

Lord *Tao* you live forever creating the whole universe.
    You *Tao* alone are just.
You steer the world with the span of your *two* hands,
    and all things obey your will.
To none have you given power to proclaim your works;
    and who can search out your magnificent deeds?
Who can measure your magnificent power?
    and who can go fully recount your mercies?
Nothing can be added to them, nothing subtracted,

it is impossible to fathom your marvels, O Lord *Tao!*
When someone finishes, it is only beginning,
and when someone stops, that person is as puzzled as ever.
What is a human being, what purpose does one serve?
what is good and what is bad for someone?
The length of one's life:
a hundred years at most.
Like a drop of water in the sea, or a grain of sand,
such are these few years compared with eternity. ....
Who can equal your goodness, O Lord, for it is incomprehensible.
Or who can fathom your grace which is without end?
Or who can understand your intelligence?
Or who can narrate the thoughts of your Spirit?
Or who of those born can hope to arrive at these things,
apart from those to whom you are merciful and gracious?

2 BARUCH 75:1–5 AND SIRACH (ECCLESIASTICUS) 18:1–10
(SEERS VERSION)

## OCTOBER 29

*Completing the Cycle: Beyond Words*

True words aren't eloquent; eloquent words aren't true.
Wise ones do not need to prove their point;
those who need to prove their point aren't wise.
The Master has no possessions.
The more he does for others, the happier he is.
The more he gives to others, the wealthier he is.
The Tao nourishes by not forcing.
By not dominating, the Master leads.

TAO TE CHING, 81 (MITCHELL)

## OCTOBER 30

---

*Completing the Cycle: Return Is the Movement of the Tao*

> Return is the movement of the Tao.
> Yielding is the way of the Tao.
> All things are born of being.
> Being is born of non-being.

TAO TE CHING, 40 (MITCHELL)

While I was still young, before I went on my travels,
I sought wisdom openly in my prayer.
Before the temple I asked for her,
and I will search for her until the end.

SIRACH 51:13 (NEW REVISED STANDARD VERSION)

# CoCreator Chants and Songs

What shall we sing in the new age? *Could there be ancient texts and tunes that still resonate with us and with the harmonies of the cosmos?*

The words of the old chants and songs are coming to light and are now available in several collections. The words are given to us without tunes because they originated long before musical notation had been invented. Most of the music was some form of rhythmic chanting.

For some time I have been reviewing the available material and have gleaned the ones that seem most useful for us now. In some instances I have attempted to make the songs more immediate by putting them into present tense and by using direct address to the Tao. I have also made some other adaptations.

We are called to cooperate with the Source of Life in the continuing process of creation, so I call these CoCreator Chants and Songs. I have arranged them in the following groupings:

- *Praising the Source (1–10)*
- *Wisdom Songs (11–17)*
- *Songs from Christ (18–24)*
- *Songs to Christ (25–32)*
- *Songs in the Spirit (33–46)*
- *Chant Dancing (47–50)*

Ways of using these chants and songs: *For best results, read or chant these songs with at least one other person. Two people or two groups can alternate* the reading or chanting. Please notice the asterisks (*), the natural breaking point within each verse. By alternating at the asterisk, you will have a greater sense of the inherent rhythm. Often the second half will echo the first or contrast with it or expand it.

The tunes of Anglican chants, plainsong, and Native American chants will work well with these songs. If you know any of these chant tunes, try them out with the words offered here or invent your own. You may also wish simply to use a monotone chant. See what works best for releasing your freedom in the Spirit.

# *Praising the Tao*

☙

### 1. *Wake up and Praise God*

Why do you sleep, soul, and do not praise the Tao?*
  Sing a new song to God, who is worthy to be praised.
Sing and be aware of how the Tao is aware of you,*
  for a good psalm to God is from a glad heart.

**PSALMS OF SOLOMON 3:1–2 (CHARLESWORTH)**

### 2. *The Lord Is My Sun*

The Light-giver is coming, to give radiance to the whole world;*
  and the morning watch appears, which is the sun's rays.
And the sun comes out over the face of the earth,*
  and retrieves radiance to give light to all the face of the earth. . . .
As the sun is the joy to those who seek its daybreak,*
  so are You my joy, O Lord;
Because You, O Lord, are my sun, and Your rays restore me;*
  and Your light dismisses all darkness from my face.
My eyes belong to You,*
  and they see Your holy day.
Ears I have acquired,*
  and hear Your truth.

The thought of knowledge I have acquired,*
　　and have lived fully through You.
I abandoned the way of error,*
　　and went toward You and received salvation from You generously.
And according to Your generosity You give to me,*
　　and according to Your majestic beauty You create me.

2 ENOCH 15:02 AND ODES OF SOLOMON 15 (CHARLESWORTH)


### 3. *Seers and Singers Go Before You*

The seers will go before You*
　　and they will appear before You.
They will praise you Lord Tao in love,*
　　because You are near and You do see.
Hatred will be removed from the earth,*
　　and with it jealousy will be drowned.
For ignorance is destroyed upon it,*
　　when the knowledge of the Tao comes upon it.
Let the singers sing the grace of the Lord Most High,*
　　and let them offer their songs.
Let their heart be like the day,*
　　and their gentle voices like the majestic beauty of the Tao!
For You give a mouth to Your creation:*
　　to open the voice of the mouth toward You, and to praise You
We praise Your power*
　　and declare Your grace. Hallelujah.

ODES OF SOLOMON 7:18–26 (CHARLESWORTH)

## 4. *I Pour out Praise to You Lord Tao*

I pour out praise to You Lord Tao*
    because I am Your own.
And I will recite Your holy ode,*
    because my heart is with You.
For my harp is in my hand,*
    and the odes of Your rest shall not be silent.
I call upon You with all my heart,*
    I praise and exalt You with all my members.
For from the East and unto the West is Your praise.*
    Also from the South and unto the North is Your thanksgiving.
Even from the peak of the summits and unto their end*
    is Your perfection.
Who can write the odes to You O Lord Tao?*
    or who can read them?
Or who can train oneself for life,*
    so that one may become whole?
Or who can press upon You, the Most High,*
    so that You would recite through my mouth?
Who can interpret Your wonders O Lord Tao?*
    Those who interpret may perish, yet that which is interpreted will
    remain.
For it suffices to perceive and be satisfied,*
    for the odists stand in serenity;
Like a river which has an increasingly gushing spring,*
    and flows to the relief of those who seek You. Hallelujah.

ODES OF SOLOMON 26 (CHARLESWORTH)

## 5. *You Are the One*

You are the Form of the formless,
    You are the Face of the bodiless,
You are the Word of the unutterable,
    You are the Mind of the inconceivable,
You are the Fountain which flows from You,
    You are the Root of those who are planted,
You are the God of those who exist,
    You are the Light of those whom You illuminate,
You are the Love of those You love,
    You are the Providence of those for whom You care,
You are the Wisdom of those You make wise,
    You are the Power of those to whom You give power,
You are the Assembly of those whom You assemble,
    You are the Revelation of the things that are sought after,
You are the Eyes of those who see,
    You are the Breath of those who breathe,
You are the Life of those who live,
    You are the Unity of those who are mixed with All that Is!

THE TRIPARTITE TRACTATE (ROBINSON, 3D ED.)

## 6. *When First the World Began*

When first the world began, You poured forth a Holy Spirit*
    on all You were bringing into being.
You make them all attest Your wondrous mysteries.*
    You show forth Your handiwork in all You make.
You reveal Your glory in all their varied shapes,*
    Your truth in all their works.

You assign to all these diverse and varied natures*
    Your glory to be made known.
Yet how can a spirit of flesh understand these things?*
    How can it conceive so great a mystery?

THE BOOK OF HYMNS (GASTER)

### 7. *You Pour out Your Spirit on Righteous and Wicked Alike*

You pour out Your Spirit on righteous and wicked alike,*
    and You judge all people according to their deeds.
Your Holy Spirit cannot pass away.*
    The fullness of heaven and earth bears witness to Your Spirit.
I know that in Your good pleasure You bestow on people*
    wisdom and discernment in abundance.
You give people communion with truth*
    and entrust us with maintaining right.
Because all these things are present in my mind,*
    I would put into words my prayer and confession of sin,
my constant search for Your Spirit,*
    the inner strength which is mine through the Holy Spirit,
my devotion to the truth of Your covenant,*
    the truth and sincerity in which I walk, my love of Your name.

THE BOOK OF HYMNS (GASTER)

### 8. *Shapen of Clay and Kneaded with Water*

I am shapen of clay and kneaded with water,*
    a bedrock of shame and a source of pollution,
A cauldron of iniquity and a fabric of sin,*

a spirit errant and wayward, distraught by every past judgement:
What can I know that has not been foreknown?
What can I disclose that has not been foretold?
All things are inscribed before You in a recording script,*
  for every moment of time,
For the infinite cycles of years, in their several appointed times.*
  No single thing is hidden, nothing missing from Your presence.

THE BOOK OF HYMNS (GASTER)


### 9. *You Bring Me Cheer, O Lord*

You bring me cheer, O Lord Tao, amid the sorrow of mourning.*
  You bring me words of peace amid havoc.
You bring me stoutness of heart when I faint.*
  You bring me fortitude in the face of affliction.
You have given free flow of speech to my stammering lips;*
  You have stayed my drooping spirit with vigor and strength;
You have made my feet to stand firm*
  when they stood where wickedness reigns.
I am but a symbol of weakness,*
  yet unto them that repent I am a source of healing.

THE BOOK OF HYMNS (GASTER, ADAPTED)


### *When Shall I Chant Songs of Joy and Healing?*

In my tent I will chant songs of joy and healing.*
  In the midst of those who fear You, I will sing the praise of Your
  name.
I will pour forth prayer and supplication always,*
  at all times and all seasons.
When daylight comes forth from its abode,*

I will chant songs of joy and healing.
When, in its ordered course, day reaches its turning point in accordance
    with the rules of the sun,*
    I will chant songs of joy and healing.
Again at the turn of the evening, when daylight departs,*
    as the rule of darkness begins,
And again in the season of night,*
    when it reaches its turning point,
When morning breaks, and when, in the presence of daylight,*
    night withdraws to its abode;
When night departs and day comes in,*
    I will chant songs of joy and healing.
Always, at all the birthdays of time,*
    at the moment when the seasons begin,
When they reach their turning points,*
    I will chant songs of joy and healing.
When they come in order due*
    according to their several signs,*
As these have dominion in the order assured,*
    I will chant songs of joy and healing.

THE BOOK OF HYMNS (GASTER)

# Wisdom Songs

⊸

## 11. *All Wisdom Comes from You, Lord Tao*

All Wisdom comes from You Lord Tao,*
 she is with You forever.
The sands of the sea, the drops of rain,*
 the days of eternity—who can count them?
The height of the sky, the breadth of the earth,*
 the depth of the abyss—who can explore them?
Wisdom, You are created before everything,*
 Your prudent understanding subsists from remotest ages.
For whom has the root of wisdom ever been uncovered?*
 Your resourceful ways, who knows them?

SIRACH (ECCLESIASTICUS) 1:1–6 (NEW JERUSALEM BIBLE)

## 12. *You Are More Mobile Than Any Motion*

You, O Wisdom, are more mobile than any motion;*
 because of Your pureness You pervade and penetrate all things.
You are Breath of the power of God,*
 and Pure Emanation of the glory of the Almighty. . . .
You are reflection of Eternal Light,*

a spotless mirror of the working of God, and an image of
Goodness. . . .
While remaining in Yourself, You renew all things;*
in every generation You pass into holy souls and make them friends
of God.

WISDOM OF SOLOMON 7 (SELECTIONS)
(NEW REVISED STANDARD VERSION)

## 13. *Wisdom, You Are Radiant and Unfading*

Wisdom, You are radiant and unfading*
And You are easily discerned by those who love You.
You are found by those who seek You.*
You hasten to make Yourself known to those who desire You.
One who rises early to seek You will have no difficulty*
for You will be found sitting at the gate.
To fix one's thoughts on You is perfect understanding,
and anyone who is vigilant on Your account will soon be free from
care,
Because You go about seeking those worthy of You*
and You graciously appear to them in their paths,
and meet them in every thought.
The beginning of wisdom is the most sincere desire for instruction,*
and concern for instruction is love for You.
And love of You is the keeping of Your laws,*
and giving heed to Your laws is assurance of eternal life. . . .
Open my ears so I may hear You speaking,*
Give me Yourself, so that I may give You myself.

WISDOM OF SOLOMON 6:12–20 AND FIRST LINE OF ODES OF SOLOMON 9
(NEW REVISED STANDARD VERSION AND CHARLESWORTH)

## 14. *I Sought Wisdom Openly in My Prayer*

While I was still young, before I went on my travels*
    I sought wisdom openly in my prayer.
Before the temple I asked for her,
    and I will search for her until the end.
From the first blossom to the ripening grape*
    my heart delights in her.
My foot walked on the straight path;*
    from my youth I followed her steps.
I inclined my ear a little and received her,*
    and I found for myself much instruction.
I made progress in her;*
    to him who gives wisdom I will give glory.
For I resolved to live according to Wisdom,*
    and I was zealous for the good, and I shall never be disappointed.
My soul grappled with Wisdom,*
    and in my conduct I was strict.
I spread out my hands to the heavens,*
    and lamented my ignorance of her.
I directed my soul to her,*
    and in my purity I found her.
With her I gained understanding from the first;*
    therefore I will never be forsaken.

SIRACH 51:13–20 (NEW REVISED STANDARD VERSION)

## 15. *My Heart Was Stirred to Seek Her*

My heart was stirred to seek her;*
    therefore I have received a prize possession.
She gave me my tongue as a reward,*
    and I will praise her with it.

Draw near to me, you who are uneducated,*
 and lodge in the house of instruction.
Why do you say you are lacking in these things,*
 and why do you endure such great thirst?
I opened my mouth and said,*
 Acquire wisdom for yourselves without money.
Put your neck under her yoke, and let your soul receive instruction;
 it is to be found close by.
See with your own eyes that I have labored but little*
 and found for myself much serenity.

SIRACH 51:13–20 (NEW REVISED STANDARD VERSION)

## 16. *No Place for Wisdom to Dwell*

Wisdom could not find a place in which she could dwell;*
 but a place was found for her in the heavens.
Then Wisdom went out to dwell with the children of the people,*
 but she found no dwelling place.
So Wisdom returned to her place*
 and she settled permanently among the angels.
Then Iniquity went out of her rooms,*
 and found whom she did not expect.
And she dwelt with them, like rain in a desert,*
 like dew on a thirsty land.

1 ENOCH 42:1–3 (CHARLESWORTH)

## 17. *Who Has Gone up into Heaven?*

Who has gone up into heaven and taken Wisdom*
 and brought her down from the clouds?
Who has gone over the sea, and found her,*

and who will buy her for pure gold?
No one knows the Way to her,*
    or is concerned about the path to her.
But the one who knows all things knows her,*
    he found her by his understanding.
The one who prepared the earth for all time*
    filled it with four-footed creatures;
the one who sends forth the light, and it goes;*
    he called it, and it obeyed him, trembling;
the stars shone in their watches, and were glad;*
    he called them, and they said, "Here we are!"
They shone with gladness for him who made them.*
    This is our God; no other can be compared to him.
He found the whole Way to knowledge, and gave Wisdom to his servant
    Jacob*
    and to Israel, whom he loved.
Afterward she appeared on earth*
    and lived with humankind.

BARUCH 3:29–37 (NEW REVISED STANDARD VERSION)

# Songs from Christ

∽

### 18. *You Cause Me to Descend*

You cause me to descend from on high,*
    and to ascend from the regions which are in the deep below;
You gather what is in the middle, and throw them to me;*
    You scatter my enemies, and my adversaries;
You give me authority over chains,*
    so that I might loosen them;
You transform by my hands the dragon with seven heads,*
    and place me at his root that I might transform his seed.
You were there and helped me,*
    and in every place Your name surrounds me.
Your right hand destroys the evil poison,*
    and Your hand levels the Way for those who believe in You.
You choose them from the graves,*
    and separate them from the dead ones.
You take dead bones and cover them with flesh.
    But they are motionless, so You give them energy for life.
You bring Your world to corruption,*
    that everything might be broken and renewed.
The foundation of everything is Your rock.*
    And upon it You build Your kingdom.

It becomes the dwelling place of the holy ones.
    Eternal is Your Way and Your face.

ODES OF SOLOMON 22 (CHARLESWORTH)

### 19. *I Am Mortal like Everyone Else*

I also am mortal, like everyone else,*
    a descendant of the first-formed child of earth;
in the womb of a mother I was molded into flesh,* . . .
    from the seed of a man and the pleasure of marriage.
When I was born, I began to breathe the common air,*
    I fell on the same ground that bears us all.
Crying was the first sound I made, like everyone else.*
    I was nursed with care in swaddling cloths.
For no king has had a different beginning of existence;*
    there is for all one way into life, and one way out.
Therefore I prayed, and understanding was given me;*
    I called on God, and the spirit of Wisdom came to me. . . .
I loved her more than health and beauty,*
    and I chose to have her rather than light,
    because her radiance never ceases.
All good things come to me along with her,* . . .
    those who get Wisdom obtain friendship with God.
May God grant me to speak with judgment,*
    and to have thoughts worthy of what I have received. . . .
For both we and our words are in his hand,*
    as are all understanding and skill and crafts.
For it is he who gives me unerring knowledge of what exists,*
    to know the structure of the world and the activity of the elements;
the beginning and end and middle of times,*
    the alternations of the solstices and the changes of the seasons,
the cycles of the year and the constellations of the stars,*

the natures of animals and the tempers of wild animals,
the powers of spirits and the thoughts of human beings,*
    the varieties of plants and the virtues of roots;
I learn both what is secret and what is manifest,*
    for Wisdom, the fashioner of all things, teaches me.

WISDOM OF SOLOMON 7:1–22 (NEW REVISED STANDARD VERSION AND
THE NEW JERUSALEM BIBLE, CONFLATED)

### 20. *I Am Serving the Tao Who Is Pleased with Me*

The Father of knowledge is the Word of knowledge.*
    Who creates Wisdom wiser than works.
And the Tao who creates me when yet I was not*
    knew what I would do when I came into being.
On account of this the Tao was gracious to me with abundant grace,*
    and allowed me to seek and to benefit from sacrifice.
The Tao has allowed me to appear to those who belong to the Tao*
    in order that they may recognize the one who made them
    and not think that they came into being by themselves.
For I show you the Way toward knowledge*
    and spread it out and lengthen it and bring it to complete perfection.
I set traces of light over the Way*
    and the light continues from the beginning to end.
For I am serving the Tao*
    who is pleased with me.

ODES OF SOLOMON 7:7–17 (CHARLESWORTH, ADAPTED)

### 21. *All Who Saw Me Were Amazed*

All who saw me were amazed,*
    and I seemed to them like a stranger.

And he who knew and exalted me*
    is the Most High in all his perfection.
And he glorified me by his kindness,*
    and raised my understanding to the height of truth.
And from there he gave me the way of his paths,*
    and I opened the doors which were closed.
And I shattered the bars of iron,*
    for my own irons had grown hot and melted before me.
And nothing appeared closed to me,*
    because I was the opening of everything.
And I went toward all my bondsmen in order to loose them;*
    that I might not abandon anyone bound or binding.
And I gave my knowledge generously,*
    and my resurrection through my love.
And I sowed my fruits in their hearts,*
    and transformed them through myself.
Then they received my blessing and lived,*
    and they were gathered to me and were saved;
because they became my members,*
    and I was their head.

ODES OF SOLOMON 17 (CHARLESWORTH)


## 22. *My Defamation Became My Salvation*

Those who saw me were amazed, because I was persecuted.*
    But my defamation became my salvation
because I continually did good to everyone who hated me.*
    They surrounded me like mad dogs, those who in stupidity attack
    their masters.
They divided my spoil, though nothing was owed them,*
    because their mind is depraved, and their sense is perverted.
But I was carrying water in my right hand,*

and their bitterness I endured by my sweetness. . . .
They sought my death but were unsuccessful,*
    and in vain did they cast lots against me. Hallelujah.

ODES OF SOLOMON 28 (CHARLESWORTH, ADAPTED FROM ODE 31)

### 23. *I Will Be with Those Who Love Me*

I take courage, become strong, and capture the world,*
    and it becomes mine for the glory of the Most High;
and the Gentiles who were scattered are coming together,*
    I am not defiled by my love for them.
Traces of light are set upon their hearts*
    They who walk according to my life become whole.
They become my people.*
    And I will be with those who love me.
Like the arm of the bridegroom over the bride,*
    so is my love over those who know me.
And as the bridal feast is spread out by the bridal pair's home,*
    so is my love by those who trust me.

ODES OF SOLOMON 10:4–6 AND 42 (CHARLESWORTH, ADAPTED)

### 24. *Receive My Way of Knowing You*

*Wisdom is singing to the soul:*

Hear the word of truth,*
    and receive my Way of knowing you.
You may not understand what I am about to say to you;*
    nor your body know what I am about to declare to you.
Keep my mystery, you are held by it;*
    keep my faith, you are embraced by it.

Understand my knowledge, know me in truth;*
    love me with affection, return my love;
do not turn your face away from me,*
    because I know you.
Before you existed, I recognized you*
    and imprinted a seal on your face.
I fashioned your members, and my own breasts I prepare for you*
    that you may drink my holy milk and live by it.
I am pleased by you*
    and I am not ashamed of you.
I will fashion your mind and heart;*
    you are my own.

ODES OF SOLOMON 8 (CHARLESWORTH, ADAPTED)

# Songs to Christ

## 25. *Open, Open Your Hearts*

Open, open your hearts to the exultation of the Lord, Tao,*
    and let your love abound from the heart to the lips
in order to bring forth fruits to the Lord, a holy life;*
    and to speak with watchfulness in his light.
Stand and be established,*
    you who were once brought low.
You who were in silence, speak,*
    for your mouth has been opened.
You who were despised, from henceforth shall be raised,*
    for your righteousness has been raised;
For the right hand *and left hand* of the Lord Tao is with you,*
    and will be your helper.
Peace was prepared for you,*
    before what may be your war.
Seek and increase,*
    and abide in the love of the Lord Tao.
You who are in the beloved;*
    you who are kept in the One who lives;
you who are saved in the One who is whole,

you shall be found incorrupted in all ages,
on account of the name of your Father. Hallelujah.

ODES OF SOLOMON 8:1–7, 20–22 (CHARLESWORTH)

### 26. *My Joy Is You, O Christ*

My joy is You, O Christ, and my course is toward You.*
    This Way of Yours is beautiful.
For there is a helper for me, the Lord.*
    You generously show Yourself to me in Your simplicity.
You become like me, that I might receive You.*
    In form You are considered like me, that I might put You on.
And I tremble not when I see You,*
    because You are gracious to me.
You become like my nature, that I might understand You,*
    and like my form, that I might not turn away from You. . . .
You direct my mouth by Your word,*
    and You open my heart by Your light.
And You cause me to dwell in Your eternal life,*
    and permit me to proclaim the fruit of Your peace.
To convert the lives of those who desire to come to You*
    and to capture a good captivity for freedom . . .
I praise You, O Lord, because I love You.*
    O Most High, do not abandon me, for You are my hope.
Freely did I receive Your grace, may I live by it.*
    Indeed my hope is upon the Lord, and I shall not fear.
And because You, Lord, are my salvation, I shall not fear.
    You are like a crown upon my head, and I shall not be disturbed.
Even if everything should be shaken, I shall stand firm in You*
    because You are with me, and I am with You! Hallelujah.

ODES OF SOLOMON 7:2–6, 10:1–3, AND 5
(CHARLESWORTH)

### 27. I Sing from My Heart to You

I sing from my heart to You, the Eternal Christ*
    to whom the Most High gives life and rebirth.
You were raised up the second time according to the flesh,*
    when You were washed in the streams of the river Jordan.
You move with gleaming foot*
    sweeping the waves.
You escape the fire and You are the first to see delightful God*
    coming in the spirit on the white wings of a dove.
A pure flower blooms,*
    fountains burst forth.
You show the Way to people;*
    and point us to heavenly paths.
You teach all with wise words.*
    and come to encounter and persuade the unenlightened ones.
You walk the waves;*
    You heal the sickness of people;
You raise the dead*
    and repel many woes.
From one wallet You give abundance of bread*
    when the house of David brings forth a shoot.
Your hands hold the whole world*
    the earth and heaven and sea.
You flash like lightning on the earth*
    as the two begotten from each other's sides once saw You
    when You first shone forth.
It all comes to pass*
    when earth rejoices in the hope of a child.

SIBYLLINE ORACLES, BOOK 6, LINES 1–20 (CHARLESWORTH)

*"The two begotten from each other's sides"* is a reference to Adam and Eve. Sybil asserts that Adam and Eve see the coming of Christ and rejoice.

## 28. *You Fill Me with Words of Truth*

You fill me with words of truth,*
    that I may proclaim You *and Your Way!*
Like flowing waters, truth flows from my mouth,*
    and my lips declare Your fruits.
You cause your knowledge to abound in me,*
    Your mouth O Christ is the true word,
    and the door of Your light.
The Most High has given You to generations,*
    who are the interpreters of Your beauty,
the narrators of Your glory, and the confessors of Your purpose,
    and the preachers of Your mind, and the teachers of Your works.
For the subtlety of Your word is inexpressible,*
    and like Your expression so also is Your swiftness and Your acuteness,
    for limitless is Your path.
You fall and You remain standing,*
    You know the descent and the Way.
For as Your work is, so is Your expectation,*
    for You are the light and the dawning of thought.
And by You the generations speak to one another,*
    and those who were silent acquire speech.
And from You came love and harmony,*
    and they speak one to another whatever is theirs.
And they are stimulated by the word,*
    and know who made them, because they are in harmony.
For the mouth of the Most High speaks to them,*
    and Your exposition is swift through him.
For the dwelling place of the Word is in human beings*
    and Your truth is love.
Blessed are those who by means of You have recognized everything,*
    and have known the Tao in all truth. Hallelujah.

ODES OF SOLOMON 12 (CHARLESWORTH)

### 29. *Your Vine Have I Planted in the Land*

Your vine have I planted in the land; may it send its roots into the
depth,*
    spread its branches into heaven and may its fruits be seen on earth.
The money which You gave me I laid on the table of the money-
changers;*
    demand it and return it to me with interest, as You promised!
With the silver coin I have gained another ten;*
    may they be added to me as You ordained!
I remitted the silver coin to the debtors;*
    may that not be demanded from me which I have remitted!
When called to dinner I have come, released from field and wife;*
    may I not, then, be cast out, but blamelessly taste of it!
I have been invited to the wedding and have put on white robes;*
    may I be worthy of them and not go out, bound hand and foot, into
outer darkness!
My lamp shines with its light; may its Lord keep it burning until he
leaves the bridal house and I receive him;*
    may I not see it extinguished for lack of oil!
Let my eyes behold you and my heart rejoice,*
    because I have fulfilled your will and accomplished Your
command!
Let me be like the wise and God-fearing servant,*
    who with careful diligence did not neglect his vigilance!
Watching all the night I have wearied myself,*
    to guard my house from the robbers, that they might not break in.
My loins have I girded with truth and my shoes have I bound to my
feet,*
    that I may not see their thongs loosened all together.
My hands have I put to the yoked plough and have not turned away
backward*
    that the furrows may not be crooked.

The field has become white and the harvest is at hand,*
    that I may receive my reward.
My garment that grows old I have worn out,*
    and the laborious toil that leads to rest I have accomplished.
I have kept the first watch and the second and the third,*
    that I may see your face and worship Your Holy Radiance.
I have pulled down the barns and left them desolate on earth,*
    that I may be filled from Your treasures.
The abundant spring within me I have dried up,*
    that I may find your Living Spring.
The prisoner whom You committed to me I have released*
    that the freed person in me may not lose trust.
The inside I have made the outside and the outside I have made inside,*
    and Your whole fullness has been fulfilled in me.
I have not turned back to what is behind,*
    but have advanced to what is ahead.
The dead man I have brought to life and the living I have put to death,*
    and what was lacking I have filled up,
that I may receive the crown of victory*
    and may the power of Christ be perfected in me.

ACTS OF THOMAS 146–47 (HENNECKE AND SCHNEEMELCHER)

## 30. *I Am Rescued from My Chains*

I am rescued from my chains,*
    and I fled unto You, O my Lord.
Your face is with me,*
    which saves me by Your grace.
And I am covered with the covering of Your Spirit,*
    and I remove my garments of skins.
Your hands raise me,*
    and cause sickness to pass from me.

And I am justified by Your kindness,*
    and Your rest is for ever and ever. Hallelujah.

**ODES OF SOLOMON 25 (CHARLESWORTH, ADAPTED)**

### 31. *Liberator of My Soul*

Liberator of my soul, I rejoice in ecstasy*
    knowing it is time for me to enter in and receive You!
I am set free from the cares of earth.*
    I fulfill my hope and receive truth.
I am set free from grief, and put on joy.*
    I become carefree and unpained, dwelling in rest.
I am set free from slavery and called to liberty.*
    I have served times and seasons, and am lifted above times and
    seasons.
I receive my reward from the requiter who gives without reckoning.*
    I unclothe myself and clothe myself, and shall not again be
    unclothed.
I sleep and awake, and shall not again fall asleep.*
    I die and come to life again, and shall not again taste of death.
I may come and be united with my kindred and be set as a flower in a
    crown.*
    I live in the Tao and on You I have set my hope.

**ACTS OF THOMAS 142B (HENNECKE AND SCHNEEMELCHER)**

### 32. *My Eyes Are upon You, O Christ*

As the eyes of a son upon his father,*
    so are my eyes, O Lord, at all times toward You.
Do not turn aside your mercies from me, O Lord;
    and do not take Your kindnesses from me.

Stretch out Your hands to me, my Lord, at all times*
   and be my guide till the end according to Your will.
Let me be pleasing before You, because of Your glory,*
   and because of Your name let me be saved from the evil one.
And let Your serenity, O Lord, abide with me and the fruits of Your love.
   Teach me the odes of Your truth, that I may produce fruits in You.
And open to me the harp of Your Holy Spirit,*
   so that with every note I may praise You, O Lord.

**ODES OF SOLOMON 14 (CHARLESWORTH)**

# Songs in the Spirit

### 33. *I Have Reached the Inner Vision*

Behold, for mine own part, I have reached the inner vision.*
    Through the Spirit You have placed within me, I come to know You,
    my God.
I have heard Your wondrous secret nor heard it amiss.*
    Through Your Holy Spirit, through Your mystic insight,
You have caused a spring of knowledge to well up within me.
    A fountain of strength, pouring forth waters unlimited,*
    a floodtide of loving kindness and of all-consuming zeal.

**THE BOOK OF HYMNS (GASTER)**

### 34. *I Will Give Free Rein to My Tongue*

By virtue of the Spirit which You have set within me,*
    I will give free rein to my tongue.
Because of Your bounteous acts,*
    because of Your forbearance toward me,
I will confess my former transgressions,*
    I will make my prayer and supplication before You,*
I will confess my evil deeds,*
    I will confess the waywardness of my heart,*

I will let Your light shine into the dark places of my heart,*
  I will receive Your bounty,*
I will allow You to redeem my soul,*
  and give free rein to my tongue.

THE BOOK OF HYMNS (GASTER, ADAPTED)


## 35. *No One Can Pervert Your Holy Place*

No one can pervert Your holy place, O my God;*
  nor can anyone change it, and put it in another place.
Because no one has power over Your holy place;*
  for You designed Your sanctuary before You made special places.
You have given Your heart, O Lord, to Your faithful ones;*
  for who shall put on Your grace and be rejected?
For one hour of Your faith*
  is more excellent than all days and years.
You have given to us Your fellowship, not that You were in need of us,*
  but that we are always in need of You.
Sprinkle upon us Your sprinklings, and open Your bountiful springs*
  which abundantly supply us with milk and honey.
For there is no regret with You;*
  that You should regret anything which You have promised;
for that which You give, You give freely,*
  so that no longer will You draw back and take them again.
For all was manifest to You as God,*
  and was set in order from the beginning before You.
And You, O Lord, create all.*
  Hallelujah.

ODES OF SOLOMON 4 (CHARLESWORTH)

## 36. *I Raise My Arms on High*

I extend my hands and hallowed You my Lord;*
    for the expansion of my hands is a sign.
And my extension*
    is the upright cross.
I raise my arms on high*
    on account of Your grace, Lord Tao!
Because You cast off my chains*
    and raise me up according to Your grace and Your wholeness.
I strip off darkness,*
    and put on light.
Abundantly helpful to me is the thought of You my Lord,*
    and Your fellowship.
I am lifted up into Your light,*
    and I pass before Your face.
I am constantly near You*
    while praising and adoring You.
You cause my heart to overflow and bubble forth through my mouth;*
    Your Spirit springs forth from my lips.
Then upon my face shines the exultation of You O Lord*
    and Your praise. Hallelujah.

**ODES OF SOLOMON 27 AND 21 (CHARLESWORTH, ADAPTED)**

## 37. *As the Wind Moves Through the Harp*

As the wind moves through the harp and the strings speak,*
    so Your Spirit sings through all parts of my body
    and I sing through Your love.
Your praise we give on account of Your name;*

our spirits praise Your Holy Spirit.
For there flows forth a stream,*
    and it becomes a river great and broad.
Indeed it carries away everything,*
    and it shatters and floats all things to Your temple.
And the restraints of men are not able to restrain the water of Your
    Spirit*
    nor even the arts of those who habitually restrain water.
For Your Spirit spreads over the face of all the earth,*
    and it fills everything.
Then all the thirsty upon the earth drink,*
    and thirst is relieved and quenched;
For from the Most High the drink is given.*
    Yes, from the Most High the drink is given.
Blessed, therefore, are the ministers of that drink,*
    who have been entrusted with Your water.
They please the parched lips,*
    and restore the paralyzed will.
Even lives who are about to expire*
    are seized from death.
And members which have fallen*
    are restored and set up.
You give power for their openness,*
    and light for their eyes.
Because everyone recognizes them as belonging to You Lord Tao*
    and living by the water of eternity. Hallelujah.

**ODES OF SOLOMON 6 (CHARLESWORTH)**

### 38. *Wings of the Spirit over My Heart*

As the wings of doves are over their nestlings, and the mouths of the
    nestlings are toward their mouths,*

so also are the wings of the Spirit over my heart.
My heart continually refreshes itself and leaps for joy,*
    like the babe who leaps for joy in his mother's womb.
Eternal life embraces me, and kisses me*
    and from that life is the Spirit which is within me.*
And it cannot die
    because it is life.

ODES OF SOLOMON 28 (CHARLESWORTH)

### 39. *My Heart Is Pruned and Flowers Appear*

My heart is pruned and flowers appear,*
    then grace springs up and my heart produces fruits for the Tao.
For the Most High prunes my heart by the Holy Spirit,*
    and uncovers my inward being, and fills me with love.
My pruning becomes my salvation,*
    and I run in the Way of his peace, in the Way of truth.
From the beginning until the end I receive knowledge.*
    And I am established upon the rock of truth, where he sets me.
Speaking waters touch my lips*
    from the generous spring of the Lord.
I drink and become intoxicated,*
    from the living water that does not die.
My intoxication is not with ignorance,*
    because I have abandoned vanity;
I turn toward the Most High, my God,*
    and am enriched by the Lord's favors.
I abandon the folly cast upon the earth,*
    and strip it off and cast it from me.
The Lord reclothes me with his garment,*
    and takes me by his light.
From above he gives me eternal rest;*

and I become like the land which blossoms and rejoices in its fruits.
The Lord is like the sun*
> upon the face of the land.

My eyes are enlightened,*
> and my face receives the dew;

My breath is refreshed*
> by the pleasant fragrance of the Lord.

ODES OF SOLOMON 11 (CHARLESWORTH)

## 40. *You Take Me to Your Paradise*

You take me to Your paradise,*
> and shower me with the wealth of Your pleasure.

I contemplate blooming and fruit-bearing trees,*
> and self-grown is their crown!

Their branches are flourishing and their fruits are shining;*
> their roots are in eternal land.

A river of gladness is irrigating them,*
> and the region round about the land is eternal life.

I adore You O Lord Tao because of Your magnificence.*
> Yes, I adore You because of Your magnificence.

Blessed, O Lord, are those who are planted in Your land,*
> and who have a place in Your paradise;

who grow in the growth of Your trees,*
> and are passing from darkness into light.

Behold, all Your laborers are fair, they who work good works,*
> and turn from wickedness to Your kindness.

Indeed, there is much room in Your paradise: nothing in it is barren,*
> but everything is filled with fruit.

Praise to You, O God, the delight of paradise for ever.*
> Hallelujah.

ODES OF SOLOMON 11 (CHARLESWORTH)

## 41. *Joy Is for the Holy Ones*

Joy is for the holy ones.*
    And who will put it on but they alone?
Grace is for the holy ones.
    And who will receive it but those who trust in it from the beginning?
Love is for the holy ones.*
    And who will put it on but those who possess it from the beginning?
Walk in the knowledge of the Lord and you will know the grace of the
    Lord generously;*
    both for his exultation and for the perfection of knowledge.

**ODES OF SOLOMON 23 (CHARLESWORTH)**

## 42. *Water from the Spring of the Lord*

Fill yourselves with water from the living spring of the Lord,*
    because it has been opened for you.
Come all you thirsty and take a drink,*
    and rest beside the spring of the Lord.
Because it is pleasing and sparkling,*
    and perpetually pleases the self.
For more refreshing is its water than honey,*
    and the honeycomb of bees is not to be compared with it;
because it flows from the lips of the Lord,*
    and is named from the heart of the Lord.
It becomes boundless and invisible,*
    and until it is set in the middle they are not aware of it.
Blessed are those who drink from it,*
    and are refreshed in the Spirit! Hallelujah.

**ODES OF SOLOMON 30 (CHARLESWORTH)**

### 43. *The Lord Tao Is Our Mirror*

Behold, the Lord Tao is our mirror.*
    Open your eyes and see them in him.
Learn the manner of your face,*
    then announce praises to his Spirit.
Wipe the paint from your face,*
    and love holiness and put it on.
Then you will be unblemished at all times with the Tao!*
    Hallelujah.

ODES OF SOLOMON 13 (CHARLESWORTH)

### 44. *My Spirit Exults in Your Love*

As honey drips from the honeycomb of bees, and milk flows from the
    woman who loves her children,*
    so also is my hope upon You, O my God.
As a spring gushes forth its water,*
    so my heart gushes forth to praise You!
My lips bring forth praise to You.*
    My tongue becomes sweet by Your anthems.
My members are anointed by spirit-filled songs.*
    My spirit exults in Your love, and my nature shines in You.
Whoever is afraid will trust in You*
    and healing will be assured.

ODES OF SOLOMON 40 (CHARLESWORTH)

### 45. *The Lord Is on My Head Like a Crown*

You Lord are on my head like a crown*
    and I shall never be without You!

Plaited for me is the crown of truth*
    and it causes Your branches to blossom in me.
For it is not like a parched crown that cannot blossom.*
    But You live upon my head, and blossom upon me.
Your fruits are full and complete;*
    they are full of Your salvation.

ODES OF SOLOMON 1 (CHARLESWORTH)

*Note: This is not a metal crown but a garland of flowers.*

### 46. I Am Awake and Rejoicing

I am awake and rejoicing,*
    I am putting on the love of the Lord.
The members of Your body are with me.*
    I am dependent on them; and they love me.
I would not have known how to love You, O Lord,*
    if You had not continuously loved me.
Who is able to distinguish Your love,*
    except one who is loved?
I love You my Beloved and I love You,*
    and where You rest, I rest with You.
I shall be no stranger,*
    because there is no jealousy with the Lord Most High and Merciful.
I am united with You, my Lover, and I am Your beloved,*
    I love You and I am Yours.
Whoever is joined to the Eternal One truly is eternal.*
    Whoever delights in Life will become fully alive.
You are the Spirit of the Lord and You are not false,*
    You teach human beings to know Your Ways.

ODES OF SOLOMON 3 (CHARLESWORTH)

# Chant Dancing

↶

### 47. Singing in the Fiery Furnace (Four Parts)

*The original scene of this song is an interesting one: King Nebuchadnezzar had ordered everyone to worship the golden statue that he had made, but Shadrach, Meshach, and Abednego refused. The penalty was to be thrown into the fiery furnace. The three, also known as Hananiah, Mishael, and Azariah, adamantly refused to worship anyone or anything other than the Lord God. Having been warned, the three were thrown into the furnace, where a fourth, an angel of the Lord, joined them and "drove the fiery flame out of the furnace . . . as though a moist wind were whistling through it. The fire did not touch them at all and caused them no pain or distress. Then the three with one voice praised and glorified and blessed God in the furnace" (Azariah 1:26b–27, NRSV).*

*What do you do when the heat is on? Praise the Lord of life! In this chant we call on all of creation to praise and glorify God.*

*Since we are rediscovering that both the masculine and the feminine are in the Source of all, the text is modified to be more inclusive.*

#### Part 1: Blessing the God of Our Ancestors

Blessed are You, O Lord, God of our ancestors:*
    praised and exalted above all forever.
Blessed are You for the name of Your majesty:*
    praised and exalted above all forever.

Blessed are You in the temple of Your holiness:*
  praised and exalted above all forever.
Blessed are You beholding the depths, and dwelling between the
  cherubim:*
  praised and exalted above all forever.
Blessed are You on the glorious throne of Your majesty:*
  praised and exalted above all forever.
Blessed are You in the expanding heavens:*
  praised and exalted above all forever.

### Part 2: The Cosmic Order Sings Praises

O all ye works of the Lord, bless ye the Lord:*
  praise him and glorify her forever!
O ye angels of the Lord, bless ye the Lord:*
  praise him and glorify her forever!
O ye heavens, bless ye the Lord:*
  praise him and glorify her forever!
O ye waters above the heavens:*
  praise him and glorify her forever!
O ye sun and moon, bless ye the Lord:*
  praise him and glorify her forever!
O ye stars of heaven, bless ye the Lord:*
  praise him and glorify her forever!
O ye showers and dew, bless ye the Lord:*
  praise him and glorify her forever!
O ye winds of God, bless ye the Lord:*
  praise him and glorify her forever!
O ye fire and heat, bless ye the Lord:*
  praise him and glorify her forever!
O ye winter and summer, bless ye the Lord:*
  praise him and glorify her forever!
O ye frost and snow, bless ye the Lord:*

praise him and glorify her forever!
O ye nights and days, bless ye the Lord:*
praise him and glorify her forever!
O ye light and darkness, bless ye the Lord:*
praise him and glorify her forever!
O ye lightning and clouds, bless ye the Lord:*
praise him and glorify her forever!

### Part 3: The Earth and Her Creatures Sing Praises

O let the earth bless the Lord:*
praise her and glorify him forever!
O ye mountains and hills, bless ye the Lord:*
praise her and glorify him forever!
O all ye green things upon the earth,*
praise her and glorify him forever!
O ye wells and springs of water, bless ye the Lord:*
praise her and glorify him forever!
O ye seas and rivers, bless ye the Lord:*
praise her and glorify him forever!
O ye whales and all that move in the waters:*
praise her and glorify him forever!
O all ye birds of the air, bless ye the Lord:*
praise her and glorify him forever!
O all ye animals, wild and tame, bless ye the Lord:*
praise her and glorify him forever!

### Part 4: Human Beings Sing Praises

O all ye people of the earth, bless ye the Lord:*
praise to the Father and glorify the Mother forever!
O all ye people of Israel and the New Israel bless ye the Lord:*
praise to the Father and glorify the Mother forever!

O all ye priests and people of God, bless ye the Lord:*
    praise to the Father and glorify the Mother forever!
O all ye men and women everywhere, bless ye the Lord:*
    praise to the Father and glorify the Mother forever!
O all ye spirits and souls of the righteous, bless ye the Lord:*
    praise to the Father and glorify the Mother forever!
O all ye holy and humble of heart, bless ye the Lord:*
    praise to the Father and glorify the Mother forever!

*You may add here, if you like, more phrases and praises.*

Let us bless the Father, the Mother, the Son and Holy Spirit: one Tao*
    Singing praises and glorifying all forever!

DANIEL 3:52–90 (AZARIAH 1:29–65); BOOK OF COMMON PRAYER,
1928 EDITION, WITH VARIATIONS FROM THE 1979 EDITION,
SELECTED WORDING FROM THE NEW REVISED STANDARD VERSION AND
THE NEW JERUSALEM BIBLE, AND OTHER MODIFICATIONS

### 48. *Hymn of the Initiants (Eight Parts)*

I will offer my praise and at all the appointed times which God has prescribed.

#### *Part 1: The Daily Round*
*After each line, the response is, "Night and Day I will offer my praise."*

When daylight begins its rule,
When it reaches its turning point at noon,
When it again withdraws to its appointed abode,
When the watches of darkness begin,
When God opens the storehouse of darkness,

When God sets the darkness against the light,
When darkness reaches its turning point at midnight,
When darkness again withdraws in face of the light,
When sun and moon shine forth from the holy height,
When they again withdraw to the glorious abode,

*Part 2: The Seasons of the Natural Year*

*After each line, the response is, "Night and day I will offer my praise."*

When the formal seasons come on the days of new moon,
When the seasons reach their turning points at the solstices,
When the seasons yield place to one another at the solstices,
As each comes round anew,
When the natural seasons come, at whatever time may be,
When, too, the months begin,
On their feasts and on holy days,
As they come in order due,
Each as a memorial in its season,

*Part 3: The Blessings of My Lips*

*After each line, the response is, "I will offer the blessings of my lips."*

When the natural year begins,
At the turning points of their seasons,
When each completes its turn,
Turning on its natural day,
Yielding each to each,
Reaping time to summer,
Sowing time to greening time,
In the natural years of weeks,
In the several seasons of the year,
With the coming day and night,

> When evening and morning depart,
> When I see how God sets their bounds,
> When facing my sin and transgression,
> When seeking the justice of God,
> Fountain of all knowledge,
> Wellspring of holiness,
> Zenith of all glory,
> Beauty that never fades,

### Part 4: Choosing the Path He Shows Me

I will choose the path God shows me and be content with his decisions.
*After each line, the response is, "I will bless Your name."*

> Whenever I first put forth my hand or foot,
> When first I go or come,
> When I sit and when I rise,
> When I lie down on my bed,
> At common meals,
> When I raise my hand,
> When I enjoy the rich fruits of the earth,
> With the sounds flowing from my lips,
> At the beginning of fear and alarm,
> When trouble and stress are at hand,
> When musing on Your power,
> When relying on Your mercies,
> When coming to know I am in Your hand,
> When in Your hand all things live,

### Part 5: I Will Praise You

Whenever distress breaks out, I will praise God, and when his salvation and wholeness come, I will join the chorus of praise.
*After each line, the response is, "I will praise You."*

Whenever distress breaks out,
When Your salvation comes,
I will heap no evil on any,
I will pursue others with good,
I will not be envious of the profit of wickedness,
I will not lust after wealth gained unethically,
I will not engage in strife with reprobate men,
I will not rest until justice is affirmed,
I will harbor no angry grudge,
I will cherish no baseness in my heart,
I will seek the fruit of holiness on my tongue,
I will open my mouth with thanksgiving,
I will banish empty words from my lips,
I will banish filth and perverseness from my mind,
I will shelter knowledge with sound counsel,
I will set a sober limit to defending my faith,
I will limit the use of force in exacting justice,
I will bind righteousness with the measuring line of occasion,
I will temper justice with mercy,
I will bring firmness to fearful hearts,
I will enlighten the bowed with sound teaching,
I will reply to the proud with meekness,
I will answer baseness with humility,

*Part 6: Hallelujah!*

*After each line, the response is, "Hallelujah!"*

To God I commit my cause:
You can perfect my Way:
You can make whole my heart:
You in Your love can wipe my transgressions away:
You are the wellspring of knowledge:

You make light burst forth:
My eyes have gazed on Your wonders:
The light in my heart has pierced the deep things of existence:
You are ever at my right hand:
You are the path beneath my feet:
You are the rock set before all things:

### Part 7: Through Your Mysterious Wonder

*After each line, the response is, "Through Your mysterious wonder."*

Light comes into my heart,
My eye has set its gaze on eternal things,
I have seen a virtue hidden from people,
I have known a knowledge and subtle love hidden from humankind,
I have seen a fount of righteousness,
I have felt a reservoir of strength,
I have known a wellspring of glory,
You have given us an inheritance,
You have joined us in communion with the sons and daughters of
     heaven,
You have formed us in one congregation, one single communion,
You have made us a fabric of holiness,
You have made us a plant evergreen for all time to come,

### Part 8: Who Are We?

*After each line, the response is, "Who are we?"*

Who can compass the sum of Your glory?
Who are we, mortals amid Your wondrous works?
Who are we, child of woman to sit in Your presence?
Who are we, kneaded of dust?
Who are we, but food for worms?

Who are we, but a molded shape, a thing nipped of the clay?
Who are we, whose attachment is to the dust?
What can we as clay reply?
What can we say, molded by hand?
What thought can we comprehend?

THE HYMN OF THE INITIATES (GASTER, ADAPTED)

## 49. *The Hymn of Christ*

Before he was arrested, . . . Jesus assembled us all and said, "Before I am delivered to them, let us sing a hymn to the Father, and so go to meet what lies before us." So he told us to form a circle, holding one another's hands. Jesus stood in the middle and said, "Answer Amen to me." So he began to sing the hymn.

Glory to You, Father, *Amen.*
*Glory to You, Mother, Amen.*
Glory to You, Word, *Amen.*
*Glory to You, Wisdom, Amen.*
Glory to You, Spirit, *Amen.*
Glory to You, Holy One, *Amen.*
Glory to Your Glory, *Amen.*

Praise to You, Father, *Amen.*
*Praise to You, Mother, Amen.*
*Praise to You Eternal Tao, Amen.*

I will be saved, and I will save, *Amen.*
I will be loosed, and I will loose, *Amen.*
I will be wounded, and I will wound, *Amen.*
I will be born, and I will bear, *Amen.*
I will eat, and I will be eaten, *Amen.*
I will hear, and I will be heard, *Amen.*

I will be understood, and I am understanding, *Amen.*
I will be washed, and I will wash, *Amen.*
I will pipe, dance, all of you, *Amen.*
I will mourn, beat all your breasts, *Amen.*
The Holy Eight sing in choir with us, *Amen.*
The Twelfth Number dances on high, *Amen.*
The entire universe belongs to the Dancer, *Amen.*
If you do not dance, you don't know what is happening, *Amen.*
I will flee, and I will remain, *Amen.*
I will adorn, and I will be adorned, *Amen.*
I will be united, and I will unite, *Amen.*
I have no house, and I have houses, *Amen.*
I have no place, and I have places, *Amen.*
I have no temple, and I have temples, *Amen.*
I am a lamp to you who see me, *Amen.*
I am a mirror to you who know me, *Amen.*
I am a door to you who knock on me, *Amen.*
I am a Way to you who travel with me, *Amen.*

*Repeat "Glory" and "Praise" sections.*

ACTS OF JOHN 94 (SEERS VERSION)

## 50. *The Thunder, Perfect Mind*

*Sophia is communicating with us and inviting us to come into union with her.*

I was sent forth from the power, and I have come to those who reflect
  upon me, and I have been found among those who seek after me.
Look upon me, you who reflect upon me, and you hearers, hear me.
you who are waiting for me, take me to yourselves.
Do not banish me from your sight.
Do not make your voice hate me, nor your hearing.

Do not be ignorant of me anywhere or any time. Be on your guard!
Do not be ignorant of me.

*The chanting begins:*

For I am the first and the last.
I am the honored one and the scorned one.
I am the whore and the holy one.
I am the wife and the virgin.
I am the mother and the daughter.
I am the barren one and many are my sons.
I am she whose wedding is great, and I have not taken a husband.
I am the midwife and I am she who does not bear.
I am the solace and I am the labor pains.
I am the bride and I am the bridegroom.
I am begotten by my husband.
I am the mother of my father.
I am the sister of my husband, and he is my offspring.
I am the slave of him who prepared me.
I am the ruler of my offspring. . . .
I am the staff of his power in his youth, and he is my rod of my old
   age. . . .
I am the Silence that is incomprehensible.
I am the Idea whose remembrance is frequent.
I am the Voice whose sound is manifold.
I am the Word whose appearance is multiple.
I am the Utterance of my name. . . .
For I am knowledge and I am ignorance.
I am shame and I am boldness.
I am shameless and I am ashamed.
I am strength and I am fear.
I am war and I am peace. . . .

I am she who is weak and I am well in a pleasant place.
I am senseless and I am wise. . . .
I am the one who has been hated everywhere and
I am the one who has been loved everywhere.
I am the one whom they call Life, and you have called Death.
I am the one whom they call Law and you have called Lawlessness.
I am the one whom you have pursued, and
I am the one whom you have seized.
I am the one whom you have scattered, and you have gathered me
    together.
I am the one before whom you have been ashamed, and you have been
    shameless to me.
I am she who does not keep festival, and I am she whose festivals are
    many.
I, I am godless, and
I am the one whose God is great.
I am the one whom you have reflected upon, and you have scorned
    me.
I am unlearned, and you learn from me.
I am the one whom you have despised, and you reflect upon me.
I am the one whom you have hidden from, and you appear to me. . . .
I am an alien and I am a citizen.
I am the substance and I am the one who has no substance. . . .
I am control and I am uncontrollable.
I am the union and I am the dissolution.
I am the abiding and I am the dissolving.
I am the below, and they come up to me.
I am the judgment and I am the acquittal.
I, I am sinless, and the root of sin derives from me.
I am lust in outward appearance, and
I am interior self-control.
I am the hearing which is attainable to everyone and

I am the speech which cannot be grasped.
I am a mute who does not speak, and great is the multitude of my
    words. . . .
I am she who cries out, and I am cast off upon the face of the earth.
I prepare the bread and my mind within.
I am the knowledge of my name.
I am the one who cries out, and I am the one who listens.
I am the Name of the Sound and the Sound of the Name.

THE THUNDER, PERFECT MIND (TEACHING PORTIONS OMITTED)
(ROBINSON, 3D ED.)

# A Taoist Eucharist

❧

The people assemble at an agreed time in a quiet place in nature, a warm and friendly home, or some other sacred space. A creative liturgist is responsible for guiding the people through the liturgy of the Eucharist and enabling free, open, and natural participation by all who are present.

As the people gather, they will normally form a circle around a central symbol. When there is a large number of people, a series of concentric circles may form in a natural way.

## A Time of Centering in Silence

When the time has come to begin, there is an opening tone sounded on a Tibetan bowl, Japanese bowl, or similar instrument, creating a sound conducive to centering.

## A Time of Dialogue Through Holy Scriptures

When all are centered and ready to listen, two or three carefully selected passages from holy writings are read, followed by a tone and time of meditation after each. A reading from one of the Gospels should always be included. Then follows a dialogue sermon or sharing focusing on how people understand the passages and how they relate the material to their life. Responses may be given in song, dance, instrumental music, other art forms, silence. The following prayer or something similar may be used before the readings begin.

LITURGIST: *Blessed are You, Tao of the universe! Open us to any teaching there may be that is sweet and plain, giving us mind, speech, and knowledge: mind, so that we may understand You; speech, so that we may expound You; knowledge, so that we may know You. We rejoice, having been illumined by Your knowledge. We rejoice because You reveal and release Yourself among us. You are always within, around, and beyond us.*

## A Time of Praying

In silence and aloud, focused attention is given to Mother Earth, the people of the earth, contemporary events around the planet, personal concerns, and individual needs. When desired, there may be praying with laying on of hands. A vessel of oil should be available for anointing with oil for healing and for releasing the Holy Spirit.

## A Time of Sharing the Peace

After the praying, or at some other point in the Eucharist, people will be invited to turn to one another with a greeting of "Shalom" or "Peace" and sharing with a handshake, hug, kiss—whatever is appropriate to the relationship in the moment.

## A Time of Offering

The people form a circle around a central altar or holy table.
The liturgist says these or other words:

*Present yourselves, your souls and bodies, to be a living sacrifice to the Tao, within whom we live and move and have our being.*
*(Romans 12:1 and Acts 17:28)*

Offerings are brought to the table, including bread that is whole and unbroken, an empty chalice, and three small vessels: one of water, another of wine, and a third with milk and honey. When appropriate, additional offerings may be made at this point.

## A Time of Making Eucharist

LITURGIST: *Blessed are You, Tao of the universe! In You we live and move and have our being! You are our Mother, Father, Teacher, and Lover! You are the Tao of ten thousand names!*

*We praise You! We give thanks to You! We offer all that we know of ourselves to all that we know of You! Every soul and heart is lifted up to You!*

*We give thanks to You for Jesus, who shows us the Way of the Tao through his life, spiritual journey, baptism in the Jordan River, and anointing with the Holy Spirit. We see You in Jesus, who expresses You fully in the Way of passionate living, relating, teaching, healing, suffering, and dying. We rejoice because we know You are continually rising in the eternal body of Christ.*

*We seek to know You totally and completely. Remove all that hinders and blocks the free flowing of Your Spirit through our bodies. Show us how to experience fully what it is to be living members of Your eternal body.*

*We dedicate and release to You our whole self—heart, soul, mind, and energy.*

RESPONSE: *Take our minds, passions, emotions, and will. Enter and cleanse the depths of our being. Empty us so that You may fill us with all that You are!*

LITURGIST: *Blessed Tao, our Father, Mother, Teacher, and Lover, You are bread of life, and You are rising in us!*

Bread is passed around the circle with each person breaking off a piece and saying to the next, "I am the bread of life."

LITURGIST: *Blessed Tao, our Father, Mother, Teacher, and Lover, You are the water of life, and You are creating us!*

Water is poured into the chalice and passed around the circle with each person saying to the next, "I am the water of life." The cup is passed until it is empty.

LITURGIST: *Blessed Tao, our Mother, Father, Teacher, and Lover, You are the milk and honey of life, and You are nourishing us!*

Milk and honey are poured into the chalice and passed around the circle with each person saying to the next, "I am the milk and honey of life." The cup is passed until it is empty.

LITURGIST: *Blessed Tao, our Father, Mother, Teacher, and Lover, You are the wine of life, and You are celebrating in us!*

Wine is poured into the chalice and passed around the circle with each person saying to the next, "I am the wine of life." The cup is passed until it is empty.

When all have received full communion, the people embrace one another, saying, "This is my body and this is my blood."

## *Dismissal*

The people form a circle.

LITURGIST: *Go now, and be more fully who you are: the living body of Christ in the world.*

RESPONSE: *Amen! Let us be who we are!*

# Appendix:
# When Does the Natural Year Begin?

‹♦›

A study of calendars and ways of reckoning time reveals a wide variety of calculations for determining when the year begins. These are based on the climate, culture, philosophy, and spiritual practices of a particular people.

From the various systems I have chosen the Celtic model, which is based on the natural year with solstices, equinoxes, and four midpoints.

The year works best for people living in the northern hemisphere; life below the equator is reversed in natural pattern.

The natural year has *fixed* dates and *movable* dates.

Fixed dates are based on the solar calendar. Four main points are

- December 21, the winter solstice. Christmas comes at the winter solstice, a few days late (December 25).
- March 21, the spring equinox. The annunciation to Mary comes at the spring equinox, a few days late (March 25).
- June 21, the summer solstice. The feast day of John the Baptizer comes at the summer solstice, a few days late (June 24).
- September 21, the fall equinox. The feast of Saint Michael and All Angels comes a few days later (September 29).

The four midpoints are

- November 1, All Saints. The year begins with the evening (October 31).
- February 1, Saint Brigid, a celebration of the feminine.

- May 1, May Day.
- August 1, Saint Lugh, a celebration of the masculine.

Movable dates are based on the lunar calendar. Most notable is Easter, which is calculated on the basis of the first Sunday after the first full moon after the spring equinox. On the basis of the date of Easter, we move backward through Holy Week and Lent to Ash Wednesday and forward for fifty days through the Easter season to Pentecost. The result is a continuous season from Ash Wednesday until Pentecost that moves as a unit according to the lunar calendar. In this book that sequence is called Ashes to Fire. Note the following:

- The earliest possible date for Ash Wednesday is February 4.
- The latest possible date for Pentecost is June 15.
- The Ashes to Fire sequence will move as a unit between those dates.

Consequently the readings in *The Tao of Jesus* are arranged as follows:

- Fixed calendar days October 31 through February 1.
- Ashes to Fire according to the year, based on Easter.
- Fixed calendar days June 15 through October 30.

The result is two free-floating seasons:

- Between February 2 and Ash Wednesday.
- Between Pentecost and June 15.

On these days, you may wish to use one or two of the CoCreator chants and songs. These are high-energy selections, designed to invigorate you while waiting for the next season to begin.

One further note: There are three particularly significant fixed dates that will land somewhere in the Ashes to Fire season.

- March 21, the spring equinox
- March 25, the annunciation to Mary

- The visitation of Mary and Elizabeth
- May 1, May Day

Special selections for each of these days are printed on pages 107–110.

## A Table for the Days That Move According to the Solar Calendar

| YEAR | ASH WEDNESDAY | EASTER | PENTECOST |
|------|---------------|--------|-----------|
| 1994 | February 16 | April 3 | May 22 |
| 1995 | March 1 | April 16 | June 4 |
| 1996* | February 21 | April 7 | May 26 |
| 1997 | February 12 | March 30 | May 18 |
| 1998 | February 25 | April 12 | May 31 |
| 1999 | February 17 | April 4 | May 23 |
| 2000* | March 8 | April 23 | June 11 |
| 2001 | February 28 | April 15 | June 3 |
| 2002 | February 13 | March 31 | May 19 |
| 2003 | March 5 | April 20 | June 8 |
| 2004* | February 25 | April 11 | May 30 |
| 2005 | February 9 | March 27 | May 15 |
| 2006 | March 1 | April 16 | June 4 |
| 2007 | February 21 | April 8 | May 27 |
| 2008* | February 6 | March 23 | May 11 |
| 2009 | February 25 | April 12 | May 31 |
| 2010 | February 17 | April 4 | May 23 |
| 2011 | March 9 | April 24 | June 12 |
| 2012* | February 22 | April 8 | May 27 |
| 2013 | February 13 | March 31 | May 19 |

* Leap years.

# Sources

❧

## Translations of the Tao Te Ching

Chan, Wing-Tsit. *The Way of Lao Tzu.* Indianapolis: Bobbs-Merrill, 1963.

Feng, Gia-Fu, and Jane English. *Lao Tzu, Tao Te Ching.* New York: Vintage, 1972.

McCarroll, Tolbert, ed. *The Tao, the Sacred Way.* New York: Crossroad, 1982.

Mitchell, Stephen. *Tao Te Ching, A New English Version.* New York: Harper & Row, 1988.

Tan, Wee Chong. *Lao Tzu and Gandhi (Friends of Jesus).* Victoria, British Columbia: Canadian College for Chinese Studies, 1983.

Tan, Wee Chong. *Lao Tzu, Tao Te Jing.* Victoria, British Columbia: Canadian College for Chinese Studies, 1992.

## Sources for Creation Myths

Hamilton, Virginia, ed. *In the Beginning: Creation Stories from Around the World.* Illustrated by Barry Moser. New York: Harcourt Brace Jovanovich, 1988.

Jin, Yu, ed. *Chinese Myths.* Shanghai, China: Juvenile & Children Publishing House, 1986.

Pritchard, James B., ed. *Ancient Near Eastern Texts.* Princeton, NJ: Princeton Univ. Press, 1955.

Reid, Bill. *The Haida Legend of the Raven and the First Humans.* Vancouver: Univ. of British Columbia Museum of Anthropology, 1980.

Roberts, Melva Jean, and Dale Roberts. *Echoes of the Dreamtime.* With paintings by Ainslee Roberts. Melbourne, Australia: J. M. Dent Pty Ltd., 1988.

Wolkstein, Diane, and Samuel Kramer, trans. *Inanna, Queen of Heaven and Earth.* New York: Harper & Row, 1983. From tablets ca. 1850 B.C.

## *Sources for Gospels and Other Holy Scriptures*

Attridge, Harold, ed. *New Testament Apocrypha: Acts and Letters.* Sonoma, CA: Polebridge Press, 1994.

Charlesworth, James H., ed. *The Old Testament Pseudepigrapha.* 2 volumes. New York: Doubleday & Co., 1983.

Cox, A. Cleveland, ed. *The Ante-Nicene Fathers.* 10 volumes. Grand Rapids, MI: Wm. B. Eerdmans, 1951.

Crane, Frank. *The Lost Books of the Bible and the Forgotten Books of Eden.* Iowa Falls, IA: World Bible Publishers, 1926.

Funk, Robert W. *New Gospel Parallels.* Volume 2. Philadelphia: Fortress Press, 1973.

Galley, Howard. *The Prayer Book Office.* New York: Harper & Row (Seabury Press), 1988.

Gaster, Theodor H. *The Dead Sea Scriptures in English Translation.* Garden City, NY: Doubleday & Co., 1976.

Hennecke, Edgar, and Wilhelm Schneemelcher, eds. *The New Testament Apocrypha.* 2 volumes. Philadelphia: Westminster Press, 1959.

The Holy Bible with Apocryphal/Deuterocanonical Books, New Revised Standard Version. Iowa Falls, IA: World Bible Publishers, 1989. Copyright by the Division of Christian Education of the National Council of Churches of Christ in the U.S.A. Used by permission. All rights reserved.

Hutchins, Robert Maynard, ed. *Great Books of the Western World.* Chicago: Encyclopaedia Britannica, 1952.

Kenneth, Brother, C.G.A. *From the Fathers to the Churches.* London and San Francisco: Collins Liturgical Publications, 1988.

Layton, Bentley. *The Gnostic Scriptures.* New York: Doubleday & Co., 1987.

Miller, Robert J., ed. *The Complete Gospels.* Sonoma, CA: Polebridge Press, 1992.

The New Jerusalem Bible. New York: Doubleday & Co., 1985.

Richardson, Cyril C., trans. *Early Christian Fathers.* Volume 1. Library of Christian Classics. Philadelphia: Westminster Press, 1963.

Robbins, Vernon K. *Ancient Quotes and Anecdotes.* Sonoma, CA: Polebridge Press, 1989.

Robinson, James M., gen. ed. *The Nag Hammadi Library in English.* San Francisco: Harper & Row, 1977; 3d ed. rev., 1988).

Scott, Burton, trans. *The Apostolic Tradition of Hippolytus.* Easton Archon Books, 1962. Reprinted with the permission of Cambridge Univ. Press, New York.

Seers Version. Author's paraphrase.

Wright, J. Robert. *Readings for the Daily Office from the Early Church.* New York: Church Hymnal Corp., 1991.

# Acknowledgments

෯

Grateful acknowledgment is given to the following for permission to reprint material:

Attridge, Harold, ed., *New Testament Apocrypha: Acts and Letters*. Polebridge Press, copyright © 1994. Used by permission.

Wing-Tsit Chan, *The Way of Lao Tzu*. Bobbs-Merrill, copyright © 1963 by Macmillan College Publishing Company, Inc. Reprinted by permission.

James H. Charlesworth, ed., *The Old Testament Pseudepigrapha*. 2 volumes, copyright © 1983, 1985 by James H. Charlesworth. Used by permission of Doubleday, a division of Bantam Doubleday Dell Publishing Group, Inc.

A. Cleveland Cox, ed. *The Ante Nicene Fathers*, 10 volumes. Wm. B. Eerdmans, copyright © 1951. Used by permission.

Frank Crane, *The Lost Books of the Bible and the Forgotten Books of Eden*. World Bible Publishers, copyright © 1926. Used by permission.

Burton Scott Easton, *The Apostolic Tradition of Hippolytus*. Archon Books edition, copyright © 1962. Used by permission of Cambridge Univ. Press.

Gia-Fu Feng and Jane English, *Tao Te Ching by Lao Tzu*. Alfred A. Knopf Inc., copyright © 1972. Reprinted by permission.

Robert W. Funk, *New Gospel Parallels*. Augsburg Press, copyright © 1985. Used by permission.

Theodor H. Gaster, *The Dead Sea Scriptures in English Translation*. Doubleday & Co., a division of Bantam, Doubleday, Dell Publishing Group, Inc., copyright © 1976. Used by permission.

Edward Hennecke and William Schneemelcher, *New Testament Apocrypha*, 2 volumes. Westminster Press, copyright © 1959. Used by permission.

Yu Jin, *Chinese Myths*. Juvenile and Children Publishing House. Used by permission.

Benjamin Jowett, trans., *The Dialogues of Plato*. Oxford Univ. Press, copyright © 1952. Used by permission.

Bentley Layton, *The Gnostic Scriptures*. Doubleday, a division of Bantam, Doubleday, Dell Publishing Group, Inc., copyright © 1987.

Tolbert McCarroll, *The Tao, The Sacred Way*. Crossroads, copyright © 1982. Reprinted by permission of the author.

Miller, Robert J., ed. *The Complete Gospels.* Polebridge Press, copyright © 1992. Used by permission.

Stephen Mitchell, *Selections from Tao Te Ching,* copyright © 1988, HarperCollins. Reprinted by permission.

New Jerusalem Bible, copyright © 1985 by Darton, Longman & Todd, Inc., a Division of Bantam Doubleday Dell Publishing Group, Inc. Reprinted by permission.

New Revised Standard Version of the Bible, copyright © 1989 by the Division of Christian Education of the National Council of Churches of Christ in the USA. Used by permission. All rights reserved.

Cyril C. Richardson, trans., *Early Christian Fathers,* Volume 1, Library of Christian Classics, Westminster Press, copyright © 1963. Used by permission.

Vernon K. Roberts, *Ancient Quotes and Anecdotes.* Polebridge Press, copyright © 1989. Used by permission.

James M. Robinson, gen. ed. *The Nag Hammadi Library in English,* copyright © 1977. HarperCollins.

James M. Robinson, gen. ed. *The Nag Hammadi Library in English,* third edition, copyright © 1988. HarperCollins.

Wee Chong Tan, *Lao Tzu and Ghandi (Friends of Jesus).* Canadian College for Chinese Studies, copyright © 1992. Used by permission.

Wee Chong Tan, *Lao Tzu, Tao Te Jing.* Canadian College for Chinese Studies, copyright © 1992. Used by permission.

Diane Wolkstein and Samuel Kramer, trans. *Inanna, Queen of Heaven and Earth.* Harper & Row, copyright © 1983. Used by permission of the authors.

J. Robert Wright, *Readings for the Daily Office from the Early Church,* Church Hymnal Corp., copyright © 1991. Used by permission.

# *About the Editor*

☙

John Beverley Butcher is the son of Harold Butcher, an English freelance journalist and lecturer, and Elizabeth Ford, an American musician and teacher. He was raised in Prescott, Arizona, and earned his bachelor of arts degree in philosophy and psychology from Harvard and his master of divinity degree from Yale. He is a Fellow of the Canadian College for Chinese Studies.

His continuing education includes work at the Graduate Theological Union, Berkeley, California, and seminars with the Guild for Psychological Studies in San Francisco. He is an associate of the Jesus Seminar. His studies center in researching the integration of Taoist philosophy, holy Scripture, archetypal psychology, and personal experience.

His travel research has taken him to holy sites in Israel and Egypt and the Celtic sites of Iona, Holy Island, and Durham, England. He and his wife, Grace, have explored Mayan ruins in Guatemala and Mexico and have visited Aborigines in Australia and firewalkers in Fiji.

Since his ordination as priest in the Episcopal church in 1960, he has served congregations in Arizona and California. He was chaplain of the Arizona State Prison and client counselor in a California halfway house for mental patients. Since 1978 he has been serving as rector of St. Peter's Episcopal Church in San Francisco.